LEADERSHIP
AND CRISIS

LEADERSHIP AND CRISIS

BOBBY JINDAL

GOVERNOR OF LOUISIANA

WITH

PETER SCHWEIZER

AND

CURT ANDERSON

Since 1947
REGNERY
PUBLISHING, INC.

An Eagle Publishing Company • Washington, DC

Library of Congress Cataloging-in-Publication Data
Jindal, Bobby, 1971-
  Leadership and crisis / by Bobby Jindal.
     p. cm.
  ISBN 978-1-59698-158-4
  1. United States--Politics and government--2009- 2. Louisiana--Politics and government--1951- 3. Jindal, Bobby, 1971- 4. Governors--Louisiana. I. Title.
  JK275.J56 2010
  976.3'064092--dc22
  [B]
  2010037857

Published in the United States by
Regnery Publishing, Inc.
One Massachusetts Avenue, NW
Washington, DC 20001
www.regnery.com

Manufactured in the United States of America

10 9 8 7 6 5 4 3 2 1

Books are available in quantity for promotional or premium use. Write to Director of Special Sales, Regnery Publishing, Inc., One Massachusetts Avenue NW, Washington, DC 20001, for information on discounts and terms or call (202) 216-0600.

Cover photo: courtesy of The Times-Picayune ©2010
   All rights reserved. Reprinted with permission.

Distributed to the trade by:
Perseus Distribution
387 Park Avenue South
New York, NY 10016

To Supriya, my best friend,
and my parents who taught me to fearlessly
pursue my dreams.

Table of Contents

CHAPTER I

DISASTER IN THE GULF

It was a misty Sunday morning, May 2, and I was standing with my chief of staff, Timmy Teepell, on the tarmac of the Louis Armstrong International Airport in New Orleans. Air Force One had just touched down on the runway. It was a tense time in Louisiana, in fact, all along the Gulf coast. It had been almost two weeks since the Deepwater Horizon oil well had blown, killing eleven workers, and now oil was spewing into the Gulf of Mexico, and this was the first time the president visited. The spill was growing in size by the hour and moving ever closer to the delicate shoreline of Louisiana. To us it felt like a slow moving invasion: you could see it coming, it was getting closer, and little seemed to be happening to stop it.

Air Force One slowly eased toward us, and moments later the White House staff emerged. A member of the advance team took Timmy aside for a private chat with White House Chief of Staff Rahm Emanuel. Moments later the president emerged, and as his feet hit the runway pavement I extended a hand of greeting. "Hello, Mr. President."

President Obama quickly put his arm around my shoulder and pulled me aside. It was then that I realized this was not going to be an ordinary greeting.

I was expecting words of concern about the oil spill, worry about the pending ecological disaster, and words of confidence about how the federal government was here to help. Or perhaps he was going to vent about BP's slow response. But no, the president was upset about something *else*. And he wanted to talk about, well, *food stamps*. Actually, he wanted to talk about a letter that my administration had sent to Secretary of Agriculture Tom Vilsack a day earlier.

The letter was rudimentary, bureaucratic, and ordinary. "We are formally requesting that you authorize under the OPA [Oil Pollution Act] the distribution of commodities to disaster relief agencies and the state. . . . " We had also sent out requests for federal assistance on fisheries failure and job assistance. In this instance, we were simply asking the federal government to authorize food stamps for those who were now unemployed because of the oil spill. Governors regularly make these sorts of requests to the federal government when facing a disaster.

But somehow, for some reason, President Obama had personalized this. And he was upset.

There was not a word about the oil spill. He was concerned about looking bad because of the letter. "Careful," he said to me, "this is going to get bad for everyone."

My first thought was: Are you kidding? We've got millions of gallons of oil lurking off shore and you're concerned about *this*? My words to him were more measured. "We haven't criticized you about food stamps, Mr. President. What I'm frustrated about is resources. We still don't have the boom and skimmers we need to fight this oil spill."

A few feet away, Rahm Emanuel and Timmy were having a similar conversation. But Emanuel was being less delicate. "If you have a problem," he told Timmy, "pick up the f—n' phone." (Rahm is well known in Washington for his inability to communicate without swearing.)

The president never raised his voice. But you could tell that he was oddly irritated and annoyed *by this particular letter*. I was truly stunned. It would be one thing if they had been angry about the failed response to the oil spill or concerned about the pending ecological disaster or frustrated with BP. There were plenty of real things to be upset about. But mad about a letter to the Ag Secretary? It was almost surreal. The White House had a sense of urgency . . . about the wrong things. *Politico* noted that "the president put his arm around Jindal 'as if he were giving him an earful.'"[1] We were contacted by a national reporter in Washington who had been told the president was upset. The White House had clearly tipped off reporters to observe closely the greeting on the tarmac.

Just as quickly as the president turned on his anger, he turned it off. Okay, press stunt over, what's next? The weather made flying by helicopter unsafe, so we drove to Venice—in separate cars—where we were meeting with local officials.

That encounter with President Obama served as a reminder to me of why Americans are so frustrated with Washington: the feds focus on the wrong things. Political posturing becomes more important than reality. In Washington they live by the motto: "Perception is reality." They worry about things they shouldn't and fail to do those things that they should focus on. It's called core competence, or the lack thereof.

Now during the oil spill some critics said that I was being hypocritical because I believe in limited government and was also demanding more federal assistance. But they miss the point entirely. I'm not an anarchist. I believe government has a role—and at its most basic level the role of government is to protect life, liberty, and property.[2] Dealing with a disaster like the oil spill certainly fits the job description. I believe that part of the reason the federal government failed to respond effectively to the oil spill (and for that matter, five years earlier during Hurricane Katrina) is precisely because government has become too big. By too big I mean not only too *expensive*, but also our federal government has become too *expansive* and strayed too far from what should be its core competency.

Today we have the federal government in Washington trying to run car companies, banks, and our entire health care system—rather than sticking to its core job of protecting America from all enemies foreign and domestic, protecting the life, liberty, and property of the American people. What we really need is for the federal government to do those things it should be doing with excellence, and stop trying to take over pieces of the private sector that it has no business in and no reasonable chance of running well.

The federal government's response to the oil spill was lackadaisical almost from the start. Shortly after the oil well blew, we asked federal authorities how they were going to prioritize and deploy resources to protect our shoreline. We grew frustrated when they would not adjust their plans to respond adequately to a crisis of this magnitude. (We ended up writing our own plans with parish presidents and other coastal leaders who know the waters like the back of their hands.) And some of the federal plans were, how can I say it? *Crazy*. During that May 2 meeting in Venice with the president, it became clear that some of the federal plans to "protect" Louisiana were dangerous. A senior Coast Guard official explained calmly that if the oil entered the marshes, the plan was to . . . *burn the marshes!* What? How about some Napalm?

If you've never been to the Louisiana coast, it is far different than Daytona Beach. It's beautiful in a much different way. Our coast is populated with countless fragile marshes and estuaries, and it is home to numerous species of wildlife. More than a few people at the meeting commented that this sounded painfully similar to the quip by the Army official in Vietnam who said they needed to destroy the village to save it. We wanted more of an emphasis on *preventing* the oil from getting into the marshes in the first place and a greater sense of urgency.

More important than the lack of workable plans, the federal government didn't even have the resources to carry out their plans. It became apparent very early on that there simply was not enough boom to protect our shoreline. Regulations required that local industry, ports, and even some defense facilities around the country maintain a certain amount of boom. It would make sense in this case, with a lack of enough boom in the Gulf region, to relax the rules around the country so boom could be redeployed to deal with this disaster. When you are fighting a war and you are running low on ammunition, you need to get whatever ammunition you have to the frontlines. It makes no sense to say, "No we can't take those bullets from this warehouse because regulations require that we keep a certain amount here." You move the ammo to the front lines! But bureaucrats don't think that way. Despite repeated requests to the federal government and the president himself, it took them too long to relax those requirements, and we lost precious time. An admiral with the Coast Guard admitted to us they had not requested skimmers from Europe since it might take them up to five weeks to arrive, even though we ended up fighting the oil for months, and, as of this writing, are still fighting it.

Getting things approved in a timely fashion proved nearly impossible. On April 30 we had requested a Commercial Fisheries Failure from the U.S. Commerce Department. It wasn't until May 24 that we finally got word from the Commerce Department that they approved our request.

When the federal government failed to deliver on the resources needed to fight this battle and win, we began developing innovative solutions like air-dropping sand bags, Hesco Baskets, and vacuum barges. Land barriers proved to be one of the most effective protection measures. Indeed, time and time again, land barriers stopped the oil that got past the skimmers and boom and served as our last line of defense to protect our wetlands. We knew there were no silver bullets to magically stop the oil, but we also knew it was important to have multiple lines of defense rather than relying on one tactic alone. So in early May we submitted a proposal to build sand berms to protect our state so that we could fight the oil miles away from our wetlands. We waited. *And waited.* The federal government refused to give us a timely answer. We heard nothing for weeks, even though sand berms are recognized as a proven oil spill response technique by the U.S. Coast Guard. We went ahead and built one berm on our own to demonstrate its effectiveness, and saw it repeatedly prevent oil from entering our wetlands. Even after the U.S. Army Corps of Engineers concluded the benefits outweighed the risks, the federal government only made BP pay for one segment. It was weeks after submitting our first plan, and multiple meetings and press conferences later, that the federal government finally decided to make BP pay for all six approved segments.

Of course, by that point, more than 100 miles of our shoreline had been oiled.

With the feds, when resources didn't arrive, or decisions were put off, another promise would be made. Jefferson Parish Council Chairman John Young captured the parallel universe of bureaucratic time reality perfectly when he explained, "Tomorrow doesn't mean tomorrow; it just means NOT today."

When the oil reached the Louisiana marshes, it was like a poison entering Louisiana's body. It stained our birds, permeated marsh grasses, and entered the ecosystem. We still don't know the full impact the spill will have on our state. For me, the point of full realization came when we took a boat ride out to Pass a Loutre. Anyone who has spent time in our bayous knows that they contain a wide array of animals that together create a symphony of sounds. But when we cut our motor that afternoon in Pass a Loutre, all we heard was a deafening silence. It was the first time in my life I was sorry I didn't hear any mosquitoes. It was as if all the life had been drained out of the marsh. The poison had arrived. The smell was awful. Sitting on the thick, heavy slick was sickening. You could literally stir it with a stick. The oil was black, toxic crude. Two members of my staff had migraines later that day, and others complained of nausea.

People in Louisiana wonder why the federal response was so slow. You would think following the withering criticisms of President Bush during Hurricane Katrina that the federal response this time would have been swift and sure. You would have thought that a White House so concerned about its image would have been all over this.

For us, the oil spill was not just a threat to our beaches. It was a threat to our way of life. The Louisiana coastline, a fragmented and complicated system of marshes, is a fragile ecosystem with all kinds of vegetation and marine life that could potentially be destroyed by even the temporary presence of oil. Commercial fishing in Louisiana is a $2 billion industry, and fishing (both recreational and commercial) creates 60,000 jobs. One-third of the domestic seafood in the continental U.S. comes from Louisiana. Again—this isn't just a few guys who happen to fish for a living, this is a top industry in our state.

I believe that a big part of the problem with the federal response was that the administration was overly optimistic and too willing to trust the so-called experts. They believed that the elite could fix everything. It struck me during our conversations how often the president mentioned that his secretary of energy, Steven Chu, had won the Nobel Prize. Good for him. But just how exactly was this medal going to fix the problem, cap the well, and keep the oil off our coastline? It became very apparent during this crisis the administration believed the bureaucrats, whether they worked in government or for BP. The press noticed that the White House was deferential to BP and their alleged expertise from the beginning. They basically believed what BP executives were telling them. I think President Obama figured that we just needed to get all the smart people in a room (that would be easy, since most of them reside in Washington) and then they would fix the problem. He trusted the bureaucrats—both corporate and federal. He hadn't been in government long enough (or in the private sector, for that matter) to know that you have to be skeptical. They always seemed to assume the best case scenario rather than preparing for the worst case scenario.

It was a pattern evident from the beginning, one that was repeated again and again. Just a day and half after the well blew, killing eleven workers, there was a meeting between my staff and the Coast Guard. Both the Coast Guard and BP informed us that there was no oil leaking into the Gulf. (This would prove to be reminiscent of Katrina, when we were assured as the storm hit that the levees were holding.) Then a couple days later word came from BP and the federal government that there was a leak—but it was a small one. Only 1,000 barrels a day. It was a very stable situation, we were told. No big deal. Soon the estimate became 5,000 barrels, then 12,000 to 19,000 barrels, then 25,000 to 30,000 barrels, and finally 35,000 to 60,000 barrels. A week after the explosion, when I asked about the impact of hurricanes on the oil, a National Oceanic and Atmospheric Association (NOAA) official assured me we would not be dealing with the oil by June 1, the beginning of hurricane season; Timmy remarked that it reminded him of five years earlier—when the Corps of Engineers assured us the floodwalls would not breach in New Orleans.

As the oil spread to our waters, both the federal government and BP seemed trapped in their own red tape. Even when the problem was obvious and visible, they were incapable of quick action. At one point we took Coast Guard Captain Ed Stanton, who was then in charge of the response in Louisiana, up in a Louisiana National Guard Blackhawk helicopter to see the oil in Timbalier Bay. We took the man in charge of the response to see the oil because BP contractors would not deploy assets. Then we flew over Cocodrie where you could see the boom and other material literally sitting on the docks, with skimmers nearby that were idle. We expected him, having seen the inaction with his own eyes, to jump on it right away and get going. But he told us it wasn't that easy. It would take at least twenty-four hours before he could get the assets deployed. Captain Stanton faced such withering criticism for the lack of movement that at one point he snapped to the incredulous media, "I guess I'm just slow and dumb." But of course it was the system that was slow and dumb, not him.

There was no accountability. Stanton and others were working under a system that was incapable of working quickly and efficiently. It was highly centralized, bureaucratic, and often unresponsive. Process mattered more than results. The Coast Guard operated under an Incident Action Plan (IAP), which was their term for planning the mission for the next day. When oil was spotted on the water, they would put together an IAP, but it would take literally twenty-four to forty-eight hours to actually get skimmer boats on site to clean it up—this means that the problem we saw one day could only be addressed a whole day later...if we were lucky. Of course, timing in a disaster situation is everything. By the time a day passed, the currents might have shifted and the oil might be miles away. Authority was too distant and too rigid to be responsive. (Doesn't that sound like a problem with the federal government in other areas, too?) What we needed were local command centers on the ground that could react and respond more quickly.

Think of it this way. When our soldiers in World War II encountered the enemy, they did the only smart thing: they attacked with the intent to kill. For the people of Louisiana, this was war. When we saw oil coming on to our coast, we did everything we could to stop it, to kill it. There was no time to call back to headquarters, to fill out some forms, or to wait for orders from Washington.

One day I remember vividly, there was thick, black crude in Bay Jimmy off of Grand Isle. We asked the Coast Guard why there were still not enough skimmers at work. They were using only a fraction of the available vessels. One problem was there was a bottleneck when it came to spotter planes and insufficient communications equipment. Apparently they simply didn't have enough air traffic control capacity. When we suggested that they request assistance from the military, and also use some of the excess vessels to provide water-based visibility, it was like a revelation. The thought had apparently never occurred to them.

People assume that BP must have been better because after all, they're in the private sector. But BP CEO Tony Hayward seemed to suffer from the same sense of hubris. On top of that, he had little sense of accountability. "What the hell did we do to deserve this?" he reportedly exclaimed to his fellow executives as the crisis unfolded. He seemed to downplay the realities of the situation at best and exhibit arrogance at worst. "The Gulf of Mexico is a very big ocean," he told reporters on one occasion. "The amount of oil and dispersant we are putting into it is tiny in relation to the total water volume." He was seemingly nonchalant about how the very way of life for tens of thousands of people in my state was at risk. Asked whether he was sleeping at night he replied, "Yeah, of course I am." When he tried to offer apologies he messed that up, too. "We're sorry for the massive disruption it's caused to their lives," he said famously. "There's no one who wants this thing over more than I do; I'd like my life back." When workers complained of feeling ill from breathing oil fumes all day, Hayward brushed it off and managed to insult our cooking at the same time. He said that the workers were feeling sick possibly because of "food poisoning." I don't know what Hayward will do after he leaves BP, but let me make a bold prediction that he has no future in public relations or brand management.[3]

Hayward obviously felt terribly inconvenienced by the oil spill. And he had little interest in hearing solutions the locals had in mind to deal with a disaster that his company had caused. During our second meeting together, Hayward came to my office, and he had a very specific mission: he wanted me to sign off on the use of subsea dispersants, chemicals that would disperse the oil near where the leak was occurring. I had no real authority here. BP could do this with the approval of the Coast Guard. But he wanted legal cover, so he pressed me to sign off on it. I said I first wanted him to show me the science that the dispersants would not have adverse affects on the Gulf. When I expressed to him the need for us to build sand berms along the coast to help keep the oil out of the marshes, he was completely dismissive. He deemed the berms as more important in protecting the state against hurricanes than oil. (He failed to grasp the concept that a hurricane surge would bring more oil deeper into our marsh, making these barriers critical protection for both oil and hurricanes.) He was so arrogant he didn't even want to listen to me make the case. He lacked the common sense even to pretend to be interested in what I was saying. He was tone-deaf and clueless. I thought to myself, I can't believe this guy runs a multi-billion dollar company. This guy would not succeed as a used car salesman.

If the oil spill crisis teaches us one thing, it is that a distant, central command and control model simply didn't work with the fast-moving and ever-changing crisis that was unfolding. Frankly, some of the best leadership and advice we got was from local leaders, like the parish presidents and fishermen. As far as I can tell, none of them has yet to win a Nobel Prize, but they know these waters. And some of the best ideas for cleanup came from locals.

Because the federal government was failing to provide the boom we needed, we came up with creative ideas—Tiger dams, Hesco Baskets, sand-drop operations, and freshwater diversions. It was a local initiative that gave us one of the best techniques for cleaning up: vacuum trucks. The federal government was having workers clean the marsh grasses with the equivalent of paper towels. We thought of the bright idea of putting a large vacuum truck, like the kind that they use to clean Port-a-Potties, on top of a National Guard pontoon boat. They were highly effective in sucking up the oil.

Another local innovation was the "jack up barge"—commonly used here to help the oil industry service rigs out in the water. The Coast Guard and BP couldn't figure out how to rapidly deploy boom in response to specific oil sightings in marsh areas and to stretch their supplies instead of trying futilely to protect the entire coast, so Plaquemines Parish President Billy Nungusser suggested that we use these barges that people could live on and supply them with lots of boom so response boats could stock up and go directly to oiled areas in the water in real time without having to come all the way back to the shore.

In Grand Isle, they started using rigid pipe to act as a high water boom to help with the oil. There was such a void in the federal response—lack of boom, lack of approval on plans to use rocks and barges to stop the oil, to name a few—that they used this pipe to hold the oil back. It served as a barrier to protect vulnerable estuaries, and was yet another innovative use of ordinary oil field equipment. Simply put, working with locals we were able to use whatever we could get our hands on to stop oil from coming into our fragile marshes and waters. We did what the federal government just couldn't: act quickly and efficiently to protect our shores. Unlike them, we were never satisfied with just doing nothing.

We quickly discovered that the only way to get things done by either BP or the federal government was to go public. The national media was very helpful in this regard. When we asked for the Coast Guard to give us their plans for deploying and prioritizing boom to contain the oil spill, we heard nothing for more than a week. So we met with the parish presidents, and the next day we had our plans posted online. We went on TV and explained our plan, and suddenly there was some action. The federal government seemed to be motivated by the potential for bad media coverage but...at least we were finally getting their attention.

During the president's second trip to Louisiana, on May 28, we were down in Grand Isle and were meeting with the parish presidents whose parishes were being affected by the spill. It was a strange presidential visit in that before the president arrived, a group of workers were bussed in to clean the beach before the president walked it. (As of this writing, as far as I know, the president has never actually seen heavy oil from the spill; my staff and I, however, went almost daily to show the world and the nation the true caliber of this disaster.) The meeting included local officials, but Billy Nungusser and St. Bernard Parish President Craig Taffaro had to crash it, even though their parishes had been heavily affected by the oil. They showed up without an invite to represent their people. That's Billy and Craig.

Before the meeting broke up, President Obama singled out Billy and me and told us to stop going on television and criticizing him. "I go home every night and I see on TV people saying I'm not doing anything," he said. "I don't need to see you guys on CNN criticizing us." For some reason he was particularly miffed that Billy was going on with Anderson Cooper. It was the oddest conversation. Actually, it was not really a conversation. It was more like a lecture. Before we had a chance to reply and explain that this seemed to be the only way to get federal action, the president adjourned the meeting. Again, the White House seemed to focus on the wrong things. I felt like we needed to be on a wartime footing against the oil, and the president was wondering, why is everybody criticizing me? The irony is that right after that exchange, someone from the White House staff came over to prepare us for the all important photo opportunity where the president would make remarks to the national press. The staff member was insistent that I stand next to the president. But before the photographers arrived, Florida Governor Charlie Crist edged me out of the way. I was happy to yield the ground.

Billy was honest and open in his views on the failure of the federal government to adequately respond to the situation. At one point he had a conversation with Coast Guard Rear Admiral Mary Landry who was upset about his criticisms and asked him to tone them down in the meeting with the president. She said he was criticizing thousands of people in the Coast Guard, but Billy told her he was only criticizing her. At the end of the meeting they patched things up. The Coast Guard admiral later asked him for a hug. "Everyone needs a hug," Billy told the admiral.

Because of his frustration with the federal response, Mayor David Camardelle of Grand Isle pushed a plan to place rocks (temporarily) in western Barataria Bay to protect some of the most sensitive and productive fishing estuaries in the world. The idea was to narrow the passes and use vacuum barges in the gaps to fight the oil from getting to our interior marshes. This defense would be especially important when the boom and skimmers were rendered ineffective by storm surges. To implement his plan, Camardelle needed the approval of the federal government. The president promised that he would get a call within hours about the plan. Weeks later they were still telling us to wait. The mayor was repeatedly told that his plan was on the verge of getting approved, so he actually had BP go buy and move the rocks.

It wasn't until July 6—weeks later—that we got an answer. It was no. And they offered no real alternative solutions.

I will let the experts debate whether the plan was a good one or not. But the fact that they took forever to give him an answer and encouraged him to believe that the plan would be approved was ridiculous.

It was enormously frustrating, and it was becoming a pattern. The federal government didn't have an adequate plan, but kept stopping us from acting. Every time one of our requested defense measures was not provided by the federal government, we came up with an alternative—just to have those alternatives get shot down.

The federal government seemed often more concerned about process than results. The vacuum barges were working very well, but on June 17 I had to go to Delta Marina in Plaquemines Parish to check on the barges which had been shut down by the Coast Guard because they needed "inspections and certifications." There was heavy oil impact in Barataria Bay where vacuum operations had been working before these "inspections." These barges had literally suctioned thousands of gallons of oil out of the marshes. Now, the federal government wanted to make sure that the barges were using the proper valves. We asked why the valves were so important. They explained that using the wrong valves might cause a little of the oil they were sucking up to drop BACK into the water! Timmy interrupted the meeting and said, "Wait a minute, you are concerned about the environmental impacts of a fraction of the oil these barges remove from the water seeping back in?" I would have laughed harder about the silliness of it all, but the stakes were too high. I demanded that the White House show a sense of urgency in getting these barges back to work, and was therefore furious to learn that the Coast Guard wasted several hours since they couldn't find phone numbers for the barge companies. They didn't realize that they and BP had approved each of the contractors; the left hand did not know what the right hand was doing. Apparently they eventually realized the absurdity of the situation, but then they wanted the barges to *return to port* so they could count the lifejackets and fire extinguishers. We pleaded with them to allow the barges to work during the inspections, to have the inspectors *go to them*, but the feds refused. (I guess it made too much sense.) After bringing the barges back to port for twenty-four hours, they eventually allowed them to resume work without inspections.

Perhaps the most iconic image of the oil spill was the workers, dressed in white Hazmat suits, wandering the coastline. But these workers were far less effective than they might have been because of federal regulations. When temperatures rose above 90 degrees (which they do approximately *every day* in Louisiana during the summer), workers were allowed to labor for only a fraction of an hour. News crews regularly caught them working for less than twenty minutes and then resting for the remainder of the hour under white tents that had been erected on the beaches. What is so frustrating about this is that at the same time the National Guard, employees of Louisiana's Wildlife and Fisheries, and private contractors were working for eight to twelve hours every day, some with bulldozers and shovels. They got what the feds still didn't: we were at war. You literally couldn't have pulled these guys off their jobs to sit in tents. Jefferson Parish Councilman Chris Roberts got it right when he told a local reporter that it was time for the feds to get a war mentality to tackle the oil spill. "Katrina would be a perfect example of that. Another example is the war going on in Afghanistan and Iraq. It's hot, they're on the sand, but soldiers don't fight for ten minutes then say, 'Timeout, we have to take our required OSHA break.' It's ridiculous."[4]

In another instance, we were building sand berms out by the Chandeleur Islands. The project had been approved by the Army Corps of Engineers, and we had started dredging. But we were told by the Interior Department that we were dredging in the wrong spot. They were wrong, and eventually we went public and suggested that the Department of the Interior needed to consult a map to see we were dredging within the area they approved. We even offered to replace the sand we were temporarily using—but they refused. Work began once again, but we lost precious time when they forced us to move equipment. Dredging had been shut down for almost a week because of the bureaucrats.

Our problems in Louisiana were compounded by the fact that the Obama administration imposed a deepwater offshore drilling moratorium. Along the Louisiana coast fishermen and the energy industry have a long history of coexisting very well together. For example, in Morgan City for the past seventy-five years we've held a Shrimp and Petroleum Festival. When President Obama announced a moratorium on deepwater offshore drilling, it was devastating news for our state. Depending on its length, the moratorium risked killing thousands of jobs and resulting in a loss of millions in wages each month. The moratorium would do nothing to clean up the Gulf of Mexico, but it could have a severe impact on our economy. Just as the threat of expanding cap and trade, higher tax rates, and the cost of health care reform are causing businesses to refrain from investing and creating jobs, the administration appeared oblivious to the impact their actions would have on private sector jobs. The companies would likely absorb the losses and try to maintain their staffs and equipment if they were assured the moratorium would be short-lived, and indeed many are trying to do just that. Businesses need predictability when making massive investments of capital. The moratorium did the opposite.

When it came to the moratorium, there seemed to be a disconnect between the White House and reality. As of this writing, the courts have ruled twice against the administration, with one judge even calling their actions "arbitrary" and "capricious." The judge said that the government's action "does not seem to be fact-specific" and that the "government's hair-splitting explanation abuses reason and common sense." When another judge asked the lawyers for the federal government whether they "considered the severe economic harm that befalls the oil industry and the workers in the oil industry as a result of the six-month moratorium," the answer came back: NO.[5]

We had regular daily talks with the White House, and it was usually Valerie Jarrett, senior advisor to the president, who participated. When the president first announced a moratorium on oil drilling in the Gulf, I mentioned to Jarrett on the phone how the moratorium could cost Louisiana thousands of jobs. Jarrett said that no, the effects would not be long lasting because there was a lot of oil under the Gulf and the oil rigs weren't going anywhere. "There will be oil there tomorrow," she told us. Senator Mary Landrieu and I had to explain to her that some of the rigs rent at $500,000 a day, and that an unpredictable moratorium could alter companies' long-term plans. If they couldn't pump oil and were sitting idle for at least six months, the rigs would simply be moved to another location. (And indeed, some of the oil rigs have been redeployed to Africa as of this writing.) Jarrett didn't seem to understand that the rigs couldn't be turned on and off with a switch—and that global competition for the production of oil is very real. The idea that she could so confidently predict the economic impact of the drilling moratorium and not actually realize that oil rigs would simply be moved was stunning.[6]

Along with the official moratorium on deep-water drilling, independent oil operators began to complain that the Obama administration had a de facto moratorium in place on shallow-water drilling. Before the spill, federal authorities were regularly issuing permits to drill in shallow water. After the spill, the issuing of permits was reduced to a trickle. Most of these shallow-water operators were not a part of "big oil"—they were small, independent producers who could lose everything. Their operations in, say, 200 feet of water had nothing to do with what happened at Deepwater Horizon. But a de facto moratorium was imposed.

The White House certainly knew that the moratorium could cost thousands of jobs. And they went ahead anyway.[7] When I raised my concerns about the moratorium with President Obama, he assumed that I was simply parroting these words because I was supposed to say them. "I understand you need to say all of this, I know you need to say this, that you are facing political pressure," he said. He didn't seem to understand that for us in Louisiana, this was the reality on the ground. This was about people losing their jobs. He responded by saying that national polls indicated that people supported a ban. The human element seemed invisible to the White House.

Why was the decision-making so bad? Were they blinded by ideology? Ideology may have played a part. But even more important (and more troubling) to me was the simple fact that the Obama administration was making big decisions about an industry they knew little about—and they didn't seem particularly concerned about the consequences. For example, they touted the fact that they secured money from BP to compensate oil rig workers for their loss of pay as a result of the moratorium. But they didn't think about everyone else who would suffer, including suppliers, caterers, shop owners, and support personnel. They boldly went about making major decisions without really understanding the consequences of what they were doing.

The Obama administration tried to cloak the moratorium with a report based on expert opinion that the safety situation in the Gulf required a moratorium. But after the report was issued, eight of the fifteen experts named said the moratorium language was not even in the draft report they had reviewed, and that they disagreed with the moratorium. They went on to say that a suspension of drilling would have a negative impact on the economy. And some even noted that the moratorium really would not do anything to make the Gulf safer.[8] Some experts have even noted the moratorium could make drilling in the Gulf less safe as the most modern equipment may be the first to leave.

I told the president that the oil moratorium amounted to a second man-made disaster. And my message was simple: Louisianans shouldn't lose their jobs because the federal government can't do its job. Our belief is that federal officials should spend their energies on getting serious about more rigorous oversight and inspection of oil rigs rather than punishing workers. The experts picked by the federal government made dozens of specific recommendations to improve safety. Experts have recommended and we have supported a temporary pause, redundant blowout preventer equipment, federal inspectors on every rig, inspections of the safety records of each company and each rig, etc. Louisianans, of all people, don't want to see another drop of oil spilled into the Gulf of Mexico or another tragic loss of life.

The president went on to assure me that anyone who lost their job would get a check from BP. When I explained that BP might not write them checks because it was the federal government that imposed the moratorium the president said, "Well, if BP won't pay the claim, they can file for unemployment." I was amazed by the level of disconnect. The people of Louisiana want to work, not collect unemployment or BP checks.

BP's response was as bad as the federal government's. Part of it was the corporate leadership. And on one level you can't really be surprised by the response of BP—they were doing what you would expect from a corporation. They were simply looking to protect their shareholders. But I was stunned that BP execs didn't go out much into the field to see exactly what was happening. One who did was Bob Dudley, who is now the newly minted CEO of BP. We took him for a boat trip to visit East Grand Terre, and I give Dudley credit for coming. But during that trip members of my staff noticed the sole of a shoe on the bottom of the boat. Not an entire shoe—just the sole of the shoe. Turns out that Dudley later admitted it was his. He had stepped in some black, toxic crude, and it had literally eaten the sole off of the rest of his shoe until it apparently came completely apart when we got into the boat. And he was as surprised as anyone that the oil was that corrosive. Dudley got on his headset and said something like, "This stuff is really bad, corrosive. It took off the sole of my shoe." He had to walk back to his car without the sole of one of his shoes. One of my aides told me, "A BP exec has now truly lost his sole."

As I look back, the oil spill has reinforced several principles I have learned through my years of dealing with crises.

1. You must lead from the front. Always.
2. Speed is everything. There must be a sense of urgency.
3. Listen to the locals. They often know more than the Nobel Prize Laureates.

4. Don't wait for federal agencies to tell you what to do... tell them what you need.

5. Keep the public informed on the details. Do it early and often and without fanfare. Transparency inspires confidence. Confidence inspires cohesion.

6. Make quick decisions when plans fail. They will fail. As the saying goes, "No battle plan completely survives the first shot."

7. Demand and expect excellence. There is no reason government cannot function in a competent manner. Refuse to accept failure.

8. Ignore the politics, focus on doing a good job. The main thing is to keep the main thing the main thing. If you do a good job, that will all take care of itself. If you don't, there is no amount of PR that will help you.

9. Read the old playbook, then throw it out and get ready to improvise.

10. Hope for the best but prepare for the worst, immediately. Assume you are at the Alamo. If you end up attacking an ant hill with a sledge hammer... that's okay. But if you end up bringing a knife to a gun fight... that's a failure. If you prepare for war and peace breaks out, great! But if you prepare for peace and war breaks out, you're in trouble!

Louisiana National Guard members are truly the unsung heroes in the oil spill response efforts. Throughout the disaster, they logged more than 2,250 flight hours during response operations, dropped more than 21,300 sandbags weighing 46 million pounds to stop oil from entering sensitive marsh areas, and stood up 24 miles of protection systems along the coast including Hesco Baskets, Tiger dams, and land bridges. I'm proud of these men and women who worked tirelessly to protect our way of life against the oil. Many of these same soldiers have served multiple tours overseas, but when duty called again, they stepped forward and honored our state, fulfilling their mission and their duty to "Protecting What Matters."

The experience of the oil spill reaffirmed my faith and trust in the common sense and wisdom of the American people. Local fishermen and coastal leaders often showed more practical wisdom than the bureaucrats and elites. They are wiser than the Establishment wants to give them credit for. They are hard-working and generous. And the core American values that I was raised on—hard work, responsibility, accountability, innovation, stewardship—are clean, sharp, and true.

CHAPTER 2

WHO DAT?

It was 2:30 a.m. at a diner somewhere outside Monroe, Louisiana, in the waning days of my first run for office. I was running to be the next governor of Louisiana.

People told me I was nuts, that I was a fool to run; I had no money, no one knew me, and I was, shall we say, an atypical candidate. When we took our first poll, I clocked in at about 3 percent of the vote. The margin of error for the survey was 4 percent. So it was statistically possible that fewer than zero voters supported me.

With the help of a ragtag group of supporters, I ran an unusual campaign highlighting detailed proposals for sweeping reform of Louisiana's fiscal policy and ethics rules. Against all odds, starting at the back of the pack of seventeen candidates, I won the primary, throwing me into a bruising runoff against Democrat Kathleen Blanco, the state's then-lieutenant governor.

Politics in the Deep South is often described as "Bible belt during the day, knife fighting after dark." That's about right, except more so in Louisiana.

With only a few days left in the contest, my media advisor Brad Todd talked me into staying awake for the final forty-eight hours of the campaign to tour the state in an RV. I will never forgive him for that.

So there we were—me, the staffers who had drawn the short straw on this insane two-day trip, and Republican National Committee Political Director Blaise Hazelwood—at a diner somewhere near Monroe. I worked the tables, talking to the few folks in the restaurant. They were puzzled. Why in the world was I here in the middle of the night? Why wasn't I sleeping? Had I been drinking? What did I think I was accomplishing? Those were all pretty good questions. Basically, they were asking in true Louisiana parlance—Who dat?

Well, I hope to answer that question in this book—not just in terms of my background, but more importantly, in terms of what I stand for, the principles and ideas that I espouse.

The national media tends to misunderstand Louisiana. You will not find a more giving, generous group of people on the face of the earth, and this extends beyond all racial, class, partisan, or religious lines. One has only to look at the response to Hurricane Katrina to understand that. The efforts of folks in north Louisiana to help their kin in the south are legendary. The faith community in particular responded with thousands of acts of sacrifice and giving.

But during my campaign, some national Democrat operatives were hell bent on dividing the people of Louisiana along any lines they could. Just a few weeks earlier, the president of the College Democrats of America, an LSU law school student named Ashley Bell (who was not from Louisiana), wrote a now famous memo to fire up the liberal troops. The memo stated:

> On Saturday—we nominated Kathleen Blanco the Lt. Governor to be our nominee to take on Bush's personal "Do Boy" Bobby Jindal.

Jindal is Arab American and the Republicans token attempt to mend bridges long burnt with the Arab American community. With your help Blanco will be the first women Governor of Louisiana an already rarity for the Deep South.

Arab? Really? And what's with the lousy grammar? I hope this person didn't actually get a law degree.

In my 2007 campaign for governor, the Democratic Party of Louisiana really stepped in it when they ran a TV ad attacking my faith. It was an amateurish and ill-advised advertisement which took my words out of context and attempted to divide the people of Louisiana along denominational lines, and to question my Christianity. The people of Louisiana completely rejected this tactic, and to their credit, many prominent Democratic elected officials publicly renounced the ad and this shameful attempt to attack my faith.

Reporters from Washington and New York often treat me as something exotic: I'm a Christian with Hindu parents; a son of immigrants who was elected a Republican governor of a southern state; a social conservative who graduated from Brown University and Oxford. Reporters often insinuate that because I attended college in the Ivy League and in England, my faith and social conservatism must be an act designed to win votes in the Deep South. When they realize these positions genuinely reflect who I am, they're often astonished.

National reporters have also often said to me, "It must have been so tough for you growing up in the Deep South." To which my response is, "Um . . . no. It was not tough, in fact it was tremendous. I'm a son of the Deep South, so you can keep your prejudices to yourself." Louisiana is my home and I'm proud of it.

I've never had it tough, but my dad did. He grew up poor in India, the only one of nine children to get beyond the fifth grade. For me, growing up middle-class in Louisiana was anything but tough. Compared to my father, I grew up in great riches, because I grew up in America.

In our house, the last thing you wanted to do was to complain about how hard you had it or how tough your life was. That was a mistake you made only once, because it would unleash from my dad a lecture covering everything from poverty, to gratefulness, to his formative years in India, to America's place in world history, to the value of hard work, to the importance of compassion, to the unique promise of the American Dream. Being subjected to that speech kept my brother and me from complaining—ever.

*   *   *

We are all prone to take things for granted—our loved ones, our jobs, our houses, all of it. It's hard not to. But the immigrant viewpoint of my parents really helps put things in perspective. My folks are the most genuinely thankful people you will ever meet.

As Americans, we take many of our freedoms for granted, including our freedom of religion. I am intensely interested in learning about a person's faith, or lack thereof. I think it says a lot about people, about their decision-making process, about how they think, about what drives them.

Everyone has at some point thought about God and matters of faith, some more than others of course. I'll tell you about my own faith journey in the next chapter, but I'll just mention here that I would best be described as an evangelical Catholic. I love the teachings and doctrines of the Catholic Church, and I have tremendous admiration for the zeal of evangelical Protestants. But at the end of the day, it's all about faith, not about religion, not about church, and not about denomination.

Sometimes a little faith can come in quite handy during a campaign. I found that out on a plane during my 2007 campaign for governor.

When you run for statewide office, there is tremendous pressure to be everywhere at once. You travel at all hours of the day and night, using any means you can find; most often by car, sometimes in a campaign bus, and sometimes via plane. But the plane trips are far from glamorous. In this case it was a flight from Shreveport to New Orleans, where I planned to give a speech and then enjoy the rare opportunity to sleep in my own bed. We were on a borrowed six-seater, single engine propeller plane, the kind where everyone wore a headset just so we could communicate with each other over the sound of the engine.

In the front seat next to the pilot was Hal Turner, head of the Louisiana Sheriffs' Association. Imagine the big, imposing, southern sheriff type—that's Hal. He was a big dude in a small plane. In the back with me was Melissa Sellers, our campaign communications director, and Kellie Duhon, our campaign political director.

Five minutes after takeoff on this late afternoon, the pilot, a guy who looked old enough to have bombed Dresden, began fidgeting nervously. He announced on the headphones that there was a problem—we had a bad alternator and were not producing electrical power. In order to preserve what power we had, he was going to shut down our GPS, our turn coordinator, and all other modern means of navigation. We would have no radio at all if we stayed aloft much longer.

At this point, Melissa muttered under her breath, "Holy crap, we are all gonna die." Except she did not say "crap."

The pilot then announced, "Well, we should turn back now and probably land in Shreveport." His tone of voice intimated that this was the only available course of action. This was followed by about fifteen seconds of silence that Melissa and Kellie insist lasted three hours. So I broke the silence.

"Are you sure? How far can we go? Is there any way we can make it to Alexandria?" I thought it was a reasonable question. After all, that would get us halfway home. Besides, we had to land *somewhere*, and it might as well be as close to home as possible. But Melissa thought I was out of my mind (which wasn't an entirely new idea among my staff). Hal shot me a strange, quizzical look. Fortunately, the Sheriffs' Association was supporting my candidacy, so Hal decided to take one for the team and keep his objections to himself.

Meanwhile, the pilot was continuing to play with the instruments, tap on gauges, and fidget with various knobs and buttons in a semi-hurried fashion. We later found out this guy had flown every kind of bird you can imagine, and was exactly the man you want at the helm in this situation.

The pilot then came on and said, "I think I can get you to Alexandria, if I conserve power and use my maps, but there is no way we can make it to New Orleans."

Melissa was now even more convinced we were going to die. She started glaring at me like it was all my fault. But I had a campaign to win, and I needed to get to New Orleans, if not for the event, at least in order to make good on tomorrow's schedule.

I told the pilot, "Okay, let's go for it."

We later learned that at that point Melissa hurriedly tried to get right with God. She began thinking that she should have called her mom more often, and wondering when she had last told her sister she loved her.

After rummaging around the floor through various books and maps, the pilot grabbed a large Atlas-looking book and plopped it on Hal's lap. As a tough-guy sheriff, Hal was pretending to be unfazed by the whole thing. But he later admitted it was just an act.

I tried not to look at Melissa, but when I did, the body language was not good. So here in the front seat we had Hal nervously holding a large map, and this elderly pilot scratching out notes on it with a pencil. In the back you had me reading the newspaper, Melissa preparing to see God, and Kellie desperately wishing for a cigarette.

We were back in the old days at this point, navigating by hand. But judging by the pilot's age, this was nothing new for him. We heard him announce into the radio that we needed to make an emergency landing in Alexandria. It wasn't particularly welcome news when he confessed he was not sure if he could get the landing gear down without electric power.

So I decided to look at my Blackberry and catch up on my reading, a move that infuriated Melissa and didn't sit so well with Kellie, either. Melissa later told us at this point she was contemplating what her funeral would be like. She wrote me a snarky note on her Blackberry, asking if I had a Bible handy or any of "those religious writings from college that got you into political trouble."

Laughing, I reached into my pocket and gave her a rosary. Melissa is not Catholic, but she clutched that rosary with both hands and curled into the fetal position.

The pilot showed me how to operate the manual crank to lower the landing gear. That was really the last straw for both Kellie and Melissa. Fortunately, my help wasn't necessary, and the pilot got the landing gear down with the remaining power.

When we cleared the final tree line, we saw emergency response vehicles with flashing lights along the landing strip, standing ready for what Melissa was sure would be a terrible crash. The pilot turned the radio back on and with the little power left, asked into the radio who the emergency equipment was for.

"It's for you," was the response. Uh-oh.

The pilot, to his great credit, set us down without incident. Melissa began hugging—a lot. First she hugged Kellie, then she hugged Hal, and then me. (I'm not a hugger.) She saved her biggest and longest hug for the pilot. I'm pretty sure she told each of us that she loved us. Then she started round two of hugging.

Our campaign team was comprised of me and a group of Protestants. There were a few other stray Catholics, including my policy director Stephen Waguespack, but not many. Before the crew back at headquarters learned of our ordeal, I fired off an email from my Blackberry that simply read, "Fyi, Melissa is now Catholic." This set off a lot of confusion back at HQ.

Ever interested in press coverage, Melissa later told us in the airport that she was thinking the headlines in the morning papers would carry news of our demise in a plane crash. Jokingly, I told her that the lead story would actually be "Congressman and candidate for Governor dies in plane crash," and that she wouldn't be mentioned until the seventh paragraph. She was not amused.

On a serious note, I did realize in the plane that we were in some trouble, though not as much as Melissa and Kellie believed. I was comforted knowing that when it's your time to go, it's your time to go. Some may see this as a fatalistic attitude, but it really is not at all. I was just aware at that moment of what I try to remember all the time: *God is in control.*

* * *

Having attended Brown University, studied at Oxford, and served in the highest levels of government, I have spent a great deal of time interacting with folks who would be classified as our country's "elites." I've found many of these folks, who predominately reside in the Boston–New York–Washington corridor, harbor a condescending view of people of faith.

Never was this more evident than in the famous slur carried in a front-page *Washington Post* story in the mid-1990s, in which a reporter dismissed evangelical Christians as being "poor, uneducated and easy to command." This is the journalistic equivalent of saying, "If you are a person of faith in America you are, de facto, stupid."

But not to worry, in the ensuing firestorm that writer was forced to clarify his comments by noting that he should have said "most" evangelical Christians are "poor, uneducated and easy to command." Oh. Thanks. I feel so much better now.

The *Post*'s ombudsman later attempted to temper the outrage by explaining that readers needed to realize most journalists don't know any of "these people." Oh. That clears it up.

To this day, it surprises me how little the national press understands about faith. When I was serving in Washington as executive director of the National Bipartisan Commission on the Future of Medicare, I had lunch with a well-known reporter from the *Post* to discuss the Commission's progress. Before we ate she saw me bow my head and say grace, ever so briefly mind you. She immediately asked me if everything was okay. She was startled and fascinated by what I had done. And the fact that it startled her startled me. She was not rude or condescending, and later we became good friends. She just didn't have any frame of reference for a person who would say grace in a public restaurant before lunch.

But some of our top national reporters *are* condescending, and it goes beyond matters of faith. I was at a cocktail party in Washington, D.C. (my first mistake), when a lady I had never met came up to me to apologize. Not for anything she had done, mind you. "I'd just like to apologize to you for all the discrimination you have had to endure," she said.

I was perplexed. She offered condemnation of my home state disguised as an apology. It was classic elitist sentiment.

But for sure, I hear more condescension toward faith than any other topic. For many of our country's elites, faith is something for the uneducated, the uninformed, and the unenlightened. It's something for us to cling to when our plane loses electrical power. It can be charming or quaint, or it can be dangerous, but either way, it's for the weak of mind, for those folks living between the coasts out there in "fly over country" who don't know any better.

I see it in diametrically opposite terms. In my view, true seeking, true intellectual curiosity, and true devotion to logic, science, and the laws of nature lead one invariably to the Creator.

The Washington press has a tough job, and they do some invaluable work, but they're prone to their own biases. This reminds me of a tiresome conversation I've had on many occasions. A journalist based somewhere in the upper east coast or in California will come to interview me for some national publication. He has somehow made it past my communications director, which is an incredible feat, so I have some respect for him right off the bat. He comes having heard rumors that I am well-educated and maybe even halfway smart.

So he invariably starts with the same line of questioning. "How could you, an educated person with a reputation as an intellectual, oppose same sex marriage?... or oppose some forms of stem cell research?... or favor the teaching of 'intelligent design'?... or be a Republican?... or not drink Frappucino?"

I'm always tempted to respond by asking, "How could a person like you possibly have made it onto my calendar?"

When I speak to national reporters, some shoot me a mock sympathetic look, as if to say, "It's okay, I know you can't really believe those things, I know you just have to say that stuff to get elected here in the Deep South." They believe one of two things must be true: either I don't really hold these socially conservative viewpoints, or I'm really not that smart. Oh well, so much for being smart.

I say what I mean and I mean what I say. It's not a political strategy. I'm just one of those people out here in America, desperately "clinging to guns and religion," as the president would say. But the Washington press figures I must be pretty dim, because if I were smart, I'd be a liberal.

Once, during my first campaign, a *New York Times* reporter came to town to interview me. He had zero interest in my background, in any aspect of my campaign, or in anything that was happening in Louisiana. He couldn't care less that I had introduced the most detailed plan ever seen in a Louisiana gubernatorial campaign.

The reporter only wanted to talk about issues that concerned him personally—issues on which he disagreed with me, like same-sex marriage, abortion, and the origins of life. Of course, I have strong views on those topics, but they were not major issues in the campaign, partly because my Democratic opponent held similar conservative views to my own on many of these questions.

Try as I may, I could not interest this guy in the big issues facing Louisiana. The voters focused on matters of taxation, budgets, job creation, and infrastructure, but the reporter was obviously bored with it all.

That night, after the interview, this reporter had dinner with a reporter from another national newspaper at an upscale restaurant in Baton Rouge. This occurred, mind you, back when reporters had decent expense accounts, before the newspaper business hit on hard times.

During dinner, the *Times* reporter hectored his colleague about how she wasn't attacking me enough for my Neanderthal views. He bragged that he was going to just savage Bobby Jindal in his article. He had it all planned out, even though he had more interviews to complete the next day, after which he was going to file a story that would be a leftist rant of the highest order.

But there was one problem: his waiter, who overheard his conversation, was a supporter of mine. So imagine the reporter's surprise when he showed up the next day to interview outgoing Republican governor Mike Foster. One of Foster's staffers pulled the reporter aside and repeated much of the dinner conversation back to him. The blood drained from the reporter's face, leaving it a shade of white considerably lighter than the parchment you are now reading.

Suffice it to say, after this confrontation, the reporter quickly left town, and when his article appeared it was actually pretty mild. He even later called the office to sort of apologize and figure out if we were going to complain to his editor. We did not.

Let this be a lesson to all reporters travelling to Louisiana; I have friends everywhere.

Seriously, to be fair, there are plenty of principled, objective journalists. But there are fewer than there used to be. (Of course, they might fire back by arguing there are a lot fewer honest politicians than there used to be. Fair point.)

Despite the kinds of run-ins I've described here, I've always had a pretty decent relationship with the press. I've held quite a few posts in government, and in each instance I've found that honesty and candor go a long way with most reporters. Over time you learn who the biased reporters are and you try to steer around them, which of course they don't like.

Some have said I've actually enjoyed pretty sympathetic press coverage over the years. Well, maybe so, but there was this one incident that didn't go so well.

I was selected to give the Republican response to President Obama's first speech to Congress in February 2009, a time when the president was still extremely popular. Republican leaders in Washington knew me or had read good things about me, so they thought I would be a good choice to give the Republican Party response.

Turns out they were wrong. I blew it.

Truth be told, even though I've run for Congress twice, run for governor twice, and served in various high profile government positions, I have never mastered the teleprompter—and that is an understatement. In fact, I hate the teleprompter. And as the country found out that night, the teleprompter hates me, too.

So here you have me, a guy who is "teleprompter challenged," versus the king of the teleprompter. Bad match up. My delivery was just awful. Even though it's never been done before, I should have just winged the response.

The press savaged my performance. I won't repeat all their snarky comments, because this is my book and I'm the one who gets to make the snarky comments here. Several reporters tried to give me an out, by asking who wrote the speech and whether I had a speech coach. That last one cracked me up. Did I have a speech coach? You're kidding, right?

The bottom line is this: it was my speech, I delivered it poorly, and I take full responsibility for it. When you screw up, it's time to man up.

Interestingly, many people who read the speech, but did not see it, thought it was great. I stand by the content of the speech—I just should have hired Russell Crowe to deliver it. I'm simply not very good at the "showman" side of politics.

Reading the speech now is kind of eerie. Delivered barely a month after Obama's inauguration, the speech warned against expanding government and against piling up debt through excessive spending. Less than two years later, the Obama administration and its Democratic allies in Congress have spent more money, wracked up more debt, and expanded government more than I ever thought possible.

CHAPTER 3

YELLOW PAGES

I came to America as a pre-existing condition. Mom had won a place at Louisiana State University's graduate school. My dad, newly arrived in America with mom and not knowing a soul, had to find a job. So he sat down at the kitchen table in early 1971 and opened up the yellow pages. Starting with the A's, he made cold calls to local businesses in his heavily accented English, eventually landing a job offer at a railroad. When he confessed to the business owner that he didn't have a car yet, in true Louisiana hospitality, the man offered to have co-workers pick him up and take him home every day. Welcome to America.

For a young couple arriving in the United States from halfway around the world, it must have been a frightening and exhilarating experience. My dad often told me, "Son, Americans can do anything." That was America's promise—and its challenge: nothing was impossible if you were willing to work hard.

My father grew up in Khanpur, a rural village in the Punjab region of India, the middle child of nine, the son of a small shopkeeper who sold medical supplies and an odd assortment of other goods. Money was tight because most people who bought things from my grandfather did so on credit or through barter. My dad grew up in a home without running water or electricity. Although he came from uneducated parents, he developed an unwavering commitment to education, eventually earning a degree in civil engineering.

My mom came from a middle-class Indian home, so she had it a little better. Her father was a banker. It may sound good, but by American standards it was a simple life. Her parents were more educated and necessities were more available, but my mother dreamt of America, the proverbial land of opportunity.

One day opportunity knocked for my parents. My father had a great job in India, but my pregnant mother was offered a scholarship to complete a graduate degree in nuclear physics at LSU. She was excited, but nervous too, because it meant leaving behind family and security for a new life in America. Finally, she reluctantly wrote to LSU explaining that she couldn't accept the scholarship because she was pregnant. LSU wrote back and promised her a month off for childbirth if she changed her mind. LSU was so accommodating, and the opportunity to come to America so thrilling, that my parents accepted. (For this reason alone, I'm an LSU Tiger fan for life!) So my parents stepped out on faith, secured green cards, packed up a few suitcases, said their goodbyes, and took off for this exotic new place called Baton Rouge, Louisiana.

They moved into student housing and quickly discovered what most Americans know: health insurance can be expensive and frustrating. They were informed that their insurance plan would not cover my mother's pregnancy. In short, I came into this world as a "preexisting condition." In healthcare, like every other facet of life, it was important for my dad to be self-reliant; he would never ask anyone for charity or help. So he went to the doctor shortly before my birth and set up an installment plan to pay the bill. When he explained to me later how he paid for my birth, I asked him, "What would have happened if you had missed a payment on me? Would they repossess?"

"Trust me," he said dryly. "If that was an option, we would have skipped a payment."

My father had grown up around extreme poverty; he'd witnessed people starving to death and dying from easily curable illnesses. He didn't take healthcare or housing or even food for granted. He lived frugally, and I remember he once told me and my younger brother Nikesh, "If there is only enough food for some of us, we'll always feed you first." As a kid in middle-class America, with plenty all around, this seemed a bizarre thing to say.

For my dad, it was all about survival. While we were never poor growing up, we were taught to make the most of every dollar. When I was small, I would stuff change into my piggy bank. To my father this made no sense. "The money should go into the bank and earn interest," he would say. Dad was always practical.

When I was four, I announced to my preschool class and anyone who would listen that my new name was "Bobby" (which I took from my favorite character on *The Brady Bunch*). My parents were puzzled. They'd already given me a name, Piyush, but Bobby stuck, and it's a testament to my parents that they never felt the nickname was somehow a rejection of our heritage. In fact, they began calling me "Bobby," too.

Nicknames are pretty common here in Louisiana. You give people nicknames and they become comfortable and familiar, like an old pair of jeans. But you have to be careful that nicknames don't take on a life of their own. We call one of our sons Boudreaux because when he was an infant we applied a lot of "Boudreaux's Butt Paste" to you-know-where.

(It's a Louisiana thing, you might not understand.) But do we really want him having to explain how he earned the name? I don't think so.

My parents managed to walk the tightrope that many immigrants face: teaching their kids about their ancestral home while embracing all that is America. While some immigrant families have kept one foot firmly planted in the "home country," my parents always raised us from the earliest days to think of ourselves not as hyphenated Americans, but simply as Americans. I don't recall them ever referring to India as "home." Louisiana was home. I remember seeing other immigrant families where the kids spent almost all their free time with people of the same background. But my parents were always going to crawfish boils and cookouts.

One of the rites of passage for kids in Baton Rouge was attending summer camp. Mom and Dad sent us to every one imaginable, partly just to get us out of the house. They were confident enough in their Hindu identity to send us to camps organized by local churches. One summer my mom enrolled me in Camp Reznikoff, a Jewish summer camp. Being the only tan-skinned gentile in the group, I decided to throw my hat in the ring when it came time to elect a group president. I picked the prettiest counselor as my campaign manager and offered free candy to anyone who would vote for me. The strategy worked and I won. (Some say I learned the essentials of Louisiana politics early.) It never would have occurred to me that I might be rejected because I was a little different from the other kids. My parents didn't raise me to think that way.

I generally avoided trouble as a kid, but like all kids, I had my moments. In high school, growing up in a college town, there was always the allure of heading off with the college crowd. But the biggest pull was New Orleans, the big city with the big reputation only one hour down the highway. We knew it was the ultimate party town and sometimes we'd take off with friends for a Saturday trip. One mom tried to scare us. "Now don't get into trouble boys, because in New Orleans they don't put you *in* the jail—they put you *under* it." That only made it all the more exciting, walking down Bourbon Street in the French Quarter and sneaking into clubs to listen to great music. It was all pretty harmless fun. Some people might not think of New Orleans as wholesome, but I have to say, I enjoyed it—and I never got arrested, never experimented with drugs, and generally lived a life that was like *Leave It to Beaver* with a Louisiana twist.

My brother and I held summer jobs as soon as we were old enough. To raise money for school activities I sold concessions at the LSU Tiger football games. We'd get to the stadium early and be there until midnight cleaning up. I can't say it was the most fun I ever had, but it was, as they say, a learning experience—especially about the ingenious ways people can sneak alcohol into a sporting event.

From my mom and dad, I learned that hard work is a virtue—it was one they practiced every day—and so was achievement. One of my father's worst insults was to say that someone "had great potential." It meant you weren't working hard enough. If you brought home a 95 on a test, he wanted to know why it wasn't a 100. Some subjects came easily to me and my brother, but we quickly learned that my dad wasn't impressed if we only had to study for an hour to ace a test. Hard work had value in itself, and I discovered from him that the harder you work at something the easier it becomes.

* * *

One thing I worked on unbeknownst to my parents—at least initially—was faith. It came fully into the open in shocking circumstances:

I was lying in a hospital bed after I totaled my dad's Toyota Corolla, which I had borrowed.

My head had crashed through the driver's side window, but at the time I was more worried about the damage to the car than to my health. I had argued with my parents to get a driver's license at a young age, and now dad's new car was totaled. I had pestered the ambulance driver and emergency room doctor for a damage report on the car; I wanted to repair the damage before my dad saw it.

Naturally, my parents couldn't have cared less about the car's condition. They were concerned about me. They had visited the accident scene on the way to the hospital, seen the blood, and feared the worst. Now, after the initial shock of the accident had worn off, my mom stood by the bed and asked me a question that put me in a painful spot: "Which God do you have to thank for your safety, Bobby?"

Growing up I was taught to pray and believe in an all-powerful God who created the universe and was present and active in our daily lives. My parents were, and remain to this day, devout Hindus. There was no Hindu temple in Baton Rouge at the time, but we had a prayer altar in our home. My younger brother Nikesh and I would say our prayers there every night—it didn't matter how tired we were. We prayed, as kids are apt to, "Dear God, if you will just give me an A in history, I'll be good to my little brother," or, "If you will just give me one more toy, I won't ask you for anything else." To us, God was like Santa Claus. I believed in and respected God, but prayer was a transaction—"I'll be good and you'll give me what I want."

But the values I learned from my Hindu parents ran deep: honesty, respect for elders, hard work, modesty, reverence, the importance of family—traditional Hindu values that meshed quite well with

Louisiana's traditional Bible Belt beliefs. I never felt culturally differ-ent from your typical Baton Rouge kid.

My parents naturally assumed I would remain a Hindu and pass the faith on to the next generation. By the time of the accident, however, my mom and dad knew I was investigating Christianity. And now, here I was, a dutiful son, about to offer an answer that would cause considerable pain to my family.

The path that brought me to that point spiritually was unique in many ways. One day, riding the bus to middle school, my best friend Kent sat down next to me. Kent was the kind of kid who got picked first for baseball and football. And in addition to being a great athlete, he was a cool guy. Everyone wanted to be his best friend, but he was *my* best friend. On this particular day he said something that struck me as very odd.

"Bobby," he said, "I sure do feel sorry for you."

I had no idea what he was talking about. He could see my confu-sion, so he continued. "I feel sorry for you because when my family and I go to heaven, I'm going to miss you when you're not there." Billy Graham he was not.

I was a pre-teen at the time, and I thought he was crazy. Who would ever say such an odd thing? I quickly changed the subject, but the conversation jolted me for a few days. Then I forgot about it, until Christmas.

In addition to his other fine qualities, Kent was one of those thoughtful, generous people who bought the best gifts for his friends. So when it was time to open his Christmas present, I ripped off the paper in great anticipation. My heart quickly sank when I opened the box and found a book inside.

"This can't be the real gift," I thought. I actually remember flipping through the pages to see if there was any money inside, and being utterly disappointed that there was none. The more I studied the "gift," the more my disappointment grew. It was not even an interesting book; it was a Bible. The practicality I inherited from my dad kicked in: *Who spends good money buying somebody a Bible?* And, *Why buy a Bible when you can get one free in any hotel room?* Sure, you might get in trouble for stealing towels. But the Bible? No way.

I was even more disappointed when I noticed that on the front cover in gold letters were the words: "Bobby Jindal." "Great!" I thought. "I can't even return it or give it to somebody else."

My journey to Christianity accelerated at the end of my sophomore year in high school when my grandfather died suddenly of a stroke. I had spent happy days visiting him in India, riding on his shoulders as a young boy, and even though he never came to America, he was a big figure in my life. His death marked the first time I had lost somebody I loved. I felt so cheated that I did not get a chance to say good-bye or tell him that I loved him. I was mad that I had wasted so much time while he was still alive, and worried if I would ever see him again. His death also set my mind racing about the biggest questions in our lives: Why are we here? Do our lives have a purpose? Does some part of us live on after death?

The idea of God as Santa Claus no longer satisfied me. Looking for answers, I read Hindu texts and talked to pastors of several different faiths. I pushed my parents to buy a copy of the *Bhagavad Gita*, one of the most important Hindu scriptures, and read all 700 verses. Then I dug out from my closet the unread Bible Kent had given me. I didn't know how my parents would react to my reading the Bible, so I found a cozy spot in the back of the closet and, armed with a flashlight, I read from Genesis through to the end. At one point, I bought *Cliff's Notes to the Bible*, to help me make sense of it. I spent countless hours sitting in that closet, but in the end I had no epiphany. I prayed desperately, promising God that if He told me He existed and how to worship Him, I would consider myself blessed beyond belief and would not ask for anything else.

God used what was most important to me to get my attention back on Him. I was a normal teenage boy, so he used a teenage high school girl to get my attention.

During my junior year in high school, while attending a math tournament in New Orleans (stop snickering), I spotted Kathy. I had a crush on her, but had never mustered the nerve to say hello. This time I did, and we ended up going to a dance and having a great time. That night we stood on the top floor of the Hyatt Hotel in New Orleans and tossed coins down into the water fountain. Things were going great. Here was this pretty girl and she was interested in me! Then I asked her a simple question that changed everything.

"What do you want to do after school?"

Now, most of my friends in Baton Rouge wanted to be doctors, or football players, or teachers, or nurses; a few might have wanted to be rock stars. But she gave me an answer I had never heard. "I want to become a Supreme Court Justice," she said, "because I want to save innocent lives."

Where'd this come from? I thought to myself. And yet, I was struck by her answer. Saving the unborn gave her a purpose in life, something that was missing from mine.

Kathy was Catholic, and out of curiosity I attended Catholic Mass with her. I didn't want my parents to know, so I was probably the only teenager in Baton Rouge who told his parents he was going to a party so he could sneak off to church. Here too, as with my first tussle with the Bible, I had no profound spiritual awakening. If anything, I was confused by the kneeling, standing, praying, and mumbled words of the priest over the altar.

I bombarded friends and pastors with questions. I read classics of Christian apologetics, books about Biblical archeology, and books like *Evidence That Demands a Verdict.* My mind kept whirring. I wanted to know how the Church worked and how decisions were made. I asked a Catholic layman, "How does one get elected Pope?" "Bobby," he replied, "don't become Catholic because you think you're going to be Pope." Perhaps he knew me too well.

My constant queries were not always welcomed. At one point a pastor pulled a friend aside and said, "Look, Bobby is just not going to become a Christian. It's not going to happen. He's so stubborn. He's got so many doubts."

My questions continued until Kent (who had given me that Bible I read in my closet), invited me to hear him sing in a church musical at Chapel on the Campus, a nondenominational church at LSU. In the middle of the performance, they showed a simple black and white film about the crucifixion. I had intensely studied that momentous event, yet watching that film I suddenly realized that Christ was on the cross because of me—my sins—what I had done, what I had failed to do. This was my epiphany. He didn't die for billions, which was so abstract, but because of me. Suddenly, God was tangible. Everything instantly came into focus. An historical moment in the Bible became a living reality. Christ had died for me, and how arrogant was I to be anywhere but on my knees worshipping Him? I don't know why God chose that moment to reveal Himself to me, but I remember exactly when it happened.

I started reading the Bible with Todd Hinkie, a youth pastor, and I realized, under his guidance, that it was not just a book of stories and obscure genealogies and laws, but a series of personal letters from God slowly revealing himself to man, to me. I spent hours in fervent prayer, repentant and grateful. In the summer of 1987 I knelt in prayer and accepted Christ as my Savior.

But for a year I postponed telling my parents. The moment of truth came after the car accident, when my mother questioned which God had saved me.

I prepared myself for the worst. I was a senior in high school and I had been accepted early admission to a unique pre-med program at Brown University; now I feared my parents wouldn't pay my tuition. I thought they might kick me out of the house. I had even quietly secured a scholarship and a job at LSU just in case.

I told the truth, and as I expected, my answer set off an emotional bomb in the family. My parents blamed themselves for being bad parents, and blamed me for being a bad son, and then blamed Christian evangelicals for, well, practicing evangelism.

My father had practical worries. Given the poverty he had seen growing up, he measured success in material terms. He lived by the idea, expressed by Maxim Gorky, that no man could consider his life worthy unless his children surpassed his abilities and achievements. Spiritual interests, particularly something new like Christianity, were a distraction or a diversion from material success. My mom worried that I might have been manipulated, that I might be the victim of a smooth-talking, corrupt televangelist, or that I might be joining some cult.

Many Christians, born and raised in Christian families, take their faith for granted. For me it was a hard-won treasure, the result of a painful and deliberate process of accepting the truth of Christ. If

Christianity is worth risking family and friends for, it is worth practicing every day, whether convenient or not.

My path to Christianity was an intellectual journey followed by a leap of faith. It took me years, and at the end of it I concluded that the historical evidence for Christianity was overwhelming: Jesus had walked the earth and had performed amazing miracles in front of thousands of people. He claimed to be the Son of God, rose from the dead in front of witnesses, and His apostles willingly gave their lives for Him because they were certain of His truth.

That struck me as reliable history. But I also discovered that you can't read yourself into faith. God is thankfully too big, too amazing to be fully comprehended by the human mind. That's why, ultimately, you have to make the leap of faith. You need to trust God and accept Him, including all the mysteries.

My parents eventually accepted my conversion to Christianity. Looking back now, I can see they initially felt I was rejecting them. When they realized I still loved them, and respected and honored them and our heritage, they relaxed. They also discovered it was not just a fad, and that I still embraced the same values they had taught me as a child. Our relationship benefitted from the fact that my parents' Hinduism proclaims there are multiple paths to God, and that there is but one God. It would have been harder for my parents if I had told them I was an atheist. When my children were baptized into the Catholic faith, which is where my spiritual journey ultimately led, my parents were on hand to celebrate the good news.

*   *   *

For my father, my requisite career path was pretty simple, reflecting the deprivations he had seen in his early life. "Son, you can grow up and become any kind of doctor you want," he told me. So when I enrolled at Brown in fall 1988, my course of study was clear. I was accepted in the university's PLME program, which offered automatic admission to Brown's medical school. In my mind I was on a fast track to becoming a surgeon.

Providence, Rhode Island, was very different from the laid-back southern culture I had known in Louisiana, and Brown was especially distinct. I assumed that many of my Ivy League schoolmates would be better educated than I was—they came, many of them, from elite Northeastern prep schools—but I soon found that a Baton Rouge education could hold its own. What I wasn't prepared for was the rabid "political correctness" of campus life. This was a campus where the College Democrats were considered the *conservatives*.

A few weeks into my freshman year (oops, at Brown you didn't use the term fresh*man*—that would be sexist) our resident advisor (who actually became a good friend) took me aside. She told me I was caus-ing great offense because, as she said, "You're holding the doors for the female students. And you need to call them *women*, not *ladies* or girls." (Actually she would spell it *womyn* because to spell the word wo*men* would be sexist, too.) She went on for about ten minutes, telling me exasperatedly, "Look, Bobby, this is not how people act up here." I glanced over at some of my dorm-mates and started to grin. *Oh, I get it. They're teasing me. This is hilarious.* But she continued with such earnestness that I realized she was dead serious. I sat there for a moment dumbfounded. "But that's how I've been raised," I finally exclaimed. "That's who I am."

I rebelled against Brown's insistence on politically correct unifor-mity. I refused to attend a mandatory new student orientation pro-gram in which, in the name of tolerance, straight men were asked to take on the identity of gay men. When the resident advisor reminded me the session was mandatory, I stood firm. "I'm not going. You can send my dad's tuition money back, but I'm not going."

Early in my first semester, Rory Kennedy, daughter of Robert Kennedy, called my dorm looking for my roommate, who was a leader in the College Democrats. When I told her he wasn't there, she said, "I was calling him to see if he wanted to go to a protest. You want to go instead?"

"Really?" I asked. "What are you protesting?" I thought it would be something serious, maybe apartheid or some other human rights issue, or even nuclear power.

"Fruit," she said. "We're protesting against fruit. We don't want people to eat grapes." I later learned the protest had something to do with Cesar Chavez, pesticides, and the United Farm Workers of America. But at that moment, it struck me as absurd. You already had other groups on campus protesting veal and red meat. Now they were protesting fruit. We had all the basic food groups covered.

"Well, in my family, we like to eat grapes," I said. "Red ones, green ones, we like them for lunch and dinner. We like all kinds of fruits. Vegetables, too." Not finding this very funny, she asked me to leave a message for a roommate. I was never invited to attend a protest rally again.

I had never been a terribly political person in high school. Sure, I watched the news and knew who was running for president. But at Brown everything was politicized to the point of absurdity—except to the folks at Brown, I was the absurd one. I was often told, "You are the first pro-life person I have ever met." I could have kept my head down and my mouth shut, but that was not my nature. Instead, I spoke up for ideas that were incredibly unpopular with my fellow students. I realized that my own beliefs were conservative, and Brown forced me to think about *why* I was a conservative.

I worked hard at Brown. I was a biology major taking twenty hours every semester, rather than the normal load of sixteen. The plan was to save money and graduate a semester early, which I did. But even with my heavy class load I was active in the College Republicans, Campus Crusade for Christ, and Intervarsity Fellowship.

Years after I left Brown, I was a guest instructor at Harvard's Kennedy School of Government. I remember once discussing diversity and pluralism at a luncheon with Harvard president Larry Summers, former Minnesota governor Jesse Ventura, and an editor from the *Washington Post*. I asked Summers, "Does it bother you that you don't have a diversity of political views in your student body and faculty? You talk about the need for racial diversity, but what about philosophical diversity? Why are conservatives underrepresented?" His answer shocked me. "You know, the reality is that many evangelical Christian families who vote conservatively don't want their kids here," he said. Then he added, "And that's probably good for them and good for us."

Imagine if he had uttered the same thing about blacks or Jews or Muslims. Perhaps even more amazing, there was no dissent in the room. No one seemed to note the irony that Harvard had been founded primarily as a Christian seminary.

Summers deserves credit for honestly expressing what many other elite academics think. He was not being malicious or combative. And I certainly do not favor affirmative action for conservatives. But there is a definite disconnect between our elite institutions, which have become liberal cocoons, and the values held by most Americans.

Still, I never regretted my three and a half years at Brown. There is truth to the old Biblical saying that iron sharpens iron. At Brown I heard some of the best, most articulate and most intelligent arguments against everything I believed in; and I found that at the end of the day, I could hold my own. In the Bible we are taught to be salt and light in the world. But you've got to be in the world to make that happen.

After Brown I hoped to go to Harvard medical school. When I was accepted I was genuinely thrilled, but I went through the application process at several other schools just in case. One was Johns Hopkins, where I was required to sit down for an interview. My interviewer didn't ask about my grades or transcripts. Instead she remarked, "I hope you're not one of those crazy pro-life Catholics." She must have looked at my volunteer activities and noticed I had been involved with several Christian ministries.

She spent the entire interview grilling me on my personal views and faith. If I had been a devout Muslim or of any other faith, this would have been considered highly inappropriate, but campus liberals seem to think Christians are fair game. Later, during my exit interview at Brown, I told them about my grilling at Johns Hopkins. The Brown administrator sided with the interviewer, though the dean was concil-iatory. "Well, there's nothing wrong with being a Christian, I just don't want you to be one of those *crazy* Christians."

*   *   *

Then something happened that changed the course of my life. I was offered a Rhodes Scholarship to attend Oxford University. When I broke the news to my dad, he asked, "Do you need to go?" He saw the scholarship as an unnecessary delay on my path to medical school. "Trust me, dad, this is a good thing," I told him.

The intellectual climate at Oxford was similar to that of Brown. The vast majority of Rhodes Scholars were politically liberal. Indeed, of the thirty-two from the United States that year, I was the only one to publicly admit not voting for Bill Clinton. The students at Oxford were amazingly bright, but often they were also amazingly ignorant of our Judeo-Christian heritage. I met an intelligent woman who had gone to Harvard who pulled me aside and asked me, "Who was St. Paul and why is he so important? And what is the difference between the Old and New Testament?" I was dumbfounded, wondering how someone educated at the best schools in the world could know so little about the fundamentals of Western civilization. When I had been interviewed for the Rhodes Scholarship, they had asked me detailed questions about the Muslim faith, who Mohammed was, and when the Koran was written. I didn't have to believe these things, but I was expected at least to know about them.

One of my courses at Oxford was a class on justice taught by Ronald Dworkin. When I enrolled I knew nothing about him. On the first day he told us the first half of the class would be lectures and the second half would be student presentations. He asked for volunteers and I raised my hand. "Okay, good," he said, pointing at me. "You can go first." After the class broke up I went to the library and read everything I could by him. To my surprise I discovered he was one of the most prominent political theorists in the world. I also found I disagreed with almost everything he wrote. *Great*, I thought. *I'm going to have to stand there and tell a world-famous political theorist why he's wrong*. But that is precisely what I did.

Given my interest in medicine, I focused my presentation on why healthcare could not be addressed properly by modern liberalism, but only by the Judeo-Christian tradition that affirms human dignity. When I finished, the other students were in a state of shocked silence.

Instead of being offended or threatened, Dworkin invited me to lunch to discuss the issues at length. It turned out he was writing a book on healthcare and asked me to help him. It was a great learning experience, and while we never managed to agree on the issue, it was a wonderful opportunity to debate important ideas and policies, policies I'm still dealing with today.

After spending two years at Oxford studying how a just society should provide healthcare, I found myself less interested in practicing medicine and more interested in making the system work better for the patient. My interests had shifted to policy, but I still told myself, and my parents, that my eventual goal was to be a neurosurgeon.

But when I had a chance to do something different, I took it. McKinsey, a global management consulting firm, was looking to recruit business associates from unconventional, non-business backgrounds. I went along with some buddies to an interview. And why not? If you made it to the second round they put you up in London at this incredible hotel. If you made it to the third round they flew you back to the United States for free.

Despite my cavalier attitude, I made it to round three. For my free trip home, I chose to go to Washington, D.C., because that was where I had the most friends. I was told to pick a different location because McKinsey's D.C. office didn't like doing non-traditional hires. But I stuck to my choice; and I told them up front I only intended to work as a consultant for a short while before I went to med school. To its credit, McKinsey hires a lot of people who don't want to be consultants long-term; the company trusts that if it can give you interesting, exciting work with other smart, motivated people, you might decide to stay. I gave myself a two-year time limit.

I made a conscious decision to learn about business and corporate management—and this was the place to do it. McKinsey consultants Tom Peters and Robert Waterman had practically defined innovative corporate management for two decades in their influential best-selling book, *In Search of Excellence.*

I worked with senior management on interesting, complex cases of highly successful companies. My previous experience had been academic—the worst thing that could happen was that I might get a bad grade. At McKinsey I applied my analytical skills to real-world problems involving the livelihoods of thousands of people. It was intense but rewarding work, as we built teams with corporate employees and helped them solve problems.

McKinsey encouraged us to tell clients that if we were not adding tangible value to the company they should fire us. We were not hired to be yes-men and women. I remember one time we were working directly with a big client, the CEO of a Fortune 500 company. Our team worked like crazy, including weekends, holidays, and even vacations. In return our director took us out sailing and kept us well-fed, even though my team perceived that the client wasn't taking our advice. I wasn't the most senior person on the team, but during a meeting with the client, I told him directly that I didn't think we were adding value, because the company was ignoring our advice.

My director on this project later called us into his office. I told him what had happened. My teammates, however, didn't back me up. I was sure I was done with McKinsey. But then I got a voicemail from the director. He said he was proud of me; I had done exactly the right thing. That's what you were supposed to do—speak up.

I was only at McKinsey for about eighteen months, but a lot of things I believed to be true about the corporate world were reinforced during my time there. I learned the difference between working hard and working smart, that what matters is results; I learned the importance of hiring rising stars, even if you might not keep them long; I learned that "personnel is policy"; and I learned to avoid micromanagement. I was also beginning to realize that I was going to have to make an important decision in my life: did I want to help hundreds of people directly and personally by being a doctor, or thousands of people indirectly through public service?

CHAPTER 4

TO EDUCATE A CHILD

I never made it to med school, but I've had plenty of opportunities to diagnose problems. At age twenty-seven, I was asked to head the University of Louisiana system, which oversees eight universities. It is the sixteenth largest system of higher education in the country.

Education has always been important to me because I had the powerful example of my father. He grew up in a home with no electricity or running water, and his parents had little formal education and spoke no English. So when at age six it was time for my dad to go to school, it was all up to his own initiative. There was no parent-teacher meeting or school bus to pick him up. His parents didn't deter him, but they didn't encourage him either.

You often hear stories about how someone's mom or dad had to walk six miles to school, uphill both ways. Well, in my father's case that was largely true. He did walk six miles a day roundtrip from his house to a small village school in northern India, and he often had to do his homework by lamplight. He was the only one of nine kids to get past the fifth grade.

The Indian education system was brutal. Every step of the way they would weed out average or below-average students, because there were a lot more students than available slots. And yet this young boy in Khanpur, carrying books from his house to a small village school, would go on to earn a degree in civil engineering.

So you can imagine that when I was growing up, there was no tolerance for complaining about school, teachers, or homework—and this is still my attitude toward education today. Parents and kids who complain about too much homework, rigorous standards, and testing for results need to realize that high expectations, while sometimes challenging, are important. We need to set meaningful expectations for the students, parents, and even the adults in the school system.

My parents made a lot of sacrifices to ensure I got a good education. By the time I was four, they were taking a portion of their modest salaries and paying tuition for me to attend Runnels, a small private school in Baton Rouge. (At that time public schools were generally not offering pre-K or any other classes for four-year-olds. After the fourth grade, I was enrolled in public schools.) Runnels, where I spent the first five years of my schooling, was more than a school; it was a community. It had a mix of students, including white, Asian, black, disabled, etc. The teachers sent their children there, and they would discipline their own kids the same way they would discipline any student. What made Runnels great was excellent teachers, an orderly classroom, and parents who cared deeply about their children's education.

Some of those teachers profoundly affected my life and the lives of many others. Mrs. Couvillion, who taught reading, was one of the toughest teachers we had. We would sit on a "magic carpet" in her class and read all sorts of books. Most of my friends didn't like her because she was demanding and set high standards, but I enjoyed the challenge. She was also popular with all the parents because of the results they saw when their kids took her class. It didn't occur to any of those parents to indulge their children's gripes about the hard work she demanded or the high standards she established.

Once we had a read-a-thon in which you had to find sponsors to pay you for each book you read, and the students who raised the most money won a prize. Ignited by Mrs. Couvillion's inspiration, I read fifty-five books before my dad finally told me to stop. "Wait a minute, how much money do I have to give?" he asked. "No, no, stop reading. That's enough. I'll go buy you a prize instead."

Mrs. Williams was my science teacher. I met her for the first time when I was dropped off at her house because she had offered to drive me to school. She was running after one of her sons with a shoe in her hand. I don't know what she did when she caught him—but it scared me to death. I decided then and there I would never misbehave in her class. Since our small school didn't have lab equipment or expensive science displays, Mrs. Williams would bring the body parts of real animals in bags to class to teach us about biology. (I think her husband was a hunter—at least I hope so.) She was smart, passionate about science, and had a great knack for creating a fun learning environment. Her love of biology became my love of biology. The moral of the story is simple: good schools start with teachers who inspire students and create expectations that challenge them.

Many of us have wonderful recollections of the neighborhood school that was a hub of community life. The school was just that: a community of teachers, parents, and administrators working together. It's a shame, but we seem to have lost some of that in America today. In my own family, we try to uphold my dad's commitment to education. I have dedicated much of my public life to improving schools in

Louisiana. And my wife Supriya, who is a chemical engineer, has established a non-profit foundation to encourage the teaching of science and math in Louisiana. She visits classrooms across the state to demonstrate science experiments to illustrate the role that math and science play in our daily lives, and to deliver interactive whiteboards and laptops purchased with private dollars.

When I took over the University of Louisiana system, I was struck by how many in the education establishment were trying hard, but were simply setting the wrong goals. The state was funding universities according to how big their enrollment was, rather than their success in educating students. In other words, the system was rewarding universities for recruiting students, but not for keeping them in school. Just as football teams don't win championships on draft day, colleges shouldn't declare victory on the first day of class. Victory is only achieved when a student graduates and begins helping to drive our economic future.

As governor I'm fighting to drive home a new priority for Louisiana colleges. It's a novel concept that will rock the educational world: graduate the kids you enroll. Pretty crazy, huh? Louisiana has the second lowest graduation rate in the South—less than 40 percent. We would never accept having the second worst football team in the South, and we shouldn't tolerate the second lowest graduation rate either.

Our reforms work like this: we're asking state colleges to enter into six-year contracts. The contracts require these schools to retain and graduate their students at a higher rate, provide a rigorous education, eliminate low-performing programs, and do a better job transitioning students from two-year to four-year schools and from four-year schools to a job. In return for accepting accountability, we grant the schools more financial flexibility and operational autonomy.

It's all driven by a simple premise: every time a school fails to graduate one of its students, it hurts the economy and sends a person into the job market with nothing more than accumulated debt and a lack of education and training. And every time we graduate a kid with a degree that doesn't actually qualify him for a job, we do much the same thing. We need to provide students with the training they need to have productive careers.

Sure, my dad graduated in civil engineering because he was good at math, but more importantly, he thought people would pay him to design things, and he thought his family would appreciate his having a paycheck and providing a roof over their heads. For him, education was a means to achieve mobility and independence, to get ahead, and to care for his family.

What makes for a good education is no secret: motivated teachers, competition, measurable results, supportive parents, classroom discipline, and the right incentives. Unfortunately, the higher education system often encourages and rewards the exact opposite of what students need to succeed and what our economy needs to grow and expand. Moreover, this establishment often just flat-out resists change, especially when suggestions come from an "outsider."

When I headed the University of Louisiana system, I remember a faculty senate president pulling me aside to complain that I was looking at education all wrong, because I was emphasizing the importance of education in developing our economy. I was ignoring the intrinsic importance of having a liberal arts education, he said. (I guess his theory was that you can't have the proverbial starving artist without the starving part—though I am not sure the hungry artists out there would agree.) Now, of course we should cherish education for the well-rounded value it brings to our lives, even if it doesn't always provide a specific economic benefit. But in terms of public policy, when we're spending taxpayer money on education, it makes sense that we direct it in ways that will help our economy grow.

The education establishment cannot rightly expect us to take dollars from taxpayers, who often earn less than the average college professor, and use that money to subsidize courses or research on professors' esoteric pet topics. The world does not need another scholarly article on something random like "The Embedding of Economic Pressures and Gender Ideals in Postsocialist International Matchmaking."[1] Taxpayers need to know that investing in education has a real purpose—that it will create better lives and more job opportunities for their children and grandchildren.

Anyone looking to reform our education system inevitably runs up against the education establishment, which is utterly opposed to prioritizing how schools and teachers perform. Because the establishment simply does not want to be held accountable, they hide behind the students, claiming some kids just can't learn, or that other teachers, classes, or schools are not preparing them for success before they arrive on a college campus. This attitude of blaming everyone else for not properly educating our kids is the establishment's version of "the dog ate my homework" excuse. Too many of these education bureaucrats are more focused on protecting their own jobs and benefits, not looking after the interests of our children.

With that priority, it's not surprising the education establishment often dismisses the legitimate concerns of parents. In the public school system, when parents are not empowered with choices, officials don't really need to listen to them. In a 1996 court case in Franklin County, Ohio, involving a parental choice initiative, an attorney for the American Federation of Teachers actually called parents "inconsequential conduits."[2] I've been called worse in my life, but that kind of arrogant disdain for parents makes my blood boil. And it reflects the attitudes of too many education professionals and bureaucrats who believe everything would be perfect if we would just stay out of their way.

Even if you don't have children in the school system, education should still matter to you. The primary building blocks of the U.S. economy are the skills and capabilities of our people. For more than two centuries, education has been the engine that has propelled us to greatness, but now we are sputtering. A strong country simply can't be sustained without a strong education system.

With our current dysfunctional education system, we risk being overtaken by other nations. Tests consistently show we are in the middle or near the bottom in academic performance when compared to other major industrialized countries.[3] Being average or below average is not acceptable. We're Americans, after all.

Our Founding Fathers saw a vibrant and effective education system as central to protecting our liberties. Thomas Jefferson warned, "If a nation expects to be ignorant and free, in a state of civilization, it expects what never was and never will be."[4] Thus, education has always been at the center of the American experiment in limited self-government. Back in 1647 the Massachusetts Legislature passed a law that required any community with fifty families or more to set up a public grammar school. Every town with one hundred or more families was required to establish a more advanced school to prepare young boys to attend Harvard. The American approach to education, traditionally involving public schools with high standards, worked. America soon developed literacy rates that were the envy of the world. John Adams, who spent many years in France, pointed out how much more literate Americans were than the French—out of 24 million French citizens, only half a million could read and write.[5]

Alexis de Tocqueville noted in his book *Democracy in America* that "the American people will appear to be the most enlightened in the world." Observing that people were expected to be well-informed and well-read, he wrote, "It cannot be doubted that in the United States the instruction of the people powerfully contributes to the support of the democratic republic."[6] Although secularists and others would like to deny it, literacy rates were so high in early America partly due to the early influence of Christianity and the Bible. As Daniel Webster observed, the Scriptures proved to be a great component in literacy, because wherever Americans went "the Bible came with them." Parents worked hard to get their kids into Harvard—and Harvard was primarily a seminary. Indeed, most of America's first colleges began as seminaries.

Teachers' union leaders and other interest groups endlessly complain that our schools lack resources—as if performance would dramatically improve if we would only throw more money into a failing system. History shows otherwise. According to the U.S. Department of Education, by the end of World War II we were spending $1,214 per student in 2001 inflation adjusted dollars. By the fifties that number nearly doubled to $2,345. By 1972 it had nearly doubled again to $4,479. By 2002, more than thirty years later, it had nearly doubled yet again to $8,745.[7] And what has happened to American education? Do I really need to answer that question?

Don't get me wrong, resources are important. In fact, in my first budget as governor I included enough money to raise the salary of Louisiana teachers to the southern average, and we've kept it at that average ever since. While good teachers should be well-paid, however, right now the U.S. education system pays its highest salaries and best benefits to teachers based simply on longevity in the classroom. One study found a high-quality teacher is only about half as likely to make it to the seven-year mark as a low-quality teacher. What this means is that too many good teachers get pushed out of the system.[8]

Pay should be tied to performance, not seniority. Is there anywhere in America (outside of government) where your salary is based solely on how long you've been there rather than results? If a teacher takes students who are three grades behind in reading and brings them up to their age level, that teacher should be rewarded. Also, we should reward teachers who are teaching a difficult or high-demand subject, or those teaching in an area where it's hard to recruit teachers.

Let me be crystal clear with regard to my admiration of teachers and the teaching profession. In politics, when you challenge the way our current education system works, you are often attacked by your opponents as "anti-teacher." That's politics for you. I am hard pressed to think of a more noble or more important calling in life than being a teacher. They are almost certainly undervalued and underappreciated in our society. In my own experience, it was the patience, thoughtfulness, and determination of teachers that gave me many of the opportunities I have had in life. Without dedicated teachers, America has no chance to thrive.

In my first year as governor, I proposed a flex pay program for teachers so that school districts could pay more to attract the teachers they need. But local school leaders said they couldn't adopt the program because the unions would make their lives miserable. You see, paying individual teachers for high performance, or because they teach a hard-to-fill subject, disrupts the herd mentality on which the union leadership thrives; the union's goal is to convince teachers that seniority is the only fair way to allocate pay. But that's hardly in the best interests of individual teachers who want to excel; it actually encourages teachers to simply follow the pack and serve out their time.

Flex pay or merit pay may inconvenience union leaders, but it's a much better model to drive outcomes in our classrooms, as well as a better model for young, motivated teachers and experienced teachers who are achieving impressive results or teaching complex subjects. Young teachers and high-performing teachers need to force their union leaders to truly represent their interests—and the best interests of our children.

In 2010, we passed a value-added teacher evaluation bill geared toward teaching and student achievement. In fact, the *Washington Post* called our education reform agenda "ambitious" because it brings accountability to schools and actually measures teachers and classrooms based on results.[9] This legislation assesses teachers fairly, based on a student's true progress over the course of a year. These data will help to identify the good teachers to reward them, and the struggling teachers to provide them the training they need to become more effective. The result will be better teachers and better student outcomes.

There are countless heroic teachers performing miracles in our schools every day—but too often they succeed despite, not because of, the way they are compensated.

* * *

Throwing money at schools has been tried many times. In a famous 1984 court case in Kansas City, Missouri, Judge Russell G. Clark used his powers as a federal judge to take over the Kansas City school district to try to rectify educational inequality. He unilaterally ordered the near doubling of city property taxes to fund lavish education spending. The school district built swimming pools and TV studios, bought computers and hired a legion of specialists. And what happened? Test scores stayed flat, the dropout rate increased, and attendance dropped. "They had as much money as any school district will ever get," reported Gary Orfield, a Harvard investigator who tracked the ten-year experiment. "It didn't do very much."[10]

Money is not the problem. The simple fact is the engine of American education is broken because it is badly designed. Our education system doesn't lack money; it lacks healthy competition, incentives to excel, and high expectations.

Have you ever wondered why our K–12 system is failing our children but our university system is the world's best? The difference is easy to explain: colleges and universities compete for students, scholars, and grant dollars. Students aren't required to attend them.

Compare that to elementary and secondary education. If your children, attend public school, their school is probably determined by your address. Why do we allow this local monopoly? Why don't we force public schools to compete just like private and parochial schools do? Today, if parents don't like their local public school they have three choices: they can home school or pay for private school tuition—if they can afford it—or they can move.

Imagine for a minute if our universities and colleges operated under the same rules as our elementary schools. If you lived in one part of Louisiana, you could only attend Louisiana State University. If you had a different zip code, your only option would be the University of Louisiana at Monroe. Students from one part of Massachusetts would go to Harvard, those from another to Boston University. In other words, universities would be guaranteed a set number of students regardless of their performance. And what if research grants were offered to universities not based on what they could do, but based on the simple fact that these schools existed? What would happen to our universities? With no incentive to compete or improve, they would quickly decay.

Competition forces school officials to focus on getting results. During his January 2010 State of the Union address, President Obama said education quality shouldn't be based on your zip code. Virginia's Republican governor Bob McDonnell said the same thing in his response. So why can't we make this a reality?

In my first year in office, we pushed legislation for a student scholarship program in New Orleans. (We also passed a modest tax deduction to help parents who are spending their own dollars for tuition and other education expenses.) The premise was simple: in New Orleans, we spend roughly $8,400 per child. If parents had a child in a failing public school in New Orleans, I proposed letting them take a maximum of 90 percent of those funds and use them to pay tuition at a participating private or parochial school. I called it a student scholarship program. It lets parents, and private and parochial schools, decide if they want to participate, and it has essentially no effect on the budget. Indeed, the average scholarship size has been much less: $4,593. Most importantly, this program targets those parents who need it most. In fact, the average income for the scholarship applications we received was $15,564.

Who in their right mind would oppose giving parents such a choice? The education establishment, of course, because they believe they are entitled to your children and your tax dollars. For trying to give parents a choice in the matter, I was charged with attacking the public schools. Well, despite that nonsense we passed the bill, and I proudly signed it into law—and the program's chief supporters have been parents.

Every year, many of these parents take time off from their jobs to tell lawmakers at the Capitol how important this program is to them and their children. You should hear these parents; some of them have tears in their eyes when they relate how they finally feel good about the opportunities they're giving their kids. They have hope in their eyes. No one should ever think these parents care any less about the quality of their child's education than more affluent parents do. I can't imagine why the education establishment refuses to learn from parents like these who are desperate for a choice. Why should wealthy families be the only ones who have choice?

* * *

In 2005 Louisiana experienced the horrors of Hurricane Katrina. Over a thousand people died; tens of thousands were displaced. Some have said there was some kind of silver lining to this tragedy. They are wrong. There is no silver lining to a tragedy this devastating. But we did have a choice as to how we would rebuild.

The hurricane delivered a knockout blow to one of the worst performing school districts in the nation. In 2003–2004, New Orleans had fifty-five of Louisiana's seventy-eight worst schools. In 2005, more than half of the 65,000 kids in New Orleans public schools did not have basic competence in math and English at the fourth, eighth, tenth, or eleventh grade levels, according to test results. Fully 74 percent of eighth graders had failed to show basic skills in English, and 70 percent scored below the basic level in math. Of the city's 108 public schools, 68 were rated "academically unacceptable" by the Louisiana Department of Education.[11] The district had lots of money, but auditors estimated the school system was running a $25–30 million deficit—they couldn't even state a precise figure because the financial books were in disarray. The Department of Education discovered that $70 million in federal money allocated to low-income students was misspent or simply missing. More than two dozen indictments for fraud, kickbacks, or theft soon followed. In 2003, the valedictorian for a New Orleans area high school got an 11 on the ACT, a score lower than 99 percent of the kids taking the test nationally. The structurally flawed New Orleans public schools let that girl down.[12]

The New Orleans Parish School Board operated like a centralized monopoly. Innovative ideas (like charter schools) were resisted and bureaucracy ruled. School administrators and teachers couldn't repair a building or implement even minor reforms without the board's authorization. Adam Nossiter, then a writer for the Associated Press, noted just months before Katrina, "In the dismal gallery of failing urban school systems, New Orleans may be the biggest horror of them all."[13]

Katrina forced the city to begin anew. Nearly two-thirds of the city's school buildings had been destroyed or damaged by floodwaters. While private schools set about to clean up and reopen quickly, public schools were mired in bureaucracy as much as mud and debris from the storm. So local leaders and the state Legislature pushed for the schools to be run by the Recovery School District that answered directly to the state. Seemingly overnight, New Orleans became the most chartered city in America, with nearly 70 percent of students in public charter schools. With this experiment, the state Legislature nullified the collective bargaining agreement between the New Orleans Parish School Board and the teacher unions. Charter schools are public schools, but they're free to develop innovative solutions to meet the needs of their students. And charter schools have no monopoly on local kids; parents can choose their child's school. Not all charter schools are great, but competition will allow parents to at least make a choice.

Every student is different. When I was growing up I was inquisitive—in fact, sometimes *too* inquisitive. I drove my mom nuts constantly asking her what some word meant. One day I read a biography of Abraham Lincoln that explained how our sixteenth president was an "inquisitive" boy. I asked her what that meant, and she told me to look it up. I was proud when I discovered the meaning. "President Lincoln was inquisitive and so am I," I told her smugly. "And you can't be mad at me for doing what the president did." For some reason she found this argument less than convincing.

Some children are naturally inquisitive, some possess a creative flair. Some are strong in math, others get lost in literature. Some are filled with potential but need someone unique to crack through a rough outer shell. Charter schools allow parents to make the right choice for their unique child, picking from schools that have been approved by state or local officials and are held accountable for their results. Because charter schools have to compete against each other, they tend to make a point of recruiting energetic teachers, focusing on academic performance, and offering creative and practical courses for students.

All sorts of charter schools have blossomed in New Orleans. Some focus on foreign language immersion. Others are based on the Montessori Model. National charter school entities, such as the Knowledge Is Power Program (KIPP), now educate more than 1,000 children in the city. In the last four years, assessment scores have improved citywide in New Orleans. Individual schools have demonstrated even more spectacular results. In 2010, the Sophie B. Wright Charter School celebrated that 62 percent of their 8th graders passed the Louisiana Educational Assessment Program (LEAP) test. This is a huge improvement from 2004–05, when the school still functioned as a regular public school, and 83 percent of 8th graders scored below "basic" on the test in English, and 76 percent scored below "basic" in Math.[14]

The New Orleans charter school system is not perfect. Initially, Louisiana law dictated that charter schools should not "be supported by or affiliated with any religion or religious organization or institution." This was unnecessarily restrictive, because federal laws already prevent publicly funded schools from engaging in religious discrimination or conducting religious instruction. But there is no reason why we shouldn't tap the expertise of churches and faith-based groups to help us reform and enhance our education system. As governor, I have worked to eliminate restrictions that have shut these groups out.

The key to success in charter schools is getting parents and the community involved, so we've tried to make parental involvement as easy as possible. We've also empowered teachers with a new law allowing a traditional school to become a charter school by a simple faculty vote. Traditional public schools often complain that comparisons to charter schools are not fair since charters face fewer restrictions and less bureaucracy. With that in mind, we passed the Red Tape Reduction and Local Empowerment Act that gives all our public schools the same flexible options charter schools have. A well-respected superintendent who headed our state association marveled, "The legislation was almost too good to be true; I thought I was dreaming." With this flexibility comes accountability in terms of student performance. Schools that don't improve will be taken over and reconstituted so their students succeed.

If we're going to have successful schools, we need to be able to define and measure success. Louisiana has won national recognition for our accountability programs that track the performance of individual students, teachers, schools, and districts, and even tie that performance back to colleges of education that prepare our teachers. States can use high stakes testing, school report cards, and other mechanisms, but the important point is that parents must have access to easily understandable, quantifiable, and objective data about how their children are doing. That is why we passed a law giving Louisiana schools letter grades. Just as students get a report card, so should our schools.

* * *

Beyond restructuring our education system through choice and competition, we need to return discipline to the classroom. Kids today should not fear going to school because bullies are on the prowl; and teachers should not worry about how to handle troubled students. We are all familiar with the terrible school shootings in places like Columbine, Colorado, and Red Lake, Minnesota. But other acts of violence and intimidation happen every day that we don't hear about. A survey a few years ago asked teachers what they needed most. Higher pay ranked beneath everyday concerns like a better teaching environment, more authority to deal with unruly students, and more parental support when they did so. Likewise, a survey by Southern Media and Opinion Research found the number one problem teachers face in the classroom is classroom discipline, followed by lack of parental support. National surveys have revealed similar concerns by teachers around the country.[15]

We need higher standards not just in academic achievement but in personal conduct—the two often go hand in hand. As governor, I pushed for and got a Teacher's Bill of Rights as well as legislation that gives teachers more authority to remove disruptive students from the classroom. Moreover, if a student is suspended, the new law requires that he make up all the schoolwork he's missed. Suspension should not be vacation. And we get parents involved, too. The law allows the courts to require parents to attend after-school and Saturday behavior intervention programs with their kids. If they don't cooperate, the parents can be fined or required to perform community service. Similarly, kids who fail to meet school attendance requirements or are constantly late can now have their driving privileges suspended.

High standards are an expression of love—I learned that from my parents and teachers. By tolerating lower standards we have hurt our children. We need to raise the bar for everyone—students, parents, and educators. It's a sad commentary on our education system that we need to import scientists and engineers because we can't produce enough of them here at home.

* * *

Finally, let me address the thorniest issue of all: equal opportunity in education. It sounds good. All Americans believe in it. Only one problem—we don't have it. If you grow up poor in a place with failing schools, your future prospects are diminished because you're probably not going to get a good education. It's that simple.

Liberals claim to champion equal opportunity in education, but most of them oppose the most effective solution: school choice. Why? While liberals hysterically claim school choice would destroy public education, their real concern is their fear of the teacher unions, which lose power to parents through school choice. Liberals also reflexively oppose any policy that might benefit religious schools.

School choice takes many forms—vouchers, tax credits, charters, student scholarships, and transfers to better public schools are a few. I favor whatever works, depending on the needs of the community. The successful methods we're using in New Orleans—charter schools and scholarship programs—could serve as a model for other cities looking to secure a good education for their poorest, most vulnerable kids. I'm for what works.

Communities with failing education systems nationwide need to act fast to expand school choice. Telling parents to wait for the failing school in their neighborhood to improve on its own is offensive and absurd. Their kids are growing up *right now*, and these kids need a good education *right now*. No amount of money will fix the problem, though school choice really can. But the Democratic Party, teacher unions, and their allies are standing in the way, blocking the schoolhouse door.

Consider this: what actually happens to a kid who is trapped in a failing school? Maybe the kid works hard and succeeds anyway. But the odds are just as good that this kid will struggle and fall through the cracks. Maybe you don't care much, since it's not your kid, but of course you *should* care, because that kid is a fellow American. And if nothing else, you should care because we need every kid to succeed in order to continue growing our economy.

Alternatively, you can think of it this way: that kid in the failing school (the one who ends up dropping out) is a problem for all of us—including you. That kid is more likely to need public assistance, sell drugs to your kids, rob a store in your neighborhood, or end up in jail—all of which affects you in one way or another.

So, take your pick. Either care about kids in failing schools out of compassion or out of self-interest, but either way, you better start caring about them.

For me, this is an urgent issue that really boils down to a few simple questions:

Does America promise equal opportunity in education? Yes.

Does America provide equal opportunity in education? No.

Will I ever give up this fight? Never.

FIRST-TIME CANDIDATE

If you ever get the urge to run for public office, take a deep breath and a few aspirin, and hopefully you'll feel better in the morning. If that doesn't work, see a doctor. If after that you still want to run, then go ahead and do it—but read this first.

I began thinking about running to be the next governor of Louisiana in 2002. I initially kept my thoughts to myself, only confiding in Supriya. That was safe because she was already used to my outlandish ideas, starting with the notion that she should go out with me. She was out of my league and hesitant to date me. But I wore her down—it only took ten years.

I first asked her out when I was in the tenth grade. She was the prettiest girl I had ever met. I liked her from afar for months, until my friends finally tired of hearing about her. They said if you like her so much—tell her, not us. I finally worked up the courage to call and ask her to the movies. She was the first girl I asked out and she turned me down flat, ostensibly because her family was moving in a few days to New Orleans (which, by the way, is only about an hour down the road). I was zero for one.

The next time I talked to her was ten years later, in 1996. I had travelled the globe by then, but I never got her out of my mind. I had recently been appointed secretary of the Department of Health and Hospitals for the state of Louisiana, and I was expected to attend a fancy Mardi Gras ball in Baton Rouge. Three days before the ball, my date backed out. She had to study for a med school exam (or so she said). Scrambling for a new date, I asked around and got Supriya's phone number. I left a strange message on her answering machine: "Hi, this is Bobby Jindal. If you're not married please call me back."

The message was so odd that she actually returned the call. We had a great thirty-minute talk, as I told her about my new job and asked if she would bail me out and go with me to the ball. She was a good sport about it and agreed.

I asked her to meet me at my parents' house, since I had not even found a place to live yet after moving from Washington, D.C. When my dad met her, that was it—he'd found the one for me, and he didn't seem too concerned about my feelings on the matter. The ball was a lot of fun, and of course she was great company. Other than the drunk lady at our table who could not pronounce Supriya's name—she finally settled for "Sabrina"—it was a wonderful night.

When I asked her for a second date, she invited me to come to New Orleans and go out to dinner with her and some of her girlfriends at Nola, one of Emeril Lagasse's famous restaurants. But I got sick that day. I was out giving a speech that afternoon, and I knew I wasn't going to make dinner. I couldn't reach Supriya—not many people had cell phones back then—so I left a message with Nola's maitre d'. Thus, I not only stood up Supriya, but her best friends as well. If you're looking for dating tips, I'm not the guy to talk to.

I spent the next few months pleading over the phone for another date with Supriya. Most times I couldn't reach her, so I would just talk to her mom. When I did reach Supriya, she was fun and pleasant, but she was always too busy for a date. Finally I asked her, "When are you *not* going to be busy?" A chemical engineer, she explained she had a big project at work and was working on her MBA in the evenings, so she wouldn't have time for months—until July. So I said fine, mark down the first Friday and Saturday in July for our second and third dates. It had taken me almost five months to get a second date so I was determined to get a third one, too.

When the day finally came, I spared no expense. We took a riverboat cruise on the Natchez Steamboat in New Orleans, followed by dinner at Bella Luna along the Mississippi River and then a stroll down Bourbon Street. The next day we drove down River Road, and I pointed out plantation homes and Supriya pointed out chemical plants.

Even though I had been professionally successful, something big was missing from my life. I knew when I found Supriya again, it was her. It was a fast, whirlwind courtship. I knew I couldn't risk losing her for another ten years. We got engaged that fall. We were in love—and still are. Even when I had to spend weeks on the road during the campaign, Supriya and I would talk frequently throughout the day even if only for a minute at a time. I didn't just marry the prettiest girl I knew ...she is also my best friend, fiercest ally, and a constant source of accountability.

* * *

Supriya and I talk to each other before doing anything really big. So we beat up my idea of running for governor a good bit before I had the temerity to mention it to anyone else.

Funny enough, one of the first people I floated the idea to was the president of the United States. It was winter 2002, and I was on Air Force One. As an assistant secretary of the Department of Health and Human Services, I was way in the back of the plane. The Navy steward came to me and said, "The president would like to see you when you are done eating." I don't enjoy eating much anyway, so I went forward right away. I wasn't sure what he wanted with me, though I had an inkling—I'd heard rumors he was thinking of asking me to work in the White House.

When I got to the front, President Bush was sitting with my boss, HHS Secretary Tommy Thompson. Eventually, Karl Rove joined us. Truth be told, a few people had started talking about me possibly running for governor, so the president probably already knew about that, even though I considered it to be a state secret.

Sure enough, the president told me he had a job offer for me, but he'd heard I was thinking of going home to run for office. I don't care what anyone says, it's some kind of difficult to say no the president of the United States of America, and it's even harder while you're sitting on his plane. But he was extremely gracious; after I confirmed that I wanted to run for governor, he simply told me I should do that, if that's what my passion was. I don't think everyone sitting there agreed, in fact I'm sure of it, but their opinion didn't matter—the big man had spoken. I went to the back of the plane before anyone could "revise and extend" his remarks, as they say in Washington. I sat down to find my seatmate had jammed everything in sight with an Air Force One logo into her purse.

Say what you want about President Bush, and plenty have, but I will always admire his generosity, candor, and honesty. He could easily have said, "No, I need you in this job, you have to do it for the good of the country." I was ready to say no anyhow, but he did not put me in that position. A true gentleman.

Admittedly, Supriya has a different interpretation of this conversation; she thinks the president let me off the hook so easily because he was sure he could quickly find someone else for the job. Of course, she's wrong.

The only other person I sought counsel from was Haley Barbour. I had gotten to know Haley a little bit and I knew three things about him. First, he had been the most successful chairman the Republican Party has ever had. Second, he is a policy wonk like me. And third, he's a southerner from our neighboring state of Mississippi, where he now serves as governor. But when I first talked to him, I was worried he would think I had lost my mind. He didn't, or at least if he did, he didn't say so. He encouraged me to explore running and put me in contact with Curt Anderson, a guy who had been his political director at the Republican National Committee, and who ended up helping my campaigns. Curt has been a close friend since.

Eventually, I made a final decision to run for governor. Many mistakenly view a political campaign as glamorous, full of adoring fans and appearances on the evening news. Perhaps it's like that when you run for president, but that wasn't my experience running for governor. Being a first-time candidate running in a field of seventeen candidates, many of whom were better-known and had more political experience than I had, was actually pretty far from glamorous.

On one campaign trip to north Louisiana, our campaign didn't have much money so we mostly travelled by car, and I stayed in people's homes whenever I could to save the price of a hotel. This trip came during a grueling part of the schedule, after we'd travelled several days without much rest. I was due to make a speech later that evening, so I decided to lie down for an hour in the nearby home of a staffer's cousin.

Looking back, I wish I'd paid more attention to the "For Sale" sign in the front yard—because just as I drifted off, the homeowner, a realtor, and some prospective buyers walked into the bedroom where I was sleeping. I'll never forget what the homeowner said: "Oh, this is Bobby Jindal, he's running for governor." The buyers, I'm sure, were thinking, "Bobby who? And if he's running for governor, why is he sleeping in your house in the middle of the day?" I kept my eyes closed and pretended to be dead. It worked and they left. Fortunately, the prospective buyers did not ask if I "conveyed" with the property.

My campaign took a long time to gain traction. The first poll we took had me in dead last with just 3 percent of the vote—and those 3 percent were probably confused. I had no network of donors and didn't have my own fortune to sink into the race. I had a strong résumé and some good accomplishments on the policy front, but absolutely no idea how to run a campaign. Oh, and did I mention my parents are from India? Or that I was thirty-one years old? So, to put it mildly, there were a few skeptics of my campaign. The son of Indian immigrants running for governor in the Deep South? In the state where former KKK member David Duke made a credible run for governor? Sounds like a novel.

But I did have one thing going for me, in addition to Supriya, and that was then-Governor Mike Foster. Mike was a risk taker who hired me as a 24-year-old to run his Department of Health and Hospitals. Additionally, he was not the product of any political machine in Louisiana. When he first ran for governor, the pundits considered his candidacy a joke, so this was a road he'd been down before.

Mike is one of those types that make this country great. He believes that in America, if you can dream it, you can do it. He's an anti-politician; a good ol' boy if there ever was one. During his two terms as governor he rarely travelled to Washington; he just flat out doesn't like the place and doesn't think much good comes out of it. Besides, as he once told me, the hunting in D.C. is no good.

Our campaign office was a small house in Baton Rouge, the former headquarters of a funeral parlor business. Some would say that's bad karma, but the rent was almost free.

On the campaign trail, I quickly learned something about myself: I really enjoy spending time with people. Some find it draining, but it energizes me. And it's crucial for being a successful candidate; if you want to serve people, you need to be genuinely interested in their concerns. If you aren't, the voters will figure that out. You can have all the money and the best commercials, but people can spot a phony.

That first campaign was a real start-up venture. We made do with what we had, waging an unconventional effort that relied heavily on exhausting travel and detailed policy ideas. The whole thing was held together with bailing wire and duct tape.

Many old pros warned me not to talk too much policy. They feared I would come off as a policy wonk, and that providing detailed plans would just give my opponents the rope for hanging me. I ignored that advice. In my view, it just wasn't honest to ask voters to support me without offering them detailed proposals. Besides, what did I have to lose? Three percent?

Unable to afford TV commercials, we aired radio ads focusing on policy, not politics. We put forward a detailed plan with more than twenty specific reforms for the state of Louisiana, including a major ethics reform package to root out public corruption, a plan to attract businesses to our state, a proposal to make it more affordable to launch a small business, and plans to reform education and healthcare. All these plans were more detailed than campaign documents are supposed to be—and all were designed to help Louisiana provide real career opportunities for our people. For too long, Louisiana had exported our most precious commodity to other states—our people. I was bent on giving our people more opportunities to prosper right here at home. Although the political hands still thought this was a dumb approach, the voters began to take notice. It turns out people are interested in what political candidates actually plan to do. Who knew?

In Louisiana we run elections a little differently. All the candidates run together in a primary, regardless of their party affiliation. If no candidate gets over 50 percent, the top two vote-getters then compete in a runoff. Of course, nobody was going to get a majority in a crowd of seventeen people that included a lieutenant governor, an attorney general, a really wealthy guy, a former and the current president of the Louisiana Senate, a former House speaker, and a former governor, so the primary was really a sprint for one of the top two slots.

Our biggest rival for Republican votes was a well-known state legislator named Hunt Downer. Hunt is a decent guy and was a worthy opponent. He was also the chosen candidate of the White House staff and the Republican Party establishment in Washington. After all, Hunt had switched parties and campaigned aggressively for President Bush. He had been speaker of the Louisiana House and served as a senior officer in the Louisiana National Guard. Potential Republican donors in Louisiana were letting me know that Hunt was the preferred guy—Karl Rove had told them so.

Expecting me to go nowhere, top Republicans in Washington thought I'd drop out of the race. When it became clear I wouldn't quit, some White House political officials contacted one of my advisors, Curt Anderson, cussed him out good, and threatened to make his life miserable. Luckily for me, Curt can be very ornery, and he told the White House staffers exactly what he thought of them. Years later a former White House staffer told me they were in complete shock that Curt didn't buckle under the pressure.

Push came to shove in the race when a group of the biggest GOP donors in our state decided to vet the various Republican candidates through personal interviews. They would then endorse one candidate, and it was assumed the others would drop out.

This goes to a larger issue that is crucial to success: loyalty. There is just no substitute for it. But loyalty is in short supply in the world of politics, which is largely populated with political transients who routinely change horses in mid-stream.

Many of my supporters initially approved of this process—they figured I would go in there and blow them away, and all the hotshots would agree I was the guy. Money would start to flow into my campaign, and we would all live happily ever after. But a trusted friend pulled me aside and suggested that, this being Louisiana politics, I couldn't count on getting an honest hearing—the process was probably rigged from the start. In hindsight, I believe some of these big donors were sincerely looking for the best candidate, but others clearly had different motives. So I think I made the right decision when I rejected the entire vetting process and moved forward with the novel idea of taking my campaign directly to the voters.

Aside from the pre-determined outcome, I didn't like the idea of all the "smart guys" getting together to pick the candidate. Letting the voters have a say seems rather fundamental in a democracy. And truthfully, some of these guys are really just horse traders whose biggest concern is making sure they have an "in" with whoever gets elected, regardless of that person's plans or ideology or even party affiliation.

*   *   *

Successful advertising requires repetition, or so the adage goes. This was a problem for me. After giving the same speech twice I would get terribly bored with it, and I still do today, to be honest. But to win an election, a candidate has to deliver the same message before twenty-five different audiences to even make a dent. People who follow politics closely tend to forget that normal folks are out there living their lives, working hard, taking the kids to soccer practice, looking after their parents, and going to movies. They are not glued to the TV anticipating the next campaign commercial. Anyone who does that is a little odd.

Speaking of odd, try asking all your friends, family members, pretty much everyone you have ever met, and thousands of total strangers for money. Now that's a real blast. I've heard a few candidates actually enjoy fundraising, but I don't want to meet them.

Governor Foster was immensely helpful on this front—his loyal contributors got my campaign off the ground. But after that, I had to sink or swim on my own. I decided to swim—but it wasn't easy.

Every year we see some wealthy folks get trounced in elections. In fact, in my successful race for the governorship in 2007 I beat two gentlemen who each spent more than $10 million of their own fortunes on the race. But while money does not guarantee victory, the lack of money does guarantee defeat. I was determined not to let this happen to me. So I steeled my resolve and despite my personal discomfort, I began asking folks to invest in my candidacy.

Our fundraising was incredibly amateurish at first, but we occasionally had some pleasant surprises. One of my first fundraisers was held at my in-laws' house. After I gave my speech, my first question was from a fairly liberal woman, a medical doctor, who asked me my position on abortion. I told her I was pro-life and we exchanged views. I remember thinking I was going to have to return all the money I had raised even before I started! But amazingly, she became a financial supporter despite our differences over abortion. It turns out she already knew I was pro-life; she just wanted to see if I would be honest about my position or if I would waffle in order to get her money.

A wealthy Florida doctor held another memorable fundraiser for us. He spent a lot of money to throw a fancy party at his beautiful estate . . . and *one* person showed up. So I decided not to give a speech. To make matters worse, I was scheduled to spend the night at his house. I don't know if I've ever been in a more awkward situation.

Our campaign would go anywhere to raise money. My dentist even hosted a fundraiser for me, which turned out to be a neighborhood crawfish boil that yielded zero dollars and zero cents.

For the first month of my campaign I was convinced the post office was inept. So many folks had told me they were sending a check, but we never seemed to receive them. You hear so many stories of corruption in politics, stories of people trying to buy candidates, particularly in Louisiana. That was no problem for my campaign, I can assure you; when folks don't think you can win, they don't bother trying to buy you off.

I learned three things about raising money in that first campaign. First, if your friends won't give, you have no chance. Luckily, my friends were generous. Second, forget all that nonsense about finding one big donor who will open the doors for you. It doesn't work that way, you have to do it yourself. Third, you have to ask for support if you want to win. If you don't believe in your ideas enough to ask for money, you should not run.

In fundraising you are asking people to commit an unnatural act—to give away their money. And not to a charity either; donors get no tax deduction. You are asking them to believe that your candidacy matters, that you can win, and that after you do win you will make their community a better place.

Our campaign had many first time donors who had never been involved in politics. We adopted a cardinal rule that was a little radical in Louisiana politics—you cannot give to my campaign if you want something in return. All you are going to get back is honest, competent government. Oh, one more thing, we had pledged radical ethics reforms to root out corruption in politics in Louisiana. Anyone who opposed that was encouraged to give to someone else. Many did.

* * *

When the dust cleared on primary night in 2003, I had come in first with 33 percent of the vote, a full 15 percent ahead of the second place challenger, Lieutenant Governor Kathleen Blanco, a Democrat. It's hard to pinpoint the reason for my victory. I think it was a combination of hard work, discipline, people power, and the power of ideas. One of the greatest things about our country is the simple fact that Americans are dreamers, we want to improve our lot in life, and we are forever optimistic that we can accomplish anything we set our minds to.

Our campaign had many volunteers, and even though we didn't organize them well, they carried us a long way. How did we develop this kind of people power? It was simple, really: voters will rally behind good ideas. They will give their time, talents, and resources if they have a cause worth fighting for.

Everyone associated with my campaign was thrilled by the primary result except one person—my dad. He was disappointed we didn't get more than 50 percent and win the whole shootin' match that night. We had just shocked the nation, but that didn't satisfy my dad. There's a story, I don't know if it's true, that when a young Bobby Kennedy told his dad he wanted to be a Catholic priest, his dad replied, "Well, that's great. We've never had a pope in the family before." That's exactly my dad.

But the Republican establishment wasn't disappointed at all. One thing about Washington political hacks—they are flexible. The day after we won the primary, I was suddenly the White House staff's new best friend.

Still, the election wasn't over. My advisors had warned me we did not want a runoff with the perfectly positioned Kathleen Blanco—she didn't have a controversial record to defend, she seemed non-threatening, and she could attract bipartisan support as a Democrat campaigning as a cultural conservative. She was widely known and I was not. She was likeable—everyone's aunt or grandma, and I was some new young guy who talked too fast and didn't look like he was "from around here."

At the very end of the campaign, Blanco went on the attack, running a TV ad that featured a voice shouting, "Wake up, Louisiana!" Displaying an unflattering picture of me, the ad warned that people were in danger of electing some guy no one really knew. The ad played to Blanco's strengths as a safe, status quo candidate, which was a good place to be at the time, pre-Katrina. In the end she beat us, 52 to 48 percent.

I am a competitive person, and I hate losing, at anything, ever. But I immediately accepted the defeat and decided to move on. I've seen losing candidates nurse grudges for years, and I really didn't want to go that route. Not enough people knew me, I figured, so I'd have to change that before my next run for public office.

My family, friends, and staff were devastated on election night. But it was a chance to prove my mettle, to be strong in a tough situation. And as I looked around the room, it was clear no one else was going to do it. As we walked onto the elevator to go down to the ballroom and make the concession speech, I told everyone, "No tears on the elevator." I felt we'd fought hard and had no reason to be ashamed. And I didn't want to hear any excuses either. My dad always taught us that life isn't fair, so quit expecting it to be; when you encounter a setback, just work harder and do better next time. Make your own breaks in life.

I'm not interested in looking backward. Being a leader in the good times is easy, but leadership is tested in times of adversity. I decided to be relentlessly positive. Make no mistake, this was a conscious decision—it never comes naturally in that kind of situation. Such is the human condition, where the natural instinct is to blame others and consider yourself a victim.

One of my advisors suggested I subtly blame the consultants, the staff, and even advisors like him. His exact words were, "You should just throw us overboard." I felt like snapping at him, "Do you guys not know anything about me?" President Truman had it right: the buck stops here.

Many observers have claimed I lost because of my Indian ethnicity. It's an easy narrative that fits various stereotypes, but I reject it completely. The people of Louisiana have always been completely fair to me—kind, generous, and just plain decent. During and after Hurricane Katrina, the whole world saw what Louisianians are really made of. When the government failed, individuals, families, churches, and businesses put everything on the line to help their neighbors—with zero regard for race or creed.

Not only do I refuse to offer excuses, I'm not real good at hearing them either. I always tell my staff not to bring problems to me. Don't simply try to kick your problems upstairs. Bring me solutions, and we will get them done. That's what my dad would do.

I had suffered a tough loss, but I put it behind me. I knew there were other opportunities to serve my state, and I found one pretty quickly. For better or worse, I joined the U.S. Congress.

CHAPTER 6

CESSPOOL OR HOT TUB?

Harry Truman famously derided the "do-nothing Congress" of his time. Well, based on my time in Congress and its actions during the first couple years of the Obama administration, I'm all in favor of a do-nothing Congress. If Truman were alive today, I expect he'd long for the "good old days" when Congress had a measure of self-restraint.

A year after I lost the governor's race, I was elected to the first of two terms in the U.S. House of Representatives. In Washington, I witnessed first-hand how America is governed by a bipartisan, permanent political class that feels entitled to special status, influence, and power. We have to break the back of this elite clique by returning Congress to the role our Founding Fathers intended for it.

When I first arrived in Congress, I got a fair amount of attention because, well, I looked a little different than your average congressman. I was easy to spot, so several hundred members and aides would greet me with "Good morning, Bobby," or "Good morning, Congressman Jindal," while I still hadn't learned their names. (My idea for requiring congressmen to wear nametags never gained traction.) After

I had been in Congress for several months, a good friend asked me, "Have you seen my friend, Congressman such-and-such?"

"White guy, mid-fifties?" I asked.

"Yep," my friend said.

"Balding, slightly pudgy?"

"Yes, that's him. When did you see him?"

"Only several hundred times," I said.

What's important in Congress, though, is not how its members look, but how they think and act—many have an unbounded sense of entitlement that I noticed as soon as I arrived in Washington in January 2005, just before President Bush's inauguration speech on the steps of the U.S. Capitol. While a huge crowd stood on the Mall for hours in the freezing cold, members of Congress went from their offices through a heated tunnel, then to their reserved seats up front. We were told to wear special "Member of Congress" pins on our lapels so the Capitol Police and Secret Service would know who we were. Walking in front of me was a veteran congressman who was not wearing his pin.

"Sorry sir, you can't go in here," a security official told him.

He threw an absolute fit, screaming, "Don't you know who I am?!"

Another officer recognized him and quickly came over to smooth things out. "Sorry," he said, "We didn't recognize you."

The congressman snapped back, "Well, it's your job to recognize us!"

These security officials were trying to protect us, and this congressman was treating them rudely. And it never seemed to bother him that while he was sitting comfortably up front, his constituents were literally out in the freezing cold, waiting in line for a turn in a Port-a-Potty.

Members of Congress receive all sorts of perks that reinforce this attitude of privilege and arrogance: special elevators, reserved parking spaces, dining rooms, etc. It's well-known on Capitol Hill that members of Congress can often get out of traffic stops simply by flashing their congressional I.D. I also remember one White House meeting when a senator threw a childish tantrum—and even threatened to oppose us on a key healthcare vote—just because the senator was not seated at the same table as the president. We rearranged the chairs and got the vote.

To be clear, not all members of Congress get caught up in this culture of privilege, but many do. Based on my three years in Congress, I can tell you that as a group, congressmen are not smarter than ordinary Americans, nor do they have unique insights or capabilities. A senator once told me a lot of the state legislators in his state would probably need public assistance if they weren't in politics. The same holds true for more than a few members of Congress. As they say, dumb people need representation too...and they surely have it in Washington.

Although congressmen are anxious to regulate more and more of the economy, you wouldn't want many of them running your business. As George McGovern admitted after he left the Senate, started a business, and went bankrupt, "I wish I had known a little more about the problems of the private sector.... I have to pay taxes, meet a payroll—I wish I had a better sense of what it took to do that when I was in Washington."[1] And he was the Democratic Party's nominee for president! Likewise, in announcing his decision in 2010 to retire from the Senate, Indiana's Evan Bayh explained, "If I could create one job in the private sector by helping to grow a business, that would be one more than Congress has created in the last six months." This was a rare moment of clarity from Washington.[2]

Still, for all its faults, Congress does have some capable, intelligent legislators. It's like that old Clint Eastwood movie, *The Good, the Bad, and the Ugly*. There are some brilliant folks, and there are some that couldn't pass a CAT scan. Some have impeccable integrity, and others will end up in jail. Some display great humility, and others are supremely arrogant.

Nevertheless, Americans don't have a high opinion of Congress right now. Polls show that only 21 percent of Americans believe Congress is doing a good job. (I want to know who those 21 percent are and find out what's wrong with them.) When it comes to ethics and morality, studies show Americans rank congressmen barely above car salesmen. (An unfair comparison, in my book—at least most states have lemon laws to protect you from dishonest car salesmen.)

Believing they're unpopular because Americans just don't understand the great job they're doing, congressmen send out more letters, fight for more pork and earmarks, and make more TV appearances. But the American people dislike congressmen precisely *because* they know what they're doing—they're spending our country into oblivion.

Congress has lost touch with the people they are supposed to serve. Many members are influenced far more by Washington than by their constituents back home. A city full of government employees, lobbyists, and government supplicants views the world differently from the rest of us. When congressmen do return home, it's for brief, campaign-style appearances. They don't have time for meaningful contact with regular citizens to learn about their everyday challenges. Before arriving in Washington, I decided to skip the reception and party scene, the sort of insider socializing that comes with being a congressman. As a wise old Washington hand once said, when you first get to Washington, it's a cesspool. But if you stay long enough, it becomes a hot tub. Well, there are plenty of people, both Democrats and Republicans, who have been soaking for too long.

In Congress, you have to resist a lot of suck-ups. You're constantly flattered by endless numbers of people—staff, lobbyists, other members of Congress, bureaucrats, media figures, and others—all of whom ultimately want something from you. Eventually, many members of Congress start spending more time with these ego-strokers, and less time with their family and friends who are still willing to speak to them honestly. And that's how they begin to lose touch with the real world.

I had to work hard to stay grounded in reality. My brother Nikesh is a lawyer in Washington, so I would crash at his place. His furnishings rightly belonged in a dorm room and the dinners were mostly microwaved, but it was all I needed. I also took every opportunity to fly to Louisiana to see Supriya and the kids. She made sure I didn't take myself too seriously. "I don't care if you're a congressman," she would tell me. "Go change your child's diaper." (When they need changing, they are always *my* children.) "And take out the trash while you're at it."

Congressmen tend to be insulated from the real world by their staffers, who often really run the show. Staffers are writing increasingly complex bills that members usually don't even read. The first federal highway act in 1956, which started our national highway system, was less than one-tenth the length of most highway funding bills passed these days.[3] Former vice president and Minnesota senator Walter Mondale once recalled about his Senate staff, "I felt sorry for them, so I would try to work with them. Pretty soon I was working for them."[4]

Some people think members of Congress are lazy. In truth, they work long hours, but too many of them frequently place their own political interests ahead of their constituents. Congress engages in a lot of political showmanship, especially in committee meetings, which often amount to political actors reciting well-rehearsed scripts for the cameras. As Arizona Senator John McCain once put it, "Washington is Hollywood for ugly people." And as C-SPAN watchers can testify, this ain't Hollywood.

In committees, congressmen ask witnesses "questions" by giving twenty-minute speeches. The witnesses are there to make a point, but you'll rarely see anyone change his mind. To attract media attention, celebrities are often invited to testify, regardless of their actual knowledge of the topic.

Floor "debates" are run in a similar way, with legislators typically talking to an empty chamber. Each side talks past the other, and speakers often refuse to yield for questions because, well, that would cut into their time in front of the microphone and the cameras.

It became obvious to me that the hearings and house floor proceedings people see on C-SPAN are more orchestrated theater than true debates that people care about. I quickly realized the most productive use of committee meetings was to catch up on some reading or send out emails on my Blackberry. Some members, I kid you not, would just sleep right through the meetings.

Members of Congress often behave like kids who at first fight over toys, and then fight just for the sake of fighting. One child doesn't care if he gets the toy, as long as his brother can't have it. If you're a parent, you know what I'm talking about. Both parties frequently care less about achieving some specific policy goal, and more about inflicting a "loss" on the other side. The problem is the American people are the ones who really lose and end up paying the bills.

Congress, in a way, is also like the Middle East—the place is plagued by ancient disputes and grievances. The prevailing attitude is, "When they were in the majority, they did this to us, so when we're in the majority, we're going to do this to them." So they keep on fighting. But remember: for all the vinegar that gets thrown around in Congress, many members are part of a permanent political class that takes care of its own. They might fight on the House floor today, but tomorrow they'll be opening a lobbying business together so they can take money from both sides.

A lot of congressmen "go along to get along," but that's no guarantee of success. I remember sitting in the locker room of the House gym when Connecticut Congressman Chris Shays walked over to then-Illinois Congressman Rahm Emanuel. Shays was a moderate to liberal Republican who tried hard—many Republicans felt too hard—to work with Democrats. But Shays had just learned the Democrats would drop millions of dollars to defeat him. "Gee," he asked Emanuel, "what's this about you pouring a million into defeating me?"

Emanuel put his hand on his shoulder and said, "It's not a million—it's twice that. Nothing personal." Shays basically abandoned conservative principles in an effort to get along with the Democrats. It didn't work.

* * *

Our country is in terrible financial shape, as we compile a massive debt for our children and grandchildren to pay. Right now, each American "owes" $45,000 on the national debt, and that figure is set to rise much higher. The 2009 budget deficit was nearly the size of the entire federal budget in 2000. And by 2012 the size of our debt will exceed our country's entire GDP. Congress recently voted to raise the debt limit to over $14 trillion. Estimates are that the debt will nearly double by 2020 to $26 trillion.[5]

To cover this spending, the federal government borrows money from foreign countries, which makes us even more dependent on the Chinese or other powers, and it prints more money, which will lead to inflation and a weaker dollar. And count on your taxes going up— *way up*. Economist Bruce Bartlett estimates, "Federal income taxes for every taxpayer would have to rise by roughly 81% to pay all of the benefits promised by these programs under current law over and above the payroll tax."[6]

We inherited from our parents a better way of life and more opportunities than they had. But our exploding debt means our children may be the first generation in a long time to have fewer opportunities. Families can't spend more than they earn and neither should their government—it's not all that complicated. What we need to do is institute a series of radical changes that I would call the "Saving Our Grandchildren's Inheritance" package.

We start by remaking Congress. First step: make being a congressman a part-time job. When Congress meets, a lot of bad things happen. Astronomical amounts of money get spent; the government takes over banks and car companies; people try to reengineer entire sectors of the economy. Elected officials inevitably feel the need to do something, and they crave the media coverage that accompanies big proposals, no matter how wasteful or destructive. As Mark Twain observed, "No man's life, liberty or property is safe while the legislature is in session."

Making Congress a part-time job would fundamentally change Washington, forcing congressmen to spend much more time back in their districts interacting with regular people. It would also encourage greater independence by young members of Congress.

Most crucially, under a part-time Congress, congressmen would no longer regard politics as their career. I remember hearing congressmen, as they accepted some dubious favor, whine, "Well, my colleagues from law school are now making these big salaries at law firms." It's as if *they* are doing *us* a favor by serving in Congress. If they want to go try to get a big salary at a law firm, fine. But public service is different—it should involve at least a modicum of sacrifice.

Why not pay members of Congress to stay out of Washington? For decades we have paid farmers not to grow crops. We should pay congressmen a decent salary and then deduct money for every day Congress meets in session. This would certainly be cheaper to the taxpayer than the cost of the schemes Congress concocts in Washington.

Plenty of solid research shows Congress feels the need to *do something* when it's in session. Looking at Congress over a 25-year period, Professors Mwangi Kimenyi and Robert D. Tollison discovered the more time Congress spends in session, the longer and more complex laws become, and the more money Congress spends. (In a related study, it was found that rain makes the ground wet.) Another study found the same dynamic in state governments: full-time legislatures—California, Illinois, Massachusetts, Michigan, New Jersey, and New York, among others—all rank near the top in per capita spending and tax burden.[7]

Here's another revealing study: two finance professors, Michael Ferguson and Hugh Douglass Witte, discovered that more than 90 percent of the capital gains in the Dow Jones Industrial Average occurred when Congress was out of session.[8] Obviously, Congress is not the only factor here. But investors, it seems, know a sitting Congress is bad for business.

I'm also a supporter of term limits. Some conservatives oppose them, and their academic arguments can be quite compelling. But we simply will not change Washington with the same people in charge year after year.

We also need to change the manner in which Congress operates. America's finances are in chaos because Congress, regardless of which party is in power, engages in irresponsible spending. We can't expect them to operate the same way every year and produce different results. So we need a series of what I would call Fiscal Sanity Initiatives if we want to turn things around.

- We need a federal balanced budget amendment. Most states already have to abide by these limits, and Washington should do the same. Certainly a supermajority could authorize temporary spending during wartime or other extraordinary events, but we need to eliminate deficits during normal times.
- We should adopt a constitutional amendment to require a super-majority in Congress to raise taxes, along with a pay-as-you-go rule to help enforce a balanced budget amendment.
- A supermajority should also be required for government spending that exceeds historical norms as a percentage of GDP. And we need automatic sunset reviews on all discretionary spending programs to help consolidate and eliminate obsolete programs. As Ronald Reagan once put it, the closest thing to eternity on earth is a government program.
- The president should have a line item veto to restrain spending and reduce the corrupting influence of earmarks.

- We need to prevent the packaging of bills in order to force congressmen to vote on individual issues. There is no reason to continue allowing consideration of huge bills with numerous initiatives rolled into one. Congressmen currently avoid accountability by claiming they didn't want to vote for all that crazy spending and those crazy regulations, but they had to, since those measures were attached to the "save puppies and apple pie" legislation they really liked.

A lot of these ideas have been discussed before, but they have not been tried in Washington. It's not that this stuff can't be done. Here in Louisiana, for example, we have shown that these ideas can work. We cut the 2010–2011 budget by 14 percent, billions of dollars, to ensure that we live within our means.

Because Congress regulates so much, spends so much, and has such large staffs, the legislative process is often enshrouded in secrecy. Favors for lobbyists are snuck into large bills at the last minute to avoid public scrutiny. In President Obama's so-called "stimulus" bill, for example, few members of Congress even knew what they were voting on; the bill literally had handwritten notes on some pages when it was passed.[9] And it turned out that the bill made it possible for AIG executives to get large bonuses. Like the American people, congressmen themselves often discover what is in a law only after it's been approved.

Furthermore, we need other reforms to increase Congress's transparency. Members often vote for bills comprising hundreds of pages that no one, including staff members, has entirely read. Of course, the American people are also kept in the dark until after these bills are approved. A lot of congressmen would probably stop introducing bills altogether if everyone could plainly see what's in them.

Despite promises from both the Democratic Congress and President Obama of a new era of transparency, the legislative process has become particularly murky since the Democrats gained control of the House, Senate, and presidency. Like the massive, ever-changing stimulus bill, the healthcare reform bills were a travesty. House members repeatedly complained about not having enough time to read the language in the thousand-page healthcare bill before they were to vote—and one-sixth of our economy was at stake.[10]

In addition to curtailing our national debt and boosting transparency, the reforms outlined above would help break up the permanent political class that spreads around money and favors to corrupt previously well-intentioned individuals. This problem plagues both Republicans and Democrats. I remember standing on the House floor listening to some colleagues discuss the charges being leveled against California Republican Congressman Duke Cunningham, who resigned in 2005 and pled guilty to bribery, mail fraud, tax evasion, and other charges. One junior colleague asked, "Hey, can you believe all that Duke Cunningham stuff?" And this senior Republican began arguing, "Well, don't buy into a lot of that hype. There's more to that story." He was trying to say, "Hey, look, he's one of our guys, so he's really not *that* guilty." I was stunned. I thought, "There's something wrong when we excuse this kind of behavior." The cesspool has become a hot tub.

The intoxicating power of Washington fuels the sense of entitlement that pervades Congress. Consider the case of the late Alaska Senator Ted Stevens, a Republican who apparently accepted gifts from an oil services company called VECO, which also organized the extensive remodeling of the senator's home. Stevens denied this was a gift, claiming he didn't even know a lot of extra work was done on his house.[11] Now let me ask you this: when was the last time any contractor did more than you paid him to do? I have yet to have a contractor tell me, "Well, I had nothing better to do today, so I threw in an extra staircase for free."

More recently, Congressman Charlie Rangel, then-chairman of the powerful House Ways and Means Committee, was plagued by scandals including tax evasion, owning three rent-controlled apartments and using a fourth as an office, and accepting corporate funded junkets.[12] Do I need to add more names to the list?

The Republican Party professed to be a party of outsiders when it took over the House in 1994. And it was. But Washington changed them. Far too many came to Washington complaining about the stench and later used it as cologne. Republicans have made excuses for behavior they would never accept from Democrats. That is part of the price of joining the permanent political class.

Even aside from cases of outright corruption, the sad truth is that serving in Congress is now often an apprenticeship program for lobbyists-in-waiting. I remember seeing former members of Congress on Capitol Hill pushing some new legislation or program for some new client of their lobbying firm. They reminisced with sitting congressmen about their days in the Chamber like aging high school football players recalling their glory days on the field. These politicians-turned-lobbyists exploit their political access to cash in on what was supposed to be public service.

Not only do former congressmen lobby, but family members of serving congressmen lobby as well. The wives of Senators Byron Dorgan and Kent Conrad are both registered lobbyists.[13] Others have children or sons-in-law who are registered lobbyists. They all promise not to lobby their own family members, but in reality these relatives invariably have instant access.

Lobbyists constantly bombard congressmen with changes they want made to the law. Let's face it, the stakes are high. With the federal government intruding into everyone's business, companies that didn't need lobbyists twenty-five years ago now need high-dollar representation in Washington, lest Congress pass some arbitrary law that devastates their business. Consider Microsoft. For years, the company properly dedicated its time to winning market share. But when the Clinton Justice Department threatened it with anti-trust lawsuits, the firm felt the need to hire a team of lobbyists to protect itself. Now you have to rent a ballroom to hold a meeting of all the Microsoft lobbyists. Wouldn't it be better for corporate America to spend its time winning customers and making the economy grow instead of currying favors or protection from Congress? Sadly, hiring a lobbyist is often the best investment a firm can make in America today. A University of Kansas study found that each dollar spent lobbying on the 2004 American Jobs Creation Act secured $220 worth of benefits. That's a 22,000 percent return on investment![14]

A few simple reforms would go a long way toward reigning in the corrupting influence of lobbying. First, we should force former congressmen to wait five years before becoming a lobbyist or government consultant or whatever they try to call it. Second, we should explicitly ban family members of congressmen or senators from lobbying at all.

Of course, Congress is unlikely to regain public confidence until it restores sanity to our nation's finances. But these changes would help send the message that members of Congress are looking out for the American people's best interests and not their own.

*   *   *

Serving in Congress used to be just that—an act of service, not a financially lucrative training ground for lobbyists.

Our Founding Fathers envisioned that being a member of Congress would be a part-time job. Pennsylvania's state constitution even had a provision calling for members of the Legislature to "have some profession, calling, trade, or farm, whereby he may honestly subsist." Otherwise, they feared legislators would come to rely on politics as a career, and they would be unable to "preserve [their] independence." Back then, farmers would literally leave their fields and go to legislate in our nation's capital.

Benjamin Franklin argued for keeping congressional pay low, because he didn't want Congress to attract lazy or greedy people. As he put it at the 1787 Constitutional Convention,

> There are two passions which have a powerful influence in the affairs of men. These are ambition and avarice; the love of power and the love of money. Separately, each of these has great force in prompting men to action; but when united in view of the same object, they have in many minds the most violent effects. Place before the eyes of such men a post of honor that shall at the same time be a place of profit, and they will move heaven and earth to obtain it.

A mere glance at Washington today reveals Franklin's foresight.

Franklin's notion of service and sacrifice was deeply embedded in our earliest political leaders. George Washington came out of retirement three times to serve his country—each time out of a sense of duty, not profit-seeking.

Look at Thomas Nelson Jr., who signed the Declaration of Independence and served in the Continental Congress before being elected governor of Virginia. Nelson lent large sums of money to support the war effort and was never repaid. During the battle of Yorktown, he even urged General Washington to fire on his own house, the Nelson House, which the British commander General Cornwallis was using as his headquarters. Nelson offered to give five guineas to the first man to hit the building.

Thomas McKean of Delaware also signed the Declaration of Independence and served in the Continental Congress. He wrote to John Adams that because of his sympathies, "the consequence was to be hunted like a fox by the enemy, and envied, by those who ought to have been my friends. I was compelled to remove my family five times in a few months." But McKean felt it was all worth it. You have to wonder how many current members of Congress, who can't even stand being inconvenienced by the police, would accept such hardship for the sake of their country.

Lewis Morris of New York was a prominent land owner who also signed the Declaration of Independence and sat in the First Continental Congress. When warned by his brother Gouvernour Morris of the danger of signing the Declaration, Morris replied, "Damn the consequences. Give me the pen." When the British occupied New York, they looted and burned down his home.

For almost two hundred years, being in Congress meant holding down another job. As recently as the 1950s, Congress was still largely a part-time institution. Aside from extraordinary times such as World War II, members arrived in Washington by train in January and left in the summer. But Congress became more ambitious in the 1960s with the explosion of government spending and regulations. The power and importance of congressmen vastly increased, as the number of Senate and House Committees and Subcommittees mushroomed to enact the Great Society programs. With all the new money suddenly sloshing around Washington, interest groups sprang up demanding their piece of the pie. And they hired lobbyists to make sure they got it. Living under the same rules they enact for others may deter members of Congress from regulating our economy to death.

Granted, a part-time Congress would face its own ethical issues. How can we avoid conflicts of interest when people simultaneously run a business and pass laws? How could we prevent businesses from hiring congressmen just for the sake of influence? The answer is simple: full disclosure. Let the voters know everything, and they can render their judgment at election-time.

Some of my former congressional colleagues will not like this chapter, but most won't have time to read it. Many of them believe every congressman has a responsibility to defend Congress's reputation. I completely agree. But the only way to defend Congress's reputation today is to reform the whole institution, returning it to the limited, honest, and transparent role for which the Founding Fathers designed it.

CHAPTER 7

IN THE EYE OF THE STORM

My three-year-old daughter was frightened and trying to put off going to bed. She had heard the weather reports, and was terrified that the storm might come to the house to get her. I told Selia to pray to God and He would keep her safe. She asked me why the children in Florida hadn't prayed. I was confused, until she explained that Katrina had hit their homes and so they must not have prayed. We were soon forced to evacuate, along with my in-laws, to my parents' home in Baton Rouge. We packed for a weekend, and ended up staying for months. One night, my daughter asked me why God hadn't listened to her prayers. I was again confused until she explained she had asked Him to keep Katrina away from her house. I told her to go to bed, stop asking Daddy such questions, and to ask Mommy in the morning since Mommy knows everything. But many Louisianians were asking themselves that same question.

In Louisiana we just call it "the storm."

I had been in Congress eight months when Katrina, a 300-mile-wide hurricane, hit Louisiana in August 2005. After around a 20-foot-high storm surge, 80 percent of New Orleans was buried underwater.

One of the five most deadly hurricanes in U.S. history, Katrina's final tally was devastating: more than 1,400 people killed, a quarter million homes and businesses destroyed, and $60 billion worth of property damage.

Finger-pointing became an art form in the wake of the storm. Everyone involved had someone to blame for what happened, for what they did and didn't do. Some blamed President Bush, some blamed Michael Brown at FEMA, some blamed then-Louisiana Governor Kathleen Blanco. The television commentators blamed anyone and everyone, it seemed, at one time or another. There was enough blame to go around at every level of government.

The truth is, no single individual can be blamed for this storm. The idea that politicians can control the weather went out of style at the end of the Dark Ages when, so the story goes, King Canute of Denmark purposefully demonstrated the limits of monarchical power by sitting on the beach and commanding the tides to stop their advance.

Aside from the amusing clique of global warming alarmists, most people realize politicians and kings can't control the weather. The only thing government can do is to prepare adequately for a natural disaster and act quickly and intelligently when one hits. When the sky splits in two, as it did in 2005 and doubtless will again, are we prepared for what comes? Do we hesitate to respond? Do we shirk our duties? Or do we act as best we can, in the interests of the people we serve, to do what needs to be done?

During Katrina, New Orleans saw some terrible acts of selfishness, malice, and lawlessness, which were the focus of most media attention. But the storm also brought out the best in countless Louisiana residents. Reporters tended to overlook the innumerable acts of selfless heroism and compassion, some of which I witnessed with my own eyes. Contrary to the impression conveyed by the media, the vast majority of New Orleanians did not rob passers-by or loot stores. No—they risked themselves, over and over again, to help their neighbors, their friends, and outright strangers. The heroic actions of everyday people saved thousands of lives—that fact must never disappear from the history of Katrina.

* * *

The phones were quiet in my office just before Katrina hit—it was literally the calm before the storm. No strangers to severe weather, Louisianans thought they were prepared, with more than one million people having already evacuated their homes. Unfortunately, many stayed behind, either unable to escape or foolishly deciding to ride out the storm. On his emergency radio, Sheriff Harry Lee of Jefferson Parish offered some good advice to everyone still in the area: "You better haul ass! Y'all should have left yesterday."

When the storm first hit, it looked like New Orleans had dodged a bullet. Katrina caused some damage, but it wasn't as bad as initially feared. Then conditions rapidly deteriorated. My staff began receiving reports that the city was filling up with water. Forensic studies later discovered the broken floodwalls were not built according to modern standards, and they lacked deep sheet pilings and the proper kind of clay.

At first federal bureaucrats inexplicably denied the floodwalls had been breached. Later they acknowledged the city was flooding but, reluctant to admit their previous mistake, told me that "technically speaking," it was not a breach. I yelled into the phone, "Look, the water's coming in. You can call it whatever you want, but the water's coming in!"

As the hours went by, the calls my staff received became more urgent and fearful. By the next day, the media were broadcasting pictures of desperate people seeking refuge in the Superdome and the convention center. Other images showed residents stuck on their rooftops. Many in Louisiana were asking the same question: if Fox News can get to these people, why can't the government?

The expected assistance just wasn't there. Michael Brown, head of the Federal Emergency Management Agency (FEMA), told us unequivocally he had "resources in place" ready to move in with water, food, and clothing in the event the levees failed (though at the time, no one really considered that likely). But these resources were nowhere to be found. The initial response was further hampered by communications problems among first responders. After New York City police and fire departments had trouble communicating on 9/11, billions of dollars were spent to improve responder communication and homeland security—but state, federal, and local officials in Louisiana still had the same problems during Katrina. They were not communicating on the same frequencies.

As reports appeared of looting and chaos began to envelope New Orleans, I met with FEMA officials to figure out where the aid was. It was one of the most frustrating situations I've ever faced in my life. When we asked about the trucks, medical supplies, and food, we were told it wasn't safe to send them in because of the looting. When I asked why they couldn't just give the food and supplies to the National Guard already on-site—since they have guns, looters wouldn't be much of a problem—FEMA officials told us such action wasn't authorized yet.

FEMA's planned response was enormous in scope but slow in execution. The sheer size of the effort, and the logistics of moving tens of thousands of troops, hundreds of helicopters, and countless supplies and resources on such short notice, was just too much for them to handle. It took more than forty-eight hours for most FEMA officials and resources to get into the state, and even longer to get into the disaster area. By that time, many of the looters and criminals were running wild. The supplies just sat there, as federal officials were paralyzed. None of them wanted to make big decisions, fearing things would go wrong and jeopardize their careers.

I had my office set up a hotline number that we broadcast over the radio. We thought we might reach people who had no televisions but did have battery-operated radios. Even this simple measure was slowed by the bureaucracy—Congress informed us we couldn't pay for the effort with our congressional funds, so we tapped campaign money to pay for it. The hotline produced calls from citizens with various emergencies: some needed power, others needed medical supplies, and others had been separated from their children. One caller told us, "I'm stranded in my house with a cell phone and radio. Please come and get me."

Another woman I met at a shelter in Baton Rouge had been separated from her adult mentally disabled child. I sent volunteers to her house to find her daughter and convince the young woman to join her mom in safety. She was scared, finding the familiarity of her home reassuring, and refused to leave. Seeing no way to convince her to leave, these generous individuals gave her provisions and checked on her regularly, providing updates to her mother until she was permitted to go home.

In some areas criminals spilled into the streets to exploit the chaos. One sheriff ran across a thug who attacked and mugged an elderly woman. "What are you going to do with me?" the thug said with a taunting laugh. "You can't arrest me." The intrepid sheriff nodded in agreement—and then duct taped the guy to a lamp post. As one of my aides told me, "It's like Mad Max."

Many top officials seemed primarily focused on meetings and press conferences. Several days after the storm, FEMA's Michael Brown met with the Louisiana principals—Governor Blanco, congressmen, staffers, and others. I sat there with my chief of staff Timmy Teepell and waited for a useful discussion while the participants engaged in small talk. I reached my boiling point when several of the key figures gathered around a TV to watch footage of one of their previous press conferences.

"Let's get out of here!" I snapped at Timmy.

We took off to go talk to my friend Harry Lee.

Harry was practically an institution in Louisiana. Born in the back-room of a New Orleans laundromat, he was first elected sheriff of Jefferson Parish in 1979, serving for decades before passing away just a few years ago. His tough tactics were sometimes controversial, but he kept crime rates low, and his constituents loved him. During Katrina, Harry became known in the national press for threatening to commandeer local Wal-Mart and Sam's Club stores to keep them open so people could get urgent supplies. Bureaucrats were trying to keep the stores closed, so Harry announced that anyone who tried to shut the stores would be arrested.

In short, Harry was the kind of guy who gets things done in a crisis.

When I was with Harry after the storm, I had never seen him so angry. He was in a makeshift office cussing somebody out on the phone. "Well, I'm the sheriff," he barked, "and if you don't like it you can come and arrest me!" He explained the problem to me: he had asked for volunteers to show up with their boats to help rescue people out of the water. Scores of people offered to help, but then some bureaucrat announced no one could go out on the water without proof of insurance and registration for their boat. People were clinging to their rooftops for their lives, and some government hack was worried about rescuers not having the proper papers! So Harry told the volunteers to ignore the bureaucrat and use an exit ramp off the interstate to launch their boats.

After I agreed with his approach, Harry got back on the phone and said, "This is Sheriff Harry Lee. You can come arrest me, and Congressman Jindal's here—you can come and arrest him, too."

Harry was also angry that some rescue teams were turned away because they wanted to bring armed escorts—the authorities had banned firearms in New Orleans. The prospect of an outbreak of lawlessness, when the government cannot guarantee citizens' safety, is the reason why many law-abiding folks buy guns in the first place. But now that we faced this exact scenario, the government wanted to take away their only real means of self-defense. To ensure such an outrageous situation won't be repeated, I had a bill passed in Congress afterward preventing authorities from confiscating guns from law-abiding citizens during a natural disaster.

I asked Harry what he needed and in typical fashion he said, "Nothing." Harry, it seemed, was always prepared. Then I got a call from Dan Brouillette, then a vice president at Ford Motor Company. "We want to help," he said. "I can get you some trucks. The keys will be in them. Don't worry about paying for them."

We went to see Sheriff Jack Stephens in St. Bernard Parish. I asked Jack what he needed. He gave me a short list:

1. Trucks
2. Medical supplies
3. Water
4. Guns
5. More ammo

I couldn't help with the ammo, but I did get him those Ford trucks. Months later Jack told me, "We're still using those trucks you got for us. And we're still waiting for the trucks the federal government promised us."

We went to the other companies and said, "You know, Ford gave us a bunch of trucks. The need is so great, can you help too?" Sure enough, they started to match Ford's assistance. Isn't American generosity great? Budweiser shipped in water and ice. Pharmaceutical companies sent much needed medications.

In the absence of clear authority, more private companies came to my staff and to me to ask what they could do. A major company called my office. With the situation deteriorating, they wanted to send a rescue helicopter for their stranded employees. But they could not identify the agency with the authority to give them the go-ahead—and despite our best efforts, neither could we. We heard alternatively that FEMA, the FAA, the Department of Transportation, and the military were in charge. Even a FEMA representative on the ground in the state's emergency operations center could not give me a straight answer.

Time was running out, and we had to make a decision. So I told the company to avoid interfering with the Coast Guard, whose rescue missions were amazingly effective, and then I gave them the go-ahead.

"You got us authorization?" they asked.

"I'm giving you your authorization right now," I told them.

Sometimes, asking for forgiveness is better than asking for permission. But this was hardly the only case when red tape triumphed over common sense. When one mayor in my district called federal officials to try to get supplies for his constituents, he was put on hold for forty-five minutes. Eventually, a bureaucrat promised to write a memo to his supervisor. In another case, evacuees on a boat from St. Bernard Parish could not find anyone to give them permission to dock along the Mississippi River. And I can't tell you how many churches told us they'd sent volunteers to make food for hungry people, only to be threatened by government officials for not following some obscure health code regulation.

With the government mired in bureaucratic sloth, private businesses, institutions, churches, and individuals filled the breach. In nearby Baton Rouge, signs began appearing on the streets: "If you need food, water, or a bed, come here." Churches put up signs on the side of the road saying, "If you need something, come here."

We saw that same spirit again when Hurricane Gustav struck in 2008. After that storm, I received an email from the Oklahoma Christian Center saying they wanted to send thousands of pounds of frozen chicken. Everyone thought it was a joke, but they were dead serious. They said, "Look, you send a truck, we'll give it to you for free." So we arranged for transportation and sure enough, the frozen chicken was cooked up and fed to thousands of people.

During Katrina, my office became a coordinator of volunteers and donations for the corporate, community, and faith-based groups eager to help. If someone needed clean water, we called the beer and soda companies. If someone needed medical supplies, we called the pharmaceutical companies. If we needed people and boats, we called the churches. And when volunteers called us wanting to help, we went down the list calling up everyone who owned a plane or a helicopter to transport them. We also organized efforts from out of state; church groups, Rotary clubs, and civic organizations began arriving to help with the relief effort. I was especially touched to see children from all over the country send backpacks and other supplies.

Officials got on the radio and explained they needed water for the thousands of people staying at the Baton Rouge convention center. Within a few hours they broadcast a new message: "We don't need anymore." So many people showed up to donate bottles of water, Gatorade, and other drinks that officials were overwhelmed.

Private individuals certainly acted with more energy, compassion, and competence than many politicians and bureaucrats. That Friday, I sat in a meeting with Governor Blanco, New Orleans Mayor Ray Nagin, several state and federal officials, and President Bush. I told the president about a sheriff in my district who had called federal officials to ask for assistance and was told he would have to email his request. The bureaucrat was just following procedure, you see, he just wanted to have a record of the request. When the sheriff mentioned that he, like the rest of his town, had no electricity, the bureaucrat suggested he call someone who could email the details—and be sure to include the part about not being able to email in the email.

Almost every other official around that table told a similar story of people in their districts trying to get help and coming smack up against a government whose primary concern was checking off all the boxes and sending people through the red tape maze.

The president continually shook his head, shocked at what he was hearing. He kept turning to tell his aides, with ever increasing seriousness, "Fix it."

At the end of the meeting, I suggested that he consider appointing General Colin Powell, Jack Welch, or someone of similar skills and prominence with the authority to cut through the red tape, someone without political aspirations who had a record of getting things done. It was clear that many of the people involved were far too concerned with covering their own rear and looking good on TV. President Bush said he'd consider it, but he's known for being a very loyal man, and he seemed reluctant to second guess the people he'd put in charge. Loyalty is rare in politics and is usually a great asset—but in this case, it did not serve us well.

The relief effort foundered until the military finally imposed a unified chain of command. And that's one of the main lessons to improve the response to a future crisis: the government needs to establish from the outset a unified chain of command with the power to override the normal process restrictions and get things done. And junior officials up and down the line need to know they are authorized to make obvious and sensible calls in an emergency. They need to be encouraged to think creatively, exercise common sense, and develop innovative ways to solve problems—like turning to private companies and charities.

The experts who predicted Louisiana would never be the same after Katrina were right—just not in the way they expected. Louisiana changed, fundamentally, in the wake of the storm—the disaster forced us to rethink our aspirations as a state and our goals for the next generation. The storm forced us not just to rebuild, but to improve as we did so—to cast off failed institutions, crack down on long-standing corruption, and make our state a better place for people and businesses alike. Katrina was a terrible blow, and there is no silver lining, but Louisiana seized the opportunity to change for the better.

After the storm we cut red tape and streamlined our state recovery processes. We also put federal recovery dollars toward local governments and rebuilding critical infrastructure, ensuring transparency and strict accountability. The primary focus was on helping our hardest-hit communities complete their recovery efforts.

There's still a long way to go, but I'm optimistic because I have seen how the great spirit of Louisiana's people shone through during a catastrophe. First responders saved and evacuated tens of thousands of people and distributed millions of Meals Ready to Eat and liters of water.[1]

To this day, an array of volunteers and organizations is helping us to rebuild. You see the generosity of the American spirit when you meet families from around the country, like my friend and now governor of Virginia Bob McDonnell, who give up their vacations to come down to Louisiana and help rebuild homes in our battered communities.

In many cases, charities, faith-based groups, and not-for-profit organizations move faster and are more flexible than federal programs. Don't get me wrong—there is a role for government, which has to build those levees and otherwise ensure our basic safety. And we must acknowledge that the National Guard responded to Katrina with stunning courage and efficiency, as did the Coast Guard, which is estimated to have rescued 33,000 people. But FEMA's centralized model simply didn't work.

Thus, we've created a bigger role for private citizens to play in future relief efforts. This builds on the tremendous efforts we saw from local restaurants, caterers, cafeterias, and schools and universities, which produced hot meals for evacuees. We are also coordinating efforts with church groups, which cooked thousands of meals for free. Many people would be surprised to learn it's cheaper (and tastes a lot better) for us to buy a hot meal from world famous chefs like John Folse or John Besh in New Orleans than for FEMA to deliver an MRE.

* * *

The story of Katrina is one of tragedy, yes—but it is also one of heroism, of the inspiring examples of individuals who sacrificed all so that others might live.

Craig Fugate, the new head of FEMA under President Obama, has argued that when disasters strike, government has to be prepared to "draft the public." "We tend to look at the public as a liability," he told the *Atlantic Monthly*. "[But] who is going to be the fastest responder when your house falls on your head? Your neighbor."[2] That's the truth. When disaster strikes, your neighbors are likely to be your best hope—and they shouldn't have to worry about a bureaucrat standing in their way.

It's not America's government that has made America great. It's Americans. It's the people who are, at their core, so incredibly uncommon. I witnessed America's incredible civic spirit countless times in the aftermath of Katrina. And this spirit goes back a long way. Alexis de Tocqueville wrote about it in the nineteenth century—about how the "countless little people, humble people, throughout American society, expend their efforts in caring and in the betterment of the community, blowing on their hands, pitting their small strength against the inhuman elements of life."

We witnessed this same spirit again just a few weeks after Katrina, when Hurricane Rita hit southwest Louisiana, completely demolishing some of our coastal communities.

Once again, masses of people turned out to help their neighbors in need. It is the same courageous spirit that has animated the American soul since our nation's founding—the spirit that dares us to explore, to build, and to take enormous risks to better ourselves, our families, and our country. When Americans see a burning building and hear cries for help, we don't run from the flames, but into them. That's why we are a nation of people who are not just free, but bravely so.

Government needs to acknowledge the incredible feats Americans can accomplish when called upon. Too often government stands not at the side of the firefighter, the police officer, the emergency responder, and the civilian volunteer—but in their path, standing in front of the burning building to say, "Stop! Don't go in there. Fill out this form first." Politicians appear on TV a lot during a crisis, but they're rarely heroic. Certainly nothing I did during Katrina was heroic. All that my staff and I did, or tried to do, was to knock down the barriers between the real American heroes and the people they were trying to save. It's a travesty those barriers existed at all.

In 2008, three years after Katrina, I was beginning my service as governor, and the first of two hurricanes entered the Gulf. Hurricane Gustav was a menacing storm with strong winds which the National Weather Service told us could be as bad as it gets, possibly even worse than Katrina. Remembering the experiences of Katrina, I quickly decided that we would evacuate all of coastal Louisiana, the largest evacuation in American history. We worked with parish presidents and coastal leaders to issue mandatory evacuations to encourage those who had the ability to evacuate themselves to do so. For the rest, we provided transportation, shelter, food, and medical attention when needed. Ambulances began transporting the medically needy from hospitals and homes to airfields. We faced many obstacles. Buses and ambulances that were promised didn't show up in time. MREs and tarps didn't come in sufficient numbers.

So we made do. For example, we commandeered school buses and deployed national guardsmen as drivers to evacuate our people. It was Sunday morning, hours before Gustav's winds would close the airspace and prevent medical airlifts. We had used the limited ambulances we had to bring patients from New Orleans area hospitals to Lakefront Airport. Governor Rick Perry of Texas dispatched six C130s from the Texas National Guard to fly continuous sorties bringing patients from New Orleans to Texas hospitals. Eventually Northern Command sent aircraft from as far away as Canada, but those first planes from Texas literally arrived just in time and helped us save lives. God Bless Texas.

The final sortie carrying the last patients lifted off less than an hour before tropical winds closed the airspace. We ended up evacuating over 10,000 medical patients across the state, the largest medical evacuation in our nation's history.

As the second hurricane, Ike, was still flooding Louisiana, I was in a high water military vehicle and headed toward Erath, Louisiana, a small town in Vermilion Parish. Many of the homes in Erath had been flooded just three years earlier, and now the water was rising again. As we approached City Hall we saw sandbags piled everywhere. Having already dispatched a fire and rescue team and the National Guard, I met with local leaders, asking them what else they needed. One of them replied, "Don't worry about us, Governor. We'll get control of the water and then we're going to go Cameron Parish because they got hit harder than we did." Even as they faced danger, they were worried about their neighbors.

I then went to Cameron Parish and found the same irrepressible spirit. I met a pastor of a church there. "Reverend, how bad is it?" I asked.

"Well, we're flooded again," he said. He explained they had spent the last three years rebuilding after getting flooded by Hurricane Rita. And now Ike had hit them just as they were about to hold their first service in their rebuilt church. Ike had done its damage. But then he added with a smile, "Don't worry about us, Governor. We'll find somewhere else to worship. Our people are okay, and that's the most important thing." And they did rebuild the church.

The pastor knew that where two or more are gathered in His name, He'll be there. It's that kind of faith, that kind of resilience, that demonstrates the best qualities of the American spirit.

Chapter 8

Converts and Immigrants

My dad is a pretty calm guy. But if you want to get him mad, just start bad mouthing America.

You see, my dad is an immigrant to this country. But like my mom, he's also a convert. They probably love America more passionately than most people born here, because they know what it's like in other countries where you are defined by your name or the status into which you're born. They've lived in a society that often treated women as second-class citizens, that had widespread, grinding poverty, and that offered less freedom than we have in America. In short, based on their personal experience, my parents don't just think America is the greatest country on earth, they know it.

While America's immigration problems are serious, they show how special this country really is. Think about it: millions of people are voting with their feet to come here. People risk their lives swimming with sharks, they dig tunnels, they risk going to prison, and they sometimes perish in the back of unventilated trucks just to get to America.

Passions are hot on both sides of the immigration issue. Some want to end immigration almost entirely, seeking to blow up the bridge behind them now that they have made it across. Others believe we don't have any real right to say who can and cannot come here, and think we should open up our borders and grant amnesty to millions of illegals who broke the law when they crossed the border.

The inscription on the Statue of Liberty, "Give me your tired, your poor, your huddled masses, yearning to breathe free," is a beautiful sentiment. I wish it were as simple to apply it today as it was in past centuries, when we welcomed to our shores just about anyone who could get here. For that matter, I wish we didn't need heavy security at airports, that we could walk freely through the U.S. Capitol, and that we didn't have to lock our doors at night. But that is not realistic in today's world, and I'm a realist who focuses on solutions.

Former Senator Fred Thompson said it well when he noted that we should be a nation of high fences and wide gates. In other words, we need to find a controlled way to continue welcoming immigrants. That approach would require three main things: first, ensure that our borders are secure—not talk about it or study it, just do it; second, enforce our existing immigration laws; and third, refocus our legal immigration policy to encourage high-skilled immigrants who embrace American values. I also think we need to continue to be a place where refugees fleeing persecution, such as those escaping Communist Cuba, can find safe harbor and a new home.

Immigration should help our country compete in the world and improve the quality of life for U.S. citizens while offering unlimited opportunities to hard-working immigrants looking for freedom. That has traditionally been the focus of our immigration policy, but over the past forty years we've developed an upside-down immigration system that tempts and even encourages unskilled illegals to sneak into the country while highly educated, law-abiding potential immigrants are turned away. In Louisiana we have a word for this: DUMB.

To the immigrants who came here legally, I say welcome. You are now lucky enough to be living in the greatest country on earth. It's often said that America is a nation of immigrants, but that's not quite right. We are a nation where immigrants become Americans. Now, I don't mean immigrants should strip off every old custom or deny their heritage. Growing up I remember my mom was always interested in what was happening in the "old country," but she was also heavily engaged in American issues. She never renounced Indian culture, but she became a rabid Dallas Cowboys fan because she loved Roger Staubach. (Don't worry, this has been remedied, and she is now a card carrying member of the Who Dat Nation.) Growing up, my parents took me to India to meet my extended family, but every summer they would also take me to the great shrines of America—national parks and monuments that offered a rich narrative of our national history.

I'm not suggesting there is a right way or a wrong way to assimilate. However, I do agree with Teddy Roosevelt that we should not think of ourselves as hyphenated Americans but simply as Americans. I don't much care what people call me, but I don't like when people ask me where I'm "really" from. I'm from Baton Rouge by God Louisiana. I am an American. Period.

Open immigration was a key concern of our Founding Fathers who, in the Declaration of Independence, charged King George III with "Obstructing the Laws of Naturalization of Foreigners" and "Refusing to Encourage their Migration hither." As George Washington explained, "The bosom of America is open to receive not only the Opulent and respectable Stranger, but the oppressed and persecuted of all nations and Religions; whom we shall welcome to a participation of all our rights and privileges."[1]

While encouraging immigrants, our Founding Fathers expected immigrants to learn our language, culture, and way of life. In the eighteenth century, when German immigrants insisted on setting up their own schools and maintaining their own language, Benjamin Franklin complained that "instead of learning our language, we must learn theirs, or live as in a foreign country."[2] Also opposing self-segregation, George Washington argued immigrants should live among native-born Americans to ensure they didn't "retain the language, habits, and principles (good or bad) which they bring with them." If immigration were done right, said Washington, "with our people, they, or their descents will get assimilated to our customs, measures and laws; in a word, soon become one people."[3]

During the nineteenth century, waves of immigrants came to America from Ireland, Italy, China, and elsewhere, each bringing something unique that has become quintessentially American. Hamburgers and pizza, which were once considered odd, are now authentically American. Hot dogs, thought to have been first introduced by a German immigrant, are now the unofficial food of Independence Day. Indeed, American greatness stems in large part from our unique, astoundingly successful immigration system—a system that now lies in tatters.

* * *

Two events occurred in the twentieth century that radically changed who came to this country. The first was the development of the American southwest. Until 1924, the United States did not even have a border patrol—the American southwest was so sparsely populated that few people sought to immigrate there. But California, Arizona, and

Texas grew rapidly in the last century, providing an immigration magnate for citizens of Mexico, which remained mired in corruption, poverty, and political instability.

This has created a unique situation—our southern border is the only place in the world where a highly developed country shares a long border with a developing country. Unable to produce enough jobs for its roughly 100 million residents, Mexico is effectively exporting its unemployment to us. As Professor David Kennedy of Stanford University notes, "The income gap between the United States and Mexico is the largest between any two contiguous countries in the world."[4] This dichotomy, occurring across an unsecured border, has created the current immigration crisis, with an estimated 10 to 12 million illegal immigrants now residing in America.

The second development was a growing disconnect between our immigration policies and practices and our nation's economic interests. Politicians on the Left seemed to want to grant amnesty to millions of illegal and largely less skilled immigrants, while politicians on the Right seemed to want to limit both legal and illegal immigration. Neither seemed to understand the important contribution legal immigration has made and will continue to make towards our nation's development.

Consider the case of Sanjay Mavinkurve, who holds an H1-B temporary visa for high-skilled workers. Born in Bombay, India, to working class parents, Sanjay grew up loving America. "I admired everything in the way America portrayed itself—the opportunity, U.S. Constitution, its history, enterprising middle class," he told the *New York Times*. He came to the United States on a scholarship and attended Western Reserve Academy, a private school near Cleveland. After scoring 1560 out of 1600 on the SAT, he went to Harvard, where he hung an American flag on his dorm room wall. Shortly after graduating with a degree in computer science, he began working as a product manager at Google, where he helped to develop Google News and the Google toolbar. But while Google may be in the Silicon Valley, Sanjay lives in Toronto, Canada. Why? Because his wife, who works in finance, can't get a visa to live in the United States![5]

Shouldn't our immigration policy increase the skill level of the American workforce? Go to any university or college in America and you'll see we are educating students from nearly every country on earth. But what do we do right after we train these students in medicine, nuclear physics, engineering, and the like? We kick them out. That's right—we turn a blind eye to millions of unskilled workers streaming over our borders, but we make sure to deport budding professionals, people who could add significantly to our nation's economy and dynamism, people who are inventing the technologies of tomorrow.

Just look at Silicon Valley. The founders of more than half the companies created there over the past fifteen years were born abroad. Immigrants created some of the biggest high tech powerhouses, such as Intel (Andrew Grove from Hungary), Yahoo (Jerry Yang from Taiwan), Sun Microsystems (Vinod Khosla of India and Andreas von Bechtolsheim of Germany), and Google (co-founder Sergey Brin of Russia). An incredible 42 percent of the engineers with master's degrees and 60 percent with Ph.Ds in engineering in the United States are foreign-born. Comprising 12.5 percent of the American population, foreign-born residents make up nearly 40 percent of high tech company founders.[6]

The 1990s saw an unprecedented wave of immigration to the United States, with the addition of 13 million foreign-born residents in the U.S., bringing the total to 32 million.[7] While the number of illegal immigrants would be drastically reduced simply by securing the border and enforcing existing law, as I explain below, an equally important reform is to overhaul our legal immigration policy to encourage immigrants with needed skills and education. We should not cut the number of legal immigrants we allow into this country—robust immigration keeps our country dynamic, unlike aging, low-immigration countries like Japan—but we can reorient it to bring in those who stand to contribute the most.

Studies show a key determinant in whether the children of immigrants will be successful in America is the educational level of their parents. One study found more than 40 percent of immigrants who enter the country poor are still poor ten years later. This is something new. Back in 1960, immigrants were much less likely to remain poor than native-born Americans. Today they are much more likely to remain poor—and taxpayers foot the bill. A stupid immigration policy will do that.

The data show that in 2004, for example, low-skill immigrant households received about $10,000 more in government benefits than did the average U.S. household, largely because they received more welfare. Low-skill immigrant households also pay less in taxes than the rest of us. In short, low-skill immigrant households receive nearly three dollars in immediate government benefits and services for each dollar they pay.[8]

Does this mean we should only allow immigrants who are highly skilled and educated to come to America? Absolutely not. While attracting high-skilled immigrants should be a special focus, our country can also benefit greatly from immigrants whose only credentials are a desire to work hard, assimilate, and chase the American Dream. But the American Dream is not to have the government take care of you. That is an American nightmare.

Hard-working, unskilled immigrants are in fact vital to America. I'm sure nearly every person reading this book has some personal experience with these kinds of motivated immigrants. Much like my parents, many of them have experienced third-world poverty, giving them a perspective most native-born Americans just don't have. These people make America a better place and a stronger nation. They should be embraced, not feared. But we need a legal, orderly system for admitting them, where their number is agreed upon by our elected representatives and then rigorously enforced. Despite all the heated rhetoric about this issue, there is actually a pretty simple way to do that.

*   *   *

Our illegal immigration crisis is causing all kinds of serious problems, especially by straining our healthcare and education systems. Some fire-breathing politicians argue we should simply deny healthcare and education to illegals and their families. But that's not the American way—we are far too compassionate to turn people away from emergency rooms or keep 6-year-old kids out of first grade.

My approach to stopping the massive wave of illegal immigration is straightforward: build a fence (partly high-tech, comprised of cameras and censors, and partly a traditional fence) and enforce the laws. When I was in Congress, I voted in 2006 for building a high-tech fence along the border and committing to systematically monitoring our border. Due to a lack of political will from nearly all parts of the government, however, the fence has not seen much progress; it is limited to a small part of the Arizona, California, and Texas borders. I also voted to prevent the federal government from tipping off the Mexican government about the whereabouts of Minuteman Project volunteers who monitor the border and report illegal immigration activity to the border patrol. Unlike some of my liberal critics, I believe we should encourage the peaceful involvement of public citizens in protecting our country and upholding the law.

Many members of Congress claim it would be impossible to secure the border. That's an amusing argument. Apparently, we can send men to the moon, we can kill terrorists with unarmed drones from half a continent away, but we can't build a big fence. Others emotionally compare a border fence to the Berlin Wall, ignoring the inconvenient fact that the Berlin Wall was meant to keep a captive people *in*, while our border fence would keep people *out* who get here by breaking the law.

Advocates of amnesty or quasi-amnesty for illegal immigrants don't know their history. In 1986 Congress passed an amnesty called the Immigration Reform and Control Act, legalizing about 3 million illegals and providing for employer sanctions for hiring illegal workers in the future. At the time, advocates promised the amnesty would be accompanied by strict border control to finally solve the illegal immigration problem. That should sound familiar, because it's the same plan and the same promise we hear from amnesty advocates today.

But instead of ending the problem, the 1986 amnesty led to an explosion of illegal immigration. The promise to secure the border wasn't kept, and the Act sent the message that if illegals can just make it across the border, they'll eventually get amnesty. Roughly two decades later, President George W. Bush and Senator John McCain pushed for a de facto amnesty for the millions of illegals who had arrived since the 1986 amnesty. Their plan was similar to the 1986 policy, except that amnesty recipients were required to fulfill a few minor requirements, like paying a fine. I know President Bush and Senator McCain had the purest of motives, opting for the course they believed was most compassionate. But I also believe any replay of the 1986 amnesty will fail.

We'd go a long way toward solving the illegal immigration problem if the federal government would fulfill its responsibility to enforce existing immigration laws, especially against employers of illegals. Federal courts have affirmed that local authorities also have the right and the responsibility to enforce these laws. In Arizona, for example, the state Legislature passed a law allowing state authorities to suspend or revoke the business license of a company that knowingly employs illegal workers. The U.S. District Court for the District of Arizona and the liberal Ninth Circuit Court of Appeals upheld the constitutionality of this law.

More recently, Arizona enacted new policies to enforce immigration laws. These have sparked various protests by left-wingers, including an attempt to boycott the entire state of Arizona. Clearly, when the federal government does not do its job, the American people take action on their own. The ultimate solution is for the federal government to fulfill its responsibility to secure our borders.

Some immigration experts argue a moderate enforcement of immigration laws, costing less than $2 billion over five years, would cut the illegal population in half. The key is not just to round up illegals, but to punish their employers. Without available jobs, millions of illegals will have little choice but to return home voluntarily.

* * *

Citizens of most countries define their identity by ethnic descent. But Americans are different. We're bonded together by ideals and values that form a common national creed. That's why all immigrants should learn English; in order to communicate these values with each other, we need a common language. Moreover, learning English is crucial for immigrants' chances of success in America. Today, an immigrant who doesn't speak English will probably experience a low standard of living and even government dependence.

Through most of our history, the need for immigrants to learn English was so widely recognized that it wasn't a topic of serious political debate. Congress even traditionally refused to admit new states if they lacked an English-speaking majority.

But in recent decades, the incentive to learn English has eroded. For example, the Voting Rights Act of 1965 required the provision of bilingual voting ballots. California and some other states also allow voting by mail in state elections using non-English language ballots. But bilingual ballots should not be needed, because immigrants since the Nationality Act of 1906 (later reaffirmed in the Nationality Act of 1940) have had to demonstrate literacy in English in order to gain U.S. citizenship.[9] Since only citizens can vote, why would anyone need a foreign language ballot?

Furthermore, just before he left office President Clinton signed Executive Order 13166, which required federal agencies to ensure people could receive communications and services from the government in foreign languages. Although well-intentioned, the policy further reduces the motivation for immigrants to learn English.

I co-sponsored a bill in Congress to declare English the official language of the United States and to establish a uniform English language rule for naturalization, to reaffirm the previous law. Understanding how vital English is to success in America, many immigrants enthusiastically supported the bill. In fact, much of the opposition to it didn't come from immigrants, but from guilt-ridden liberal elites who believe that encouraging English unjustly imposes American values on immigrants.

According to this philosophy of multiculturalism, we should not try to spread our values because our culture is no better than anyone else's—and in many ways, it's supposedly much worse. This view is popular among liberal academics at elite universities and professional "civil rights activists." But in my experience as both the son of immigrants and as a governor, the vast majority of immigrants reject this nonsense. They know life in America is better—that's why they came here in the first place.

I have no problem imposing American values on people who want to become Americans. Freedom, hard work, self-reliance, and rugged individualism are values all Americans should embrace. If immigrants reject these values, well, it's a big world out there.

* * *

The reasons we must secure our borders are really beyond dispute.

First—the safety of our citizens. Our porous borders tempt terrorists to sneak into America. Additionally, many border communities are imperiled by the violence, drug smuggling, and other crimes committed by vicious Mexican drug cartels that now threaten to spill over the border.

Second—the cost to our citizens. As I noted before, America is the most generous nation on earth. We care for our poor and needy, and we do the same across the world through government foreign aid as well as private charity and humanitarian assistance. But we cannot allow millions of illegal immigrants to sneak into our country and eventually end up on government assistance.

Third—the cost to our culture. Robust immigration is a great benefit to America, but immigrants have to come here legally and they have to be not just immigrants, but converts. When we accept immigrants who see America as a mere resource to exploit for their personal gain, we spread a debilitating welfare mentality that chips away at the traditional can-do attitude that has made America great.

The truth is, with the exception of Native Americans, we are all immigrants to this country. Some came hundreds of years ago, some hundreds of hours ago. My mom and dad came to America to work hard and chase the American Dream. And in the end they caught it. Becoming converts to the idea of America, they are now middle-class Americans. Make no mistake, many Americans helped them along the way, by hiring them to work, loaning them a car, and teaching them the ways of America. But they never accepted welfare, nor did the idea ever cross their minds.

Determined, highly motivated immigrants helped make this country great. And they will continue doing so—if we reform immigration.

CHAPTER 9

THE MOST BORING GOVERNOR IN LOUISIANA'S HISTORY

You could hear the snickers in the crowd. "Did he just say he's going to clean up corruption in Louisiana? Sure he is, and I bet he thinks the Saints will win the Super Bowl, too! The poor young fella."

During my runs for governor in both 2003 and 2007, many Louisianians thought it was quaint, perhaps even charming, that I pledged to crack down on the corruption that has made our state famous for over a century. It's not that folks didn't want clean government; they just thought it was terribly naïve to think we could ever achieve it.

You could see it in their faces. Some of the older ladies on the campaign trail looked like they had to restrain themselves from patting me on the head. I think a few of them wanted to adopt me. The state's grizzled political veterans were less charitable, taking me for a dreamer, a fool, or both.

A former Louisiana congressman has often remarked that at any given time half the state of Louisiana is under water and the other half is under indictment. Indeed, you could fill a small library with books about, shall we say, the "colorful" history of political corruption in my state. Although our poor reputation on this issue is long-standing, once in a while we manage to outdo ourselves.

One of the most famous examples occurred in 1991, when our race for governor came down to a battle between Edwin Edwards, a former congressman and governor famous for his corruption scandals and gambling debts, and David Duke, a former leader of the Ku Klux Klan. That was like having a choice between being shot or stabbed— either way, it's not going to turn out well. Much of the country was transfixed by this weird campaign, which produced unusual slogans like the pro-Edwards motto, "Vote for the Crook, It's Important." In the end, a majority of folks did just that. Edwards returned to the governor's mansion, served out his term, and a few years later was sentenced to ten years in prison on corruption-related charges.

More recently, another Louisiana politician grabbed national headlines for corruption. Bill Jefferson, a man whom I served alongside in Congress and whose congressional district was adjacent to mine, was convicted of taking bribes after the authorities found $90,000 hidden in his freezer. He gave new meaning to the term "cold hard cash."

And remember, for every high-profile case like Edwards or Jefferson, there are many more local corruption stories that don't get a lot of attention outside Louisiana. In February 2010, former state senator Derrick Shepherd was sentenced to three years in jail for money laundering. Worse still, three of our last four insurance commissioners ended up in prison.

I sure don't have room here to cover the whole history of Louisiana's colorful politicians. But I would be remiss if I didn't mention the granddaddy of them all, the Kingfish, the one, the only, Governor and Senator Huey Long. This guy takes the cake . . . and Lord knows what else.

In addition to being a tremendously talented politician and what many call a socialist, Huey Long wrote the book on patronage, packing the state government with his own network of political supporters. Offended by his corruption, cronyism, and his efforts to begin taxing refined oil to pay for his social programs, the state Legislature in 1929 moved to impeach Huey on eight charges, including bribery, seeking to intimidate the press, and misuse of state funds.[1]

When news of the plan to impeach the governor leaked out, Long's handpicked Speaker of the House quickly moved to adjourn the session. After that, a massive fistfight broke out on the House floor, an event known as "Bloody Monday." (It was a fitting name, in light of reports that some legislators used brass knuckles.) It wasn't one of our state's better moments, but hey, at least it was before YouTube was invented.[2]

The House eventually did impeach the "Kingfish," but he stopped the effort in the state Senate by convincing fifteen senators (just one more than he needed) to sign a statement vowing they would not vote to convict Long regardless of any evidence.

Having grown tired of endless critical news stories, Long founded his own newspaper in 1930, *Louisiana Progress*, which he used to trumpet his achievements and to trash his opponents. Companies receiving state contracts were expected to buy ads in the paper, and Long even tried to pass a law forbidding the publication of "slanderous material"—in other words, negative stories about him. (My staff has repeatedly suggested I try the same thing, but so far I've managed to fight them off.)

As colorful a politician as Huey Long was, my favorite Louisiana character is Huey's brother, Earl Long. Serving multiple terms as governor, Earl became famous for carrying on a multi-year affair with a stripper, Blaze Starr. Less well-known is that Earl Long, while serving as governor, was involuntarily confined to a mental hospital. His wife, the first lady known as Miz Blanche, is said to have played a major part in having the governor committed—owing in part to his ongoing affair with the stripper.

But the story gets better. Nothing in Louisiana law required Earl to step down as governor, so he ran the state by phone from the mental hospital. He fired the head of the state hospital system and replaced him with one of his own political supporters. Long was then immediately diagnosed as having no mental illness and later released from the hospital. He began wearing a large button that read, "I'm not crazy."

You just could not make this stuff up. And if you did, no one would believe it. I know many people who fervently insist most politicians should be committed to mental hospitals. Imagine how chagrined they would be to learn that, in Louisiana at least, even that will not stop a politician.

* * *

So it was against this backdrop of bribes, cronyism, strippers, fist-fights, and mental institutions that I pledged right after being elected in 2007 to try to be Louisiana's most effective and most boring governor of all time. My wife immediately told me that I would have no trouble with the boring part.

To be fair, Louisiana does not have a monopoly on government corruption. I saw for myself that Washington, D.C., has its share—and then some. I served in Congress at the tail end of the Republican revolution that began in 1994 when the Republicans took control of the House of Representatives for the first time in over forty years. By the time I got there in 2005, the revolution was running on fumes. The new thinking and idealism that had fueled the Republican renaissance had given way to a desperate attempt to amass and retain power. This led to a series of ethical lapses by congressmen—not strictly Republicans, but plenty of Republicans for sure.

The party that had a decade earlier stormed into Washington to change it had become changed by it. Of course these are generalities, and they don't apply to everyone, but they do apply to far too many. And the Republican Party was much too slow to condemn their own. You can't slam the other party when one of their guys breaks the rules and turn a blind eye when one of yours does it. The public sees that for what it is: hypocrisy.

Ethical lapses were not the only reason Republicans lost control of Congress, but they played a big part. In my short three years in the House we saw one of our own, Duke Cunningham, nailed for taking bribes from defense contractors. Another Republican, Bob Ney, pled guilty to corruption charges. And Republican Mark Foley was discovered to have been sexually harassing male high school students in the House page program.

Of course, with 435 members of the House and 100 members of the Senate, you're always going to have a few bad apples. And with all the temptations of power in Congress, corrupt people, shall we say, will always be well-represented there. But the key issue is how seriously we try to prevent corruption, and how we deal with it when it's discovered. Personally, I'm for throwing the book at elected leaders who cheat, steal, enrich themselves, and otherwise exploit their position for personal gain.

I had made fighting corruption a centerpiece of my 2003 campaign for governor, and I stressed the issue again in my successful 2007 campaign. The problem in Louisiana has not only been that elected officials were breaking the rules, but that the rules were too lax. This created what I would call systemic corruption, otherwise known as business as usual.

Cleaning up corruption in our state is not just some do-gooder crusade. There is also a tangible benefit: jobs. People don't want to invest their money or start companies in a state they don't trust. For years, companies have admired Louisiana's workforce, climate, natural beauty, and plentiful energy resources, but have been chased away by fears they would not get a fair shake or that they would be subject to a shakedown. In a 2004 Louisiana State University survey, 945 out-of-state business CEOs were asked what could be done to make Louisiana more business friendly; eradicating corruption was tied as the top recommendation.

During my 2007 campaign, I introduced a detailed plan for ethics reform based on five pillars.

1. *You cannot be both a lobbyist and a legislator.*

Our state has a part-time Legislature that sits in session less than one-quarter of each year. Over the years too many legislators had been allowed to augment their income by working as lobbyists or as "consultants" for lobbying firms. In my view, this was an inherent conflict of interest that cost us business and hurt our reputation.

2. *Legislators should be required to submit to financial disclosure.*

The best way to prevent corruption is to mandate transparency. Statewide elected officials in Louisiana were required to submit financial disclosure forms, but legislators, local officials, and other state appointees were not. Some complained they would not serve if they had to fully disclose their income, assets, and debts. I responded that they should not let the door hit them on the way out. You can now go online and see full disclosure for these officials.

3. *You cannot serve in government and do business with the government at the same time.*

It had become routine for legislators or their family members to own or be part owners of businesses that work for the government. In my view, you can do business with the government or you can serve in the government, but you cannot do both. You are elected to serve the public, not yourself.

4. *Lobbyists must fully disclose all their actions.*

The public has a right to know who is lobbying whom and for what.

5. *Don't do the crime if you can't do the time.*

When the penalty for breaking ethics laws is a small fine or a slap on the wrist, the whole system becomes a joke. Severe offenses must be punished by expulsion and/or criminal charges.

After I became governor, many in our state capitol were startled to learn this wasn't just empty campaign rhetoric. In fact, when we first announced our ethics platform in 2007, some reporters didn't cover the event because they thought it was just a meaningless pledge.

It's said that Speaker of the House Tip O'Neill had the same reaction to President Reagan's election in 1980. A year into Reagan's first term, O'Neill reportedly told the president they had assumed his campaign promises to reduce government and cut taxes were just rhetoric. He said they were shocked to find out he really meant it. Now that is a great compliment.

In my first month as governor, I called a special session of the Legislature, and we completely rewrote our ethics laws along the lines of my proposals. As a result, we've finally begun to change our century-long reputation for corruption. The Center for Public Integrity says we have gone from 44th to 1st in the country in terms of legislative disclosure laws.[3] And we have gone from the bottom 5 to the top 5 on the Better Government Association's "Integrity Index."[4]

Still, there's more work to be done. In fact, I warned folks that the new rules could result in many more politicians getting prosecuted, creating the perception that things are actually worse than ever. But make no mistake—the casual toleration of corruption is a thing of the past.

*   *   *

It's a bit sad that ethics in government has become such a pressing topic. Conducting one's business in an ethical manner, be it public service or any other pursuit, should be seen as standard practice, not as some wonderful virtue. Being ethical is only a minimum requirement for a politician. I can only laugh when politicians brag that they have never been involved in corruption. So what? I should hope not. That hardly seems like grounds for support.

Unfortunately, the public today often expects the worst from politicians. Can you blame them? Certainly corrupt politicians have been with us for all of human history. That said, we are on a strong bipartisan run of "men behaving badly" in the past few years. Bill Clinton was just the tip of the iceberg. In just the past year or two, New York Governor Eliot Spitzer resigned after getting caught with prostitutes; New Jersey Governor Jim McGreevey stepped down over a homosexual affair; South Carolina Governor Mark Sanford was censured for "hiking the Appalachian Trail"; Idaho Senator Larry Craig was caught toe tapping in a bathroom stall; Nevada Senator John Ensign preyed on his staffer who also happened to be his best friend's wife; and New York Congressman Eric Massa resigned amidst allegations he had sexually harassed his male staff. I could go on—but this is plenty.

And of course, there's the saga of morally bankrupt former North Carolina Senator John Edwards. Here's a guy who had a real shot at becoming president. And while he pursued that goal he was breaking his marriage vows as his wife courageously battled cancer. He stared into the camera every day, lied through his near perfect teeth, and convinced a staffer to claim paternity of his "love child." Again, you just can't make this stuff up.

I've heard many people blame the sordid transgressions that marred Bill Clinton's presidency for causing a moral decline in America. But I don't think one person can cause a moral decline, nor can one person improve our society's moral condition. The way I see it, we often get the politicians we deserve. True, this unethical behavior sometimes comes out of the blue. But in the case of Bill Clinton, for example, Americans already knew a lot about his . . . er . . . unusual personal history during his first presidential campaign—and we elected him anyway.

It should be noted that unethical behavior is by no means confined to politics. It's all around us, in big business, on Wall Street, in athletics, in entertainment, in the legal profession, in education, and even in the clergy. If you're looking for prominent Americans who act badly, you can find them everywhere. Golf comes to mind . . .

During his playing days, former basketball star Charles Barkley famously declared, "I am not a role model." That's not true, because it wasn't his decision to make. You don't choose to be a role model. That choice is made by the young people who admire you and try to emulate you. Our kids get it. Our kids instinctively know to respect those who protect us, those who wear our nation's uniform, those who run towards danger, not away from it, so that we can be safe. One day, I returned to the Mansion shortly after being sworn in as governor. I arrived before the kids had gone to bed, and my three-year-old son Shaan came running to the door yelling, "Daddy is home!" He hugged my legs, and I picked him up to see him face to face. He excitedly asked me to show him my badge. Confused, I told him I didn't have a badge. He asked, "Aren't you a state trooper dad?" I told him, "No, I am the governor of the great state of Louisiana." He gave me a disappointed look that only a son can give a father and asked, "Well, do you think you might become a state trooper some day?" I told him I would work on it.

All people—regardless of their job or role in society—have the responsibility to notice when they are viewed as a role model and live up to that responsibility. No excuses. That admiring kid of today could be a political leader, athlete, parent, or teacher of tomorrow.

I believe leaders gain people's confidence by earning it, not by demanding it. And the only way to earn the opportunity to lead is by example. The real test for leaders, and indeed the real test for all of us, is to answer this question: are my actions designed to help others or to help myself? Taking advantage of others, or exploiting powerful positions to enrich ourselves or to feed our own appetites, is the opposite of real leadership. Real leaders focus on one thing: service. Effective leadership is "servant leadership."

Becoming involved in unethical behavior can be a slippery slope. It often begins by denying the temptation exists—that is, to believe you are so great a person that you could never possibly stoop to corruption. Humility is the key to keeping a proper perspective on power, and is thus one of the most important character traits we should look for in our elected leaders.

So, yes, it's true, I am indeed hoping to be the most boring governor in the history of Louisiana. I don't believe we should elect politicians to entertain us. We have movies, music, sports, books, plays, and Mardi Gras for that.

That said, I also want to aim high and try to be Louisiana's most effective governor ever. The public is desperately seeking competence from elected leaders. I won't be perfect, but I will strive for excellence, and I will pursue it with everything I have.

DO WE REALLY WANT TO BE LIKE EUROPE?

When you look in the mirror in the morning, what do you see? Do you see a victim?

Is the person staring back at you a helpless victim of fate, incapable of making the important decisions that steer his or her life? Are Americans like you and I so incompetent and powerless that we are unable to assume the responsibilities other generations of Americans have met?

Over the course of my life, I've been told numerous times that I should think of myself as some sort of victim. I was told by teachers and elites that if I didn't see myself as a victim, I needed to be awakened to my true state of existence. Because of how I was raised, these conversations would usually prompt me to break out in laughter.

Now President Obama and many of the advocates of bigger government in Washington are having the same conversation with America. We all need help. Or, as my staffers, might put it, "They think Americans have become wusses."

This is the tug-of-war going on in America today. Two different sides are pulling on the rope. The side that wins will determine what sort of country our children grow up in, and whether we continue to be the greatest country the world has ever seen.

Tugging on one side are those of us who believe that what *made* America great is what *makes* us great today: freedom and all the things that come with it—individualism, self-reliance, limited government, and personal responsibility. These are the sort of values I'm raising my children with. Pulling on the other end are those who see Americans as sheep, lost and helpless souls unable to find their way around our complex world without the enlightened guidance of what David Brooks of the *New York Times* calls "the educated class." How can Americans get along without a much wiser elite to guide us? Our future, they say, lies in becoming more like Western Europe, with the government playing a larger role in our lives. We sheep, they tell us, can't get along without sheepherders.

Now the debate is not exactly presented in that way. President Obama and those on the other side of the discussion don't call us "sheep" or admit they want to take America the way of Europe. Instead, they beguile us with promises of safety. They promise government-run healthcare, automatic wage increases, environmental regulations, and expanded social welfare programs. They overflow with guilt about our unmet collective responsibilities and economic inequality, and promise to "spread the wealth around." They cloak their arguments in compassion: If you care about the elderly, poor, disabled, disadvantaged, single moms, unemployed, middle-class, homeless, children, fill-in-the-blank—then you will of course support their agenda.

That's what we hear every day from the White House. And that's exactly the argument I heard on the House floor every day that I served in Congress. If you care, you better vote for more government spending. If you oppose more spending, it means you don't give a damn.

As a result, Republicans in Congress often fall into the "Democrats Lite" trap: we taste just as bad as the Democrats, but we are less filling. The Dems want to spend several bajillion dollars to help some unfortunate group of people, and the Republicans, fearing being painted as uncaring, decide to go along. To maintain some shred of principle, however, we propose to spend a little less—maybe half a bajillion. And away we go. Now we are in a bidding war with the Obama White House and the Democrats in Congress. The minute we are in a contest with a Democrat in Congress to see who can spend more tax dollars—we are goners. That, my friends, as Senator John McCain would say, is a war Republicans will never win. Remember, Democrats really *like* spending. To paraphrase Muhammad Ali, they will beat us so bad we will need a shoe horn to put our hat on.

Trying to outbid Democrats not only won't work, it is wrong. As tempting as it may be to try, we can't produce a no-fault, no-pain society. It's not possible, and the costs to our liberties would be incredibly high. What Benjamin Franklin wrote in 1775 should be spoken out loud by every congressman before they cast a single vote: "They who can give up essential liberty to obtain a little temporary safety, deserve neither liberty nor safety."

What our government can guarantee is our freedom, the liberty that is the miracle of America. That freedom, if we preserve it, is what guarantees both our prosperity and our safety. As many have noted, that liberty has allowed roughly 4 percent of the world's people to create approximately 20 percent of the world's wealth and prosperity. That liberty has allowed millions of Americans to create strong families, prosperous communities, and a powerful and generous country. It has allowed generations of Americans to roll up their sleeves and achieve their dreams. It has allowed us to build the miracle of

America, the strongest, safest, and most successful country man has ever known.

My parents reminded me about this almost every day when I was growing up. They knew what living in a less free society was like. They knew what it was like to grow up in a society where the circumstances of one's birth could easily outweigh the substance of one's efforts and accomplishments in determining one's fate. Today we need to hold on tight to that rope and pull. We might get tired, we might get rope burns, but we need to fight for freedom and protect it. The U.S. Constitution is a brilliant document—but it works only so long as we, the American people, *want* to be free. Freedom is rare in human history. We can't assume it will come up with every sunrise. It won't last, unless it lives within each of us and we each stand up to keep America strong.

I'm not embarrassed to confess that as a governor responsible for the safety of nearly 4.5 million people, the threat of terrorism keeps me up at night. I worry about the random act of violence in a shopping mall or a madman deploying the nearly unlimited power of the atom. The single greatest threat to our freedoms isn't external, however. Islamic terrorists can't rob us of our liberty. America is too big and powerful for them. No, the biggest threat to our freedom comes from within our borders, not beyond them. It comes when we are tempted to bargain away, little by little, the liberties other Americans have fought and died to place in our hands.

When times are tough, that temptation grows. Left-wing Democrats who offer to wrap a blanket around our shoulders can sound comforting. I remember as a student reading both George Orwell's *1984* and Aldous Huxley's *Brave New World* about totalitarian governments in the future. Huxley's vision frightened me more. Orwell saw Big Brother as controlling people through fear and force. Huxley imagined that people gave up their freedoms because they *liked* to be taken care of.

Don't get me wrong. I firmly believe each and every one of God's children has an obligation to care for those who can't care for themselves, and government has an essential role in that. There are times government can and should lend a hand. In Congress, I cast a few votes along those lines that irritated my fellow conservatives.

However, it is always our obligation to see if we can meet America's challenges from the bottom up, at the local level, as individuals in our communities, through the private sector, churches, and charitable institutions, without first turning to the heavy, expensive, and inefficient hand of big, old, slow, top-down, industrial-age government in Washington. We don't need so many czars in the White House!

A surprising number of Americans do not see any connection between the growth of government and the loss of freedom. It just doesn't compute for them. They figure that government is supposed to protect them, therefore bigger government means more protection.

So let me bypass political correctness and say exactly what I mean: the more you pay in taxes the less free you are—the less free you are to do what you want with your money, to start a business, to chase your dreams, to chart your own course, to live the way you want and make your own way in this world.

When government grows too large, we begin to lose pieces of our freedom.

Big government programs that try to take care of everyone are like cement. When Washington pours them, they set and last forever. Their heavy weight crushes innovation, kills competition, chokes our work ethic, erodes responsibility, and suppresses the rugged individualism fundamental to the unique experiment that has made America a great nation.

The American experiment with freedom has survived wars and economic setbacks in the past. We've faced threats to our freedoms, both internal and external, before. Why is the threat so great right now? In my mind it's simple: the American character qualities of self-reliance and independence have been eroded. Many have bought the collectivist idea that Americans are victims of fate who can only be saved by all-knowing, all-spending, all-powerful politicians and bureaucrats. As a result, we have some people in this country who've been told they don't have to grow up because government will always be there to take care of them. So they haven't grown up. They expect someone else to pay their bills or give them "free" healthcare. They've become adult children who avoid personal responsibility and assign others the blame for their own failures.

Of course we all know people who face real tragedies or setbacks in their lives. There *are* real victims in our society, and we have a moral responsibility to help them. But frankly, people we should be helping today often get overshadowed by those who undeservedly portray themselves as victims. We have people suing corporations over ridiculous claims of "abuse." Spill some hot coffee in your lap? Sue the restaurant. Do you have "offensive body odor?" Maybe you can qualify as handicapped under one state's Fair Employment Act. (This was tried in Wisconsin.) The political scientist Aaron Wildavsky took all of this to its logical absurdity and calculated that given all the new claims of victimhood out there in America today, victims now account for 374 percent of the U.S. population. No wonder the lines are so long for government benefits: on average, we have nearly four times as many "victims" as we do living, breathing Americans!

Bad things can and do happen. We need to protect and help genuine victims of life's misfortunes. The goal should be to give them a leg up—not a hand-out. In my experience, the real victims in our society often want to overcome the challenges in their lives—not wallow in them. As Thomas Sowell has put it, "Victimhood is something to escape, not something to exploit."[1] Yet, a modern-day Benjamin Franklin would cause a firestorm today if he once again said, "I think the best way of doing good to the poor, is not making them easy in poverty, but leading or driving them out of it."[2] Franklin, the father of bifocal eyeglasses, still saw America with 20/20 vision.

As soon as Obamacare passed, there were news reports of health insurance companies getting calls from people asking about their "free healthcare." There used to be a stigma attached to seeking public assistance. If you have never seen the movie *Cinderella Man*, you need to. It's the true story of champion boxer James J. Braddock, who when he was down on his luck during the Great Depression, with no heat and no food to feed his family, applied for public assistance. He received $24 a month from the Hudson County Relief Agency of New York. But when Braddock got back on his feet and back in the ring, he actually went back to the welfare office and paid every single penny of it back. Why? He didn't have to. The government required no such thing, but his conscience required it.[3]

But American culture is changing. There used to be a stigma about being dependent on the government. Increasingly we have a culture of entitlement, where individuals feel they are owed and forget that government does not create the benefits it bestows. Government simply takes from us with one hand and gives with another, wasting a portion in the process.

All too often the sales pitch for bargaining away our freedoms for security comes from intellectuals and people in the elite who have an ill-disguised contempt (or little respect) for the American people. They operate with a basic premise: Americans are just not smart enough to govern themselves. This has been the cry of those who lust for power throughout history. Both fascism and communism were developed and created by intellectuals who believed people were too dumb to take care of themselves. Even the apartheid system in South Africa was laid out in detail by the social psychology department of Stellenbosch University with the claim that it would be beneficial for everyone: let us take care of you![4]

Here in the United States the message is more subtle and less threatening. "Trust us to meet your needs. Trust government to guarantee your security." It is a tempting and dangerous sales pitch. First, we know these intellectual elites can't deliver the security they promise. Is there any problem in your life you would trust politicians and bureaucrats to tackle? Is Washington doing anything more efficiently or inexpensively? What problem has Washington fixed lately?

Never have so many smart people been out of touch with America's problems. The "genius" of a few political leaders is no substitute for the combined wisdom of the American people. Those who would run our schools, businesses, and every aspect of our lives, often with the best of intentions, want us to believe that they can get together in Congress, write a few thousand pages of law, and simply right highly complex wrongs. They can make our problems evaporate! The truth is, of course, the increasingly complicated and interconnected nature of our lives in today's fast-moving Age of Communications makes our problems much too complex for bureaucrats and politicians in far-away Washington to understand or even measure. They don't have the local understanding, innovative spirit, and adaptive ability that Americans have always used to meet this nation's great challenges and create its unmatched progress and prosperity.

Take Social Security and Medicare. The 2009 Social Security and Medicare Trustees Reports show the combined unfunded liability of these two programs has reached nearly $107 trillion dollars.[5] That is roughly seven times the size of the U.S. economy. When we get about halfway through this century, one third of the wages workers earn will be needed just to pay Social Security and Medicare benefits—that's before we pay our teachers, provide for our national defense, fix a single pothole, or find a way to pay for Obamacare. One survey revealed that our young people were more likely to believe in UFOs than in the solvency of the Social Security system! I would have to agree with them, though politics has made me wish for the discovery of more intelligent life on other planets. Franklin D. Roosevelt designed the Social Security System to be funded by the Social Security Tax and not out of general funds. "No dole," he said, "mustn't have a dole."[6] He wanted the people getting it to pay for it. Our only chance of preserving these programs is to take action now.

We declared war on poverty more than forty years ago. We have spent trillions in fighting it. Yet the poverty rate today is basically unchanged. We've fought an expensive war on poverty and we are poorer as a nation than if we had never fired a shot. Yet many in Washington still feel the Land of the Free should become the Land of the Free Lunch.

Don't get me wrong. I believe in some safety nets. But safety nets can, and often do, create "moral hazards" when they encourage irresponsible behavior. It took the federal government decades to figure out that if welfare subsidizes out-of-wedlock births, you get more

out-of-wedlock births! And government programs that promise us
"safety" are always oversold and cost more than estimated. In 1996
Congress passed a farm law expected to cost $47 billion. The final
price tag: $118 billion. When Medicare Part A was passed in 1965, it
was expected to cost $9 billion by 1990. It cost $67 billion that year.
The entire Medicaid system, which was designed as a state-federal program for the poor, costs 37 times more than it did when it was
launched—even after adjusting for inflation![7] If a private company
offered to do something for you but failed to deliver in such an
abysmal way, they would be sued for false advertising and fraud. When
big government fails, all we get is, "Let's go back to the drawing board
and raise taxes."

The problem with the intrusive power of old-fashioned, industrial-
age government is not just that it doesn't work. It also undermines
who we are as Americans. Once we start to accept the premise that we
can't take care of ourselves, the basic thesis of self-government begins
to erode, like sand dissolving under our feet. If we can't take care of
ourselves, how can we be expected to take care of the business of self-
governance?

Western Europe is often presented as an idyllic model for utopian,
collectivist schemes. If we could only be more like Europe, our problems would go away. Europe is evidence that we need a government-
run healthcare system, a big-brother-controlled employment system,
and an expansive social welfare state. But where is Europe today? The
Euro always seems to be on the verge of collapsing, many countries
have abrogated their economic sovereignty, and Europeans have far
less control over their own futures than they did just two generations
ago. In the European Union many of the rules are now being written,
not by elected officials, but by *unelected bureaucrats*. If you don't like

the rules, too bad. There is nowhere to go when those making the rules are not directly accountable to the people. Scholars call this the "administrative state," when unelected bureaucrats become the real powerbrokers. I have another word for it: tyranny.

The move away from greater political freedom is the natural consequence of a paternalistic state. Alexis de Tocqueville warned about the corrosive effects that paternalistic thinking would have on the American people. The government has a role to play in protecting us, he wrote, but its mindset should be that of the parent who seeks to prepare their children for adulthood. We should encourage *independence* from the government. But de Tocqueville warned that some would be tempted to keep people "in perpetual childhood" by promoting *dependence* on the government.[8]

The biggest push for the greater intrusion of government is in the area of economics and business. Some argue the government is supposed to "redistribute" the wealth, control businesses, and restrict the economic activities of people. Forget for a minute whether or not this is just. Restricting economic freedoms limits our political freedoms. History teaches that the two are intimately entwined. Economic freedom disperses political power and distributes it among the people. With a free market system we separate economic power from political power, so that each may offset the other. As the late Nobel Prize-winning economist Milton Friedman put it, "Historical evidence speaks with a single voice on the relation between political freedom and a free market. I know of no example in time or place of a society that has been marked by a large measure of political freedom, and that has not also used something comparable to a free market to organize the bulk of economic activity."[9] Economic independence is what allows people to protect their political rights and freedoms. Once the powerful hand of government subsumes our economic independence, it immediately becomes more difficult to stand up to that government. The natural logic of capitalism requires democracy. Synchronously, if we over-restrict capitalism, our democratic logic is disrupted. Economic freedom and political freedom are indivisible. As President Gerald Ford said, "A government big enough to give you everything you want is big enough to take away everything you have."[10]

Too many people in Washington believe they can restrict our economic freedom without limiting our political liberties. They see the private sector as a threat, dangerous unless controlled. I was struck by the words President Barack Obama used in his memoir to describe his feelings on taking the only job in a private business he has ever held. Looking back on his brief stint at a financial consultancy, he says he felt "like a spy behind enemy lines."[11] Furthermore, he has surrounded himself with few people in Washington who have any experience in the private sector. Around 20 percent of his Cabinet appointments have private sector experience, far below any other recent president. For fellow Democrats Lyndon Johnson and Bill Clinton, that figure was well over 30 percent.[12] Private businesses are the enemy? Far from it. They not only create American wealth, they are critical to our political freedoms. The economic independence of each and every American, rich or poor, is at the heart of the American experiment in self-government.

Don't get me wrong. Private businesses are plenty capable of doing the wrong thing. Wall Street has proven that. But the private sector lacks the coercive powers government wields. McDonald's can't force us to buy their hamburgers. Starbucks can't force us to buy their coffee. Businesses can only be successful in a free market if they provide services or goods that people want. The more people want them, the more the business will sell.

Our Founding Fathers saw the Constitution as codifying pre-existing rights—not creating those rights. And they considered government to be the biggest threat to a people's liberties. Were they correct? During the twentieth century, in peacetime, governments across the world killed some 170 million of their own people. (Thirty-eight million died in war.[13]) We should all be concerned about the power of big business, but I'm far more concerned about the unchecked power of government.

A paternalistic government not only threatens our political independence, it also affects our character. Do I believe that we have a responsibility to others? Of course. Whenever possible, however, that responsibility should flow through our communities, not through government, especially at the federal level. It's an amazing paradox, but there is considerable evidence that shows the more you believe the federal government should help other people, the less likely you are to help yourself or others. A few years ago, Syracuse University professor Arthur C. Brooks wrote a book called *Who Really Cares*, which demonstrated that those who are skeptical of big government are actually more charitable. A paternalistic view of society leads to the conclusion that individuals can't really change things, only government can. Professor James Lindgren of the Northwestern University School of Law also looked at research on charitable giving and discovered that "those who wanted the government to promote income leveling were less likely to be generous themselves."[14]

What we need in America today is to trust *ourselves*—not look to others to take care of us. I have complete faith in the common sense and character of the American people. To paraphrase the late writer William F. Buckley, I would rather be led by the first one hundred names in the Baton Rouge, Louisiana phone book than the faculty of Harvard University. We need to remind ourselves that America is a collection of individuals, brought together with a common outlook and heritage of freedom. That is what makes us great.

As the Nobel Laureate in economics F. A. Hayek put it, the "unchaining of individual energies" has given us prosperity, freedom, and liberty. Only individuals create and dream. Individuals have rights and responsibilities. As a society, we thrive when people take responsibility for themselves and those around them. We bloom when we allow individuals to work hard and enjoy what they can achieve.

At their most extreme, collectivists believe, "The individual is nothing in relation to the course [of time], the species is everything." (Adolf Hitler said that.) As Americans who love the United States, however, we cannot ever allow our society to drift to the opposite extreme where, "The individual is everything. The group is nothing." We have personal freedom, but we also have personal responsibilities, to both ourselves and those around us. In my family, our need to care for others, not just our families but strangers, too, springs from our Christian beliefs. The greatest commandment, which envelopes so many others, is the voluntary obligation to "love your neighbor as yourself." Government coercion is a poor and dangerous substitute for that appeal to our better angels. As Winston Churchill said just over 100 years ago, the good Lord taught us to believe "all mine is yours," not "all yours is mine." Christian charity is about giving, not taking.

Here in Louisiana, when the storms have come, we have seen the incomparable generosity of the American spirit. I'll never forget what I saw: people standing on rooftops begging to be rescued. Hospitals meant to save lives, suddenly helpless to preserve them. Families torn apart for all time by the relentless force of the rising waters. A monumental failure of government contributed mightily to what we saw during those grim days in 2005. We will see other storms come to our state but, as governor, I've worked to make sure those tragic events never visit Louisiana again. I've also put everyone in the state on notice that all of us, as individuals, must take greater responsibility for preparing for the storms life brings us. All of us must be responsible for meeting the needs of the truly disadvantaged, people with physical or mental limitations. People who can take responsibility for themselves should not expect someone else do so. We will help you when catastrophe comes, but you better not sit there and just wait for someone to pull you out when you could climb out, or pick you up when you could stand on your own two feet.

Today we have taxpayer dollars going to banks, investment houses, and automakers, and financial firms that are judged "too big to fail." Our government is supposed to be a "partner" with these businesses. As one businessman told me, that's like an alligator having a chicken as a partner for dinner. I believe big government should not be picking and choosing which companies we will bail out or rescue. That political competition lets the best lobbyists determine the winner.

Government's role is to serve as an objective referee and make sure companies abide by the rules, compete fairly, and obey the law. We don't want the referee tilting the football game. But when the federal government starts bailing out individual businesses, that's exactly what it does. Of course, if you think there aren't enough backroom deals and corruption in Washington now, then let's give big government officials the chance to pass out more cash, loans, and contracts.

When you give Washington not hundreds of billions, but trillions of dollars to hand out, you create corruption on steroids. Some will use their power and privilege to enrich themselves. Others will enrich their political allies. Either way, with new trillion dollar pots of gold to lust after, I'm sure corruption is growing, even now, in Washington. Consider the words of Harry Hopkins, who oversaw both the Works Progress Administration (WPA) and the distribution of funds from the Federal Emergency Relief Act (FERA) under FDR during the Great Depression. "I thought at first I could be completely non-political," Hopkins is quoted by Robert E. Sherwood in the definitive *Roosevelt and Hopkins: An Intimate History*. "Then they told me I had to be part non-political and part political. I found out that was impossible, at least for me. I finally realized that there was nothing for it but to be all-political."[15] When trillions of dollars are sloshing around the Treasury, awaiting direction from the privileged few, we know what will happen: people who walk into public service with nothing will walk out with the taxpayers' gold in their pockets. And businessmen who walked in with empty pockets will walk out millionaires because of who they knew, not who they served. Look at the list of the most corrupt countries in the world today and you will see that centralized economies are at the top of the list.

In his 1958 book *The Affluent Society*, John Kenneth Galbraith said that with a home, car, television set, and a family member in college, Americans had reached their economic pinnacle. Stanford University Professor Paul Ehrlich warned us in the 1970s that the immediate future would bring widespread famine, shortages, and despair. He wrote in his book *The Population Bomb*: "By 1985 enough millions will have died to reduce the earth's population to some acceptable level, like 1.5 billion. . . ." In his book *The End of Affluence*, Ehrlich said Congress would be dissolved "during the food riots of the 1980s."[16] In 1977 Jimmy Carter warned, "We could use up all of the proven reserves of oil in the entire world by the end of the next decade." Of course, there were no food riots in America in the 1980s. Our oil reserves expanded, they did not evaporate, despite our still growing dependence. And at last count there were approximately 6 billion people on earth, including, surprisingly, Paul Ehrlich.

Yet today there are still some people who want to harp on America's limits. They still say that our best days are behind us. These big government advocates tell us their failures are the best Americans can do. Forget cooking up anything new—let's just divide the old American pie into smaller, equally unsatisfying pieces.

That is all bunk. It's not a sunset, but a sunrise, that still starts America's day.

As Ronald Reagan said, "I do not believe in a fate that will fall on us no matter what we do. I do believe in a fate that will fall on us if we do nothing."[17]

Western European nations did not decide one day to embrace what they now call "democratic Socialism." It has happened little by little, piece by piece, program by program. I'm certainly not suggesting that this European style socialism willfully pursues the economic rationalization and social interventionism of a completely planned economy. I also would never claim that our European friends do not each have many strengths and positive attributes. I am suggesting that they have in many ways taken a turn for the worse over the past sixty years to the degree they have exchanged the dynamic potential of a free people for the false security of a planned society. Perhaps they are happy with their trajectory and direction? Older, less dynamic societies on the downhill side of their national lifespans might be content with redistributing instead of creating. They might be satisfied managing their declines. That is something our country is still too young and promising to do. Our liberty, like our country, is ever-young and prepared to meet the challenges of a new day.

I do not want to see America follow Europe's trajectory and I do not believe that most Americans do either. I don't want to see us pay more in taxes, expand our government, erode our freedoms, or become weaker in the world. Americans don't need to become more like Europe. But we will if we do not change course.

Big government may be broken, but America isn't broken. Washington may be unable to solve America's problems, but if we bring real change to Washington there isn't any problem America can't solve, any goal we can't reach, any frontier we can't conquer. Whatever Americans can dream, we can achieve.

I believe America should remain the greatest country in the world. When I was a kid, that was safe to say and aspire to. Not so today. There are many political leaders in America today who don't like the sound of that. They cringe at the thought of American exceptionalism and superiority. It strikes them as unsophisticated, unrefined, kind of "cowboyish." They think our aspirations of leadership are arrogant evidence of a fundamental intolerance of other nations and their cultures. They believe America should be content to settle into our place as just another country in the family of nations. They are ashamed we would seek to be the greatest country in the world.

I am not ashamed. I am proud that America is exceptional. Global leadership is not a responsibility America can discard. It is a responsibility we must cherish. America is the hope of free peoples everywhere. Without American leadership the world around us would be more dangerous and less prosperous. The stronger America is, the safer the world is. We have a moral responsibility to make our country stronger and unashamedly export our ideals of freedom, democracy, and self-determination to all who would fulfill the divinely inspired potential of every living soul on this planet.

And Americans are not victims. When you look in that mirror tomorrow morning, I hope you see what I see: the strength of the greatest country on earth.

CHAPTER II

REAL CHANGE FOR HEALTHCARE

Imagine for a moment you are standing in a quiet hospital room holding your three-month-old son in your arms for what could be the last time.

He is looking up at you with his beautiful, innocent brown eyes. And you stare down into his tiny face and wonder how you, his parent, are so powerless to save him that you need to entrust his life to a complete stranger. Despite having done all you can do, you are scared. And the helplessness you feel doesn't stop the crushing weight of responsibility that comes with being a parent deeply in love with your new child.

The time has come to hand him over. You are paralyzed; you love him too much to let him go, but your love for him has led you here, to this strange place full of technology and experts—and other scared families. All you want at that moment is for someone to tell you everything will be all right and that your boy is going to be healthy.

But reality sets in. He is in the hospital. He needs help. And there is no other way. You must swallow your fears for the moment—just long enough to gently pass your little boy into the hands of the anesthesiologist who will prepare him for surgery. No amount of reason can dull the feeling that a part of you is being torn away as she takes your son through the large operating room doors and out of sight.

For me, this was not a hypothetical situation. I was standing in that hospital room in 2004, holding my second child, Shaan, in my arms. And let me tell you—letting him go at that moment was one of the hardest things I've ever done.

We had no reason to suspect there was anything wrong with Shaan when he was born only a few months earlier. The birth had gone smoothly, and he looked like any other healthy baby. But a week later, during a regular checkup, Shaan's pediatrician detected a heart murmur. Later that morning, we took Shaan to a pediatric cardiologist who diagnosed him with a serious heart defect, which would prevent him from breathing or eating normally without becoming exhausted.

My immediate reaction was that I'd give anything and everything to trade places with Shaan. I was devastated for him, devastated that this innocent little boy had this burden. When we see horrible tragedies happen to other people, we never think it will happen to us or to those we love. Of course, we feel compassion for children afflicted with disease or chronic health problems, and we pray for them and their families. But trust me, it is never truly real until it happens to your own child.

The cardiologist said the problem might fix itself, but if it didn't— and in Shaan's case it did not look like it would—he would need life-saving open-heart surgery. The doctor then gave us one of the toughest prescriptions imaginable: waiting. Three grueling months of it. The wait would increase Shaan's chances of surviving a heart surgery, if he could keep breathing until then. In the meantime, we would have to watch our son waste away. We watched his strength gradually leave him until he would sleep for hours and it took all his strength just to breathe. We watched his growth slow to a halt as it became harder to get him to eat. We watched him become more and more dependent on medications, and we watched him go into the intensive care unit. Weighed down by the consuming sense that we were failing Shaan, we struggled to accept the reality that there was very little we could do to ease his pain.

I was running for Congress at the time, so I canceled campaign appearances to focus first and foremost on Shaan. We spent weeks of the waiting period trying every medical option short of surgery. Every option failed, but we refused to sit still, even after we had come to terms with the cold, hard truth that heart surgery was the only path. There was no one in Baton Rouge who could perform the procedure, so our pediatrician referred us to Boston Children's Hospital, one of about half a dozen centers in the country that specialize in these kinds of cases.

From the minute we learned of Shaan's illness, Supriya left nothing to chance and took nothing for granted. A successful engineer, Supriya has an amazing zeal for data and a logical approach to problem solving. I have to say, as proud as I was of her, she really drove the doctor crazy with technical questions even during one of our first visits. They had been talking for a while before I got there, and when I arrived, the doctor looked at me and said, "Please tell me you are not an engineer. I don't think I can handle two of you."

Supriya immersed herself in research on pediatric cardiology, learning about the endless intricacies of the procedure and all possible alternatives. Seeking precise numbers and facts, she would come to the doctor's office each week with spreadsheets and a new list of questions.

She was highly organized and far more studious than any medical student I had ever seen. I think she probably could have performed the surgery herself.

I focused my time searching for the best surgeon. One thing I learned is that we can know the details of any procedure, and we can pepper the doctors with every technical question. But let's face it—once the doctor is behind those operating room doors with your child, there is no turning back. The only power you have as a parent at that point is to make sure you chose the right person to trust—the person who will put your child to sleep, hold his tiny heart in his hands, and use the power God gave him to heal.

The Bible says that God loves you, He knows everything about you, and He will take care of you. From knowing every hair on Shaan's head to providing for even lesser beings than a beautiful human child, I knew, no matter what, God had a plan. I also believe God gives us the tools to help guide our course, and I was determined to use everything He gave me. Yet, with the outcome of Shaan's illness unclear, and with my layperson's inability to completely understand the available information, I was shaken to my core.

*   *   *

Now imagine you are in my place again, standing in that room in Boston Children's Hospital with your little son in your arms and the anesthesiologist standing by to take him through those doors past the point of no return. Only this time, you didn't get the surgeon you wanted; after your painstaking work to find the best surgeon and the best treatment, your choices were denied by some far-away bureaucrat.

Let's be clear. Government intrusion into the healthcare system creates this scenario every day. When federal or state bureaucrats who control Medicare and Medicaid determine the rates they pay to providers based on politics, lobbyists, and federal or state-wide budgets rather than on real market-driven principles, it creates shortages of doctors who will treat those patients.

Under the Democrats' healthcare "reform," government intrusion is set to grow much worse.

Look at the much-vaunted Medicaid system, which will add around 16 million people under President Obama's healthcare reform. Even now, before this huge expansion, getting a doctor is so difficult that many people simply opt to get treated in an emergency room. One example we saw was a grandmother caring for a young, autistic child. The woman, a Medicaid recipient, was struck with a brain tumor. Yet no specialists would take new Medicaid patients. Her primary care doctor told her to drive three hours to another city and go to the public hospital emergency department, tell them she has a brain tumor, and get them to find a doctor for her. In light of these kinds of horrifying situations, we are implementing some of the most sweeping reforms of our Medicaid system in Louisiana's history.

The single most important question in healthcare is often overlooked: who do we want controlling our healthcare decisions— patients and their doctors, insurance middle-men, or government bureaucrats?

I'm passionate about healthcare because, for me, it's personal. Before Shaan became ill, I had begun to devote my professional life to healthcare issues, having served as secretary of Health and Hospitals in Louisiana, executive director of the National Bipartisan Commission on the Future of Medicare, and as an assistant secretary of the U.S. Department of Health and Human Services. I had studied healthcare policy in both America and around the world. But no book, study, or commission can replace the firsthand experience that comes with encountering the system yourself for your own child's sake.

I believe everyone has a right to affordable healthcare. We are all created in God's image, and that makes us valuable, independent of our economic worth or the contributions we make to the economy. It is a question of human dignity granted to us by our Creator.

But with equal passion I believe this goal cannot be achieved through a government-run system. Government healthcare is top-down: decisions are politicized and are indifferent to the needs of individuals. Medicare and Medicaid have proven that when there is no free marketplace with transparency and consumer engagement, we get an inflexible system that wastes money, reduces choices, and produces poor outcomes. In 2009, the federal government admits around $50 billion was wasted simply on improper payments in Medicare alone.[1]

When government sets prices, shortages result. Consider that in the next twenty years, the number of Americans over the age of fifty-five will double, while at the same time there is a projected shortage of more than 125,000 doctors by 2025. More doctors are already refusing to accept Medicare, and the Medicaid program is imperiled even before it enrolls millions of new patients under Obamacare.

In a government-run system, choices, either directly or indirectly, are made *for* you without your consent. America is built on choice—where we live, what we eat, what we drive, and with whom we associate. Yet oddly, when it comes to healthcare, choice is usually an afterthought. Disagree? Go online and try to find out which physicians have the best outcomes. It's nearly impossible to find that information. If choice were paramount in our system, those data would be readily available and the public would be demanding it. But instead, we have a system where we are told what we need and expected to comply.

My view is pretty straightforward: the more important the decision, the more important it is that you have choices. This goes for the poor as well as the rich. Poor people have few healthcare choices: typically, they either get Medicaid or nothing. The poor are often criticized for neglecting their healthcare, but this is the natural result when people are automatically relegated to a poorly functioning, top-down healthcare program with few choices.

Some supporters of government-run healthcare seem to believe the poor need this kind of command and control healthcare structure because they can't be expected to be responsible for their own care. I disagree. Poor people are poor, not stupid. In my experience in public policy, a poor woman, just like anyone else, will responsibly care for herself and her children whenever she has plenty of choices and easy access to information. I certainly trust a mom to do the right thing more than I trust a nameless, faceless bureaucrat.

There is also the question of proximity—both physical and emotional—in making decisions. The best decisions are made when the decision-maker is close enough to the problem to understand it and has a strong, personal stake in getting it fixed. But when the decision-maker is an insurance or government bureaucrat too far removed from the situation to feel the full weight of responsibility, you can bet you won't get the compassion of a father or mother fighting for their son's life.

Without a doubt, our lifestyle choices are the primary driving factor behind the overall poor state of health in America. But the answer is not a government diktat, which can never replace the sound judgment of an educated consumer. And not only is government control ineffective, it's un-American. People just don't want the government to tell them how to live their lives. I work out at the gym, but I also eat chocolate chip cookies and the occasional McDonald's hamburger. My health would be better off without the cookies and burgers, but it's my choice and my right to eat them.

The government's role should center on providing market-based incentives for sound healthcare management, especially for children. That has been the focus of my reforms in Louisiana to ensure parents get well-child checkups for their children and that people with diabetes get their blood sugar tested regularly. We also provided market-based incentives to physicians to improve immunization rates for children, which resulted in our rates jumping from 44th in the nation to 2nd, according to the Centers for Disease Control.

I'm amazed by the envy some Americans feel toward the health systems in other countries—systems that supposedly function for the overall social good, but often at a great cost to the individual. Great Britain, which has a centrally run National Health Service (NHS), is plagued with shortages and long waiting periods. British newspapers are filled with stories about babies being delivered in hospital bathrooms, parking lots, and in hallways due to a lack of nurses or beds. Individuals who need simple operations, such as for cataract surgery, have to wait years for the procedure; some have even gone blind waiting for this fifteen- to twenty-minute operation.[2]

The waiting list to see a dentist in Britain is so long that thousands of people resort to do-it-yourself dentistry. George Daulat of Scarborough, England, for example, contacted twenty public NHS dentist offices to have four painful teeth removed. After they all put him on a waiting list, he was forced to pull them out with pliers, using vodka to dull the pain. Don Wilson of Kent, used fishing disgorgers—the tool used to get a hook out of the back of a fish's mouth—to pull his painful teeth. Some have attached their own crowns using superglue.

The British government estimates more than 2 million people who want treatment for mouth ailments can't get a dentist.[3]

In Canada, the shortage of doctors is so severe that some doctors have held lotteries to reduce their caseload. Canadians who have been diagnosed with brain tumors need to wait up to eight months to be treated. A woman in Winnipeg with clogged arteries was put on a three-year waiting list for surgery. She died before the surgery was performed. "This tragedy could have been avoided," her son told one newspaper. "My mother trusted the system with her life, it failed her."[4]

When Canadian Karen Jepp was pregnant with quadruplets, there wasn't one hospital in Canada with space in its neonatal unit to treat four premature babies together. She ended up being treated in Great Falls, Montana.[5] Similarly, a four-year-old child in Canada was diagnosed with cancer, but when doctors wanted to check if it had spread, they faced a two-and-a-half year wait for a simple MRI scan. This is not unusual in Canada—the average wait there for an MRI scan is sixteen months.[6] A Slavic immigrant living in Ontario was diagnosed with a cancerous lesion and was told he would have to wait more than fourteen weeks for surgery. He chose instead to return to his homeland to have the procedure done there within the week. "I felt very bad," he said. "I couldn't believe that in a rich country, you had to wait so long."[7]

Anecdotes, yes. But when you see them over and over again, you begin to wonder whether this is the direction in which our own healthcare system should be going. Government-run healthcare seems free, but it's not—it's rationed care paid for by taxpayers. Yet Obamacare will expand bureaucratic, government-run programs like Medicaid without reforming them to make room for market mechanisms.

The Left touts the expansion of Medicaid as a way to increase "access" to healthcare, but coverage in a failed system does not equate to access. Consider that even though Louisiana has led the nation with a 95 percent "coverage" rate for children, the majority of children in our Medicaid program still do not receive well-child checkups. Fewer than 5 percent of covered adults had a preventive visit to a doctor. These people have "coverage," but they still don't access the system. To fix this problem, we are overhauling our entire Medicaid program in order to ensure real healthcare access, not just access on paper. The Obama administration, unfortunately, has chosen a different course.

We should closely study foreign healthcare systems—despite their many flaws, we can still learn from the things they do well. But America offers far better treatment and has much faster innovation than any other system. There is a reason foreign monarchs, politicians, and other elites, including the sitting premier of a Canadian province,[8] still come from around the world to receive medical care in America. America's healthcare system needs reform, as discussed below. But that should not obscure the fact that at its best, American healthcare is the world's greatest.

* * *

But sometimes, even in the best of circumstances, the system is out of reach. That was the case during the birth of our third child. Our first two kids were born without much difficulty—at least for me. Like most men, I neither comprehend nor can imagine the pain of childbirth.

Childbirth has never been easy for Supriya. I suppose any woman would respond, "No, duh." When Selia, our first child, decided she was coming into the world, Supriya beeped me on my pager. When I found a landline she told me, "I'm on my way to the hospital. They say I'm in labor. Come home now." I responded with perhaps the dumbest thing I've said in my marriage: "Are you sure you are in

After saving their money for a few years, my parents purchased their first new car in 1973, a Chrysler Dodge Dart. That's me standing next to it.

I celebrated my fourth birthday at McDonald's. Because of my precocious behavior, someone labeled my hat "Manager."

Me with my proud parents, after I was recognized on the House and Senate floors at Louisiana's State Capitol for my academic achievements.

I enjoy it when my family can accompany me on the campaign trail. In 2007, Supriya and I rode a fire truck through my childhood subdivision for its annual Fourth of July parade.

Invigorated by the people I met while campaigning for governor, I committed to restoring ethics and honesty to government.

I have had the privilege of personally thanking thousands
of veterans from Louisiana. We passed legislation to create
the Louisiana Veterans' Honor Medal to recognize their
heroic service. (Photo courtesy of Louisiana National Guard)

I cherish the opportunity to welcome our troops home.
Here, I was greeting members of the 927th Engineer
(Sapper) Company, 769th Engineer Battalion, who were
returning from a year-long deployment in Afghanistan.
(Photo courtesy of Louisiana National Guard)

Having been raised in a household that prioritized education, I continue to work for systemic education reforms that include expanding school choice and rewarding great teachers.

On January 14, 2008, with Supriya and our family at my side, I was sworn in as Louisiana's fifty-fifth governor. Immediately following my inauguration, as I had promised the voters, we adopted comprehensive ethics reforms.
(Photo courtesy of *The Advocate*, January 15, 2008, Capital City Press, Baton Rouge, LA)

My chief of staff Timmy Teepell and I just after going duck hunting. Louisiana truly is a sportsman's paradise — for those of you who haven't tried it, come on down!

Supriya and I celebrating the Saints' win in Super Bowl XLIV. The victory served as a powerful example of the faith, perseverance, resilience, and teamwork that embodies New Orleans.
(Photo courtesy of the Associated Press, February 8, 2010)

Congratulating quarterback Drew Brees, with his wife and son, moments after the Saints won the Super Bowl. I am proud of Drew, Coach Payton, and the entire team — they're not only NFL champions, but they're also actively involved in the community.

We arrived in Pass a Loutre to find our worst fears had come true, as the vibrant sounds of birds and wildlife were silenced by thick oil.

To keep the oil from entering our marshland, Louisiana's National Guard built a land bridge along Elmer's Island, west of Grand Isle. Here, we are on the land bridge observing the oil that was kept out of the marshland.

Perhaps my toughest battle every year is getting all three of my kids to smile for our family Christmas picture. In this photo from Christmas 2009, Shaan is 5, Slade is 3, and Selia is 7.

As I saw firsthand while serving in Congress, our democracy is the greatest form of government on earth today. But our government is also an oversized and inefficient bureaucracy in need of comprehensive reform.

labor?" I'll leave it to your imagination how the rest of that conversation went. Thankfully, God gave us a beautiful, healthy daughter after
thirty-six hours of labor and the gift of having us be together to welcome her into the world.

Our second child, Shaan, took twenty-four hours. In both these
instances my job was pretty simple: let the doctor and the nurses do
their work and don't take any inappropriate pictures. However, the
birth of our third child, Slade, was a little different. He only took
thirty minutes, but the process was . . . unusual.

Supriya went to bed that night with stomach pains, but she said she
was fine. After all, she had already been to the hospital with false labor
twice in the past week, and she had seen her doctor earlier in the day.
But she woke me up that night and told me, "My stomach's hurting.
This isn't right." We quickly grabbed our clothes from the closet, and
I called her parents to come watch the other two kids. But in an
instant, Supriya went into full labor.

I called 911 for an ambulance and gave them all our information.
I was a congressman at the time, and when the dispatcher heard my
name he started laughing. He thought it was a prank call.

Supriya started screaming in pain. She had opted for the epidural
route in both her previous pregnancies, thinking, "God, if you wanted
me to do this naturally, you wouldn't have made drugs." She told our
doctor before the birth of our first child, "I want the epidural in the
parking lot. Is that clear?"

But on this night there was no epidural, and the ambulance was
nowhere in sight. As Supriya kept screaming, I tried to calm her down
by telling a few jokes. (Bad idea, guys.)

"You know, if you want to stop teenage girls from having sex, show
them a video of this," I cracked.

She glared at me. "You're making jokes? REALLY?!"

Supriya and I (more her than me) delivered Slade right there on the bathroom floor. I was tying the umbilical cord off with an old shoelace when the paramedics arrived. Childbirths on TV shows are always beautiful—the babies come out pink and cute and wrapped in a blanket. Sometimes, real life is a little different. Slade came out sort of off-color and covered with, well, while I'm certain there's a technical term, let's just call it "goo."

"How does he look?" Supriya asked me when he first emerged. "How does the baby look?"

"He looks great," I lied. What I wanted to tell her was he didn't look done—and that maybe we needed to put him back in.

By this time, Supriya's father and a police officer who had been nearby arrived at the house. I found out later these two brave men heard Supriya screaming and looked at one another. "Well, I'm not going in there," said one.

"Well, if you're not going in there, I'm not going in there," replied the other.

When I handed Supriya our child for the first time, her pain instantly vanished. It was one of the most amazing moments of our lives; I don't think I have ever loved my wife more. Now all she cared about was her newborn child. People later asked me if I panicked. "No," I would tell them, "all I did was catch the baby."

Later, the doctor had the hardest time figuring out the billing for our insurance. "I didn't deliver the baby," she said.

Slade's birth was a reminder to me of the greatness of God and the gift of life. Again, God had given Supriya and me the strength together to bring our own child into the world.

*   *   *

Every American cares about healthcare because it's a life and death issue that determines how we care for our society's most vulnerable people. As I said earlier, it's personal.

The federal government is uniquely *unsuited* to manage healthcare. Washington is full of big proposals dealing with national policy. A lot of these policies are geared toward hitting macro-level targets, like Obamacare's goal of 16 million new Medicaid enrollees. And often, few have really contemplated the unintended consequences of these policies on an individual level. Is this a chance we should be taking with our healthcare system—something so personal, and yet also representing one-sixth of our economy?

Our Founding Fathers created a federal system because they understood everyday political issues should be handled at the most local level possible. The national government was meant to handle large-scale problems like national defense, not to dictate which medical procedures individuals can get and at what cost.

Government is most likely to threaten your life and liberty when it sees you as a number instead of a person. It's not that Congress has bad intentions—it's got its share of corrupt members, but the majority in each party means well. And it's not that bureaucrats are inherently lazy, dishonest brutes, either. But the bureaucracy is designed to behave slowly, dispassionately, and without regard to the individual circumstances of each person its decisions effect. And that is where government can become disconnected from the individuals it is supposed to serve.

Here's a simple illustration of the incredible inertia and bureaucratic disconnect that characterizes our healthcare system. While I was an

assistant secretary at the U.S. Department of Health and Human Services, I convinced Secretary Tommy Thompson to cut the paperwork
and red tape that burden medical professionals. There was a form that
was supposed to measure the quality of a home healthcare agency. The
evaluation contained some rather odd questions: How often do you
have sexual relations? How often is foul language used in the home?
Asking why irrelevant, intrusive questions like these were necessary,
we were told some researcher theorized they were correlated with better healthcare outcomes. We followed up: Did the data prove it to be
true? We received a stunning answer: We don't know, that researcher
doesn't work here anymore. They were asking the questions only
because they were supposed to ask the questions!

Americans want healthcare reform that reduces costs, improves outcomes and real access, and puts consumers in control. It's useless for
us to bury our heads in the sand and pretend reform isn't necessary.
The Democrats have chosen a reform program based on a massive
expansion of the size and scope of the federal government. Republicans have offered a variety of ideas and plans with a consistent theme
of smaller government and a robust private sector.

I reject the claim among some Republican strategists that healthcare is a Democrat issue. It may seem that way, because prominent
Democrats such as the late Senator Ted Kennedy worked doggedly
toward a specific vision of reform. I disagree with that vision—a
single-payer government scheme—but at least they know where they
want to go. They're winning this battle because conservatives have
failed to present our own clear, consistent vision for reform.

You could see this even before the debate over Obama's healthcare
bill, back when we were discussing SCHIP expansion. Democrats said
they wanted to cover more kids. Republicans opposed the plan by say-

ing they wanted to cover more kids, but not as many as the Democrats. That's not a winning argument. Republicans should have argued we wanted children to have coverage too, but instead of relying on a government-run system that crowds out existing private coverage and wastes taxpayer dollars, we should introduce tax credits, voluntary purchasing pools, and other private sector incentives.

Healthcare is not a Democrat or Republican issue. It's an American issue, and we need to apply tried and true American principles to fix it. But make no mistake—despite all the strengths of our system, we urgently need reform. How will we provide good, dignified care for persons with developmental disabilities as their current caregivers age? As the population of Americans over fifty-five nearly doubles in the next twenty years,[9] how will we ensure there are enough doctors to care for them? As healthcare consumes a growing percentage of our GDP, how do we reduce costs while also expanding real access?

As I said before, I believe healthcare is a right. The issue is not whether or not to expand and improve healthcare—especially for the poor and other vulnerable groups—but whether the instrument of reform will be the government or the private sector. In my view, the government's role should be ensuring a robust marketplace that is competitive (so consumers have choice), transparent (so consumers can make informed decisions), accountable (so resources are leveraged to reward good clinical outcomes rather than simply paying for the process of care), effective (by engaging consumers in making good health choices for themselves and their families), and accessible (so healthcare is affordable). Moreover, the system has to be based on sound, proven economic principles—the government simply cannot suspend the law of supply and demand. When government inserts itself into a marketplace and makes bureaucratic decisions about paying for services, the inevitable result is shortages and fraud.

So the government can play a constructive role, but it should be a limited one, consistent with the view of our Founders, that maximizes the participation of states, local communities, and individuals. When Washington politicians claim their plans provide "choice," they imply *they* are giving us this choice and so they are on "our" side. Folks, I believe the choice is inherently *yours*, and no one has a right to take it away.

Perhaps the most surreal element of the Democrats' healthcare bill is the bizarre notion that an expanded federal role with a trillion dollar price tag will save money. This argument contradicts the fundamental principles of the American economy, in which competition and choice have always been the drivers for lower cost and innovation. Why do cell phones work better but cost less than they did fifteen years ago? Why are the flat screen TVs on which America watched the Saints win the Super Bowl larger, better, and cheaper than only a few years ago?

The fact is, scientific advancement is not linear. The pace of innovation is growing so rapidly that in twenty-five years, we won't even recognize a lot of today's cutting edge technology. The government is not responsible for this. Rather, companies are investing in research and development because they want better, lower-cost technology that will attract more customers. Sure, the government participates in research, but its most useful role is in leveraging the capacity and efficiency of the private marketplace.

An outsized government role damages the healthcare marketplace. For example, government-run Medicare and Medicaid are so dominant in the healthcare market that their government-driven payment policies spill over into the private market, as some private payers link their own payment policies to them. And Medicare and Medicaid don't pay based on outcomes—they pay based on volume. These one-size-fits-all policies are harmfully rigid, since not every doctor, hospital, or patient is the same.

Let's consider a few examples. If one neurosurgeon is much more accomplished and skillful than another, should the two be paid the same? Of course not, but that's the government's policy—it pays for the procedure rather than the outcome, because it lacks the apparatus or capability to respond to real market conditions.

Let's apply this example to the car market. Imagine that the government ran the entire auto industry (I know, I know, the government would *never* take over private car companies), and it charged the same price for a Cadillac and a Chevy. Most people, of course, would buy the Cadillac. Well, the guys making Cadillacs will eventually figure out they don't need to invest heavily in making a better car, because they don't get paid for it. So quality would deteriorate. We are seeing this same thing play out in medicine. More doctors are choosing not to serve Medicaid patients, more doctors are choosing not to care for high risk cases, and fewer people are going into primary care medicine.[10] We must stop paying for process and instead leverage the private marketplace to help us recognize and encourage value.

Dartmouth College has done some fascinating research showing there are huge differences in how much money is spent on patients in different parts of the country based solely on the historic spending patterns for process—not outcomes. In Manhattan and Miami, for example, Medicare patients receive far more expensive and more aggressive treatment than similar patients in places like Rochester, Minnesota, or Salt Lake City, Utah. But here's the interesting thing:

patients in Manhattan and Miami don't do any better than the others. In fact, their outcomes are often *worse*. A 2006 study by the Dartmouth Center for the Evaluative Clinical Sciences (CECS) concluded that in these high-use regions, "patients with the same disease have higher mortality rates, very likely because of medical errors associated with increased use of acute-care hospitals."[11]

Let's look at birth outcomes as another example. In 2009, there were more than 10,000 premature deliveries in Louisiana, and Medicaid funded more than two-thirds of them. A healthy, full term delivery costs Medicaid less than $4,000, while a premature delivery costs more than $33,000. So in Louisiana, we paid more than $212 million for the poor outcomes. Additionally, we know that premature kids have three times the likelihood to develop cerebral palsy. Perversely, everyone gets paid for this bad outcome.

What are the incentives in the funding system to go upstream and reduce the number of poor birth outcomes? In a system where providers are paid more for more services, doctors are actually penalized financially if they choose to do fewer procedures. Similarly, a hospital can only survive financially if more people are admitted. The funding system is so upside down that we actually pay more if a hospital patient gets an infection or some other bad outcome. In Louisiana, our proposals have sought to bring sensibility to how we pay for services.

America's health system also lacks consumer engagement. When consumers do not share in the cost of the care, when they have no "skin in the game," they have little incentive to make decisions that help reduce costs. Consider two sectors of the healthcare system where costs have *not* exploded over the past fifteen years: plastic surgery and laser vision surgery. Why? Because neither one is traditionally covered by third parties such as health insurance plans or the federal government. The people receiving the services pay for them directly, and they are price and quality sensitive.

We need to remind ourselves that health insurance is *insurance*. The purpose is to cover treatments that we normally couldn't afford by pooling risk across time and a large number of people. But we often think of it as something like prepaid dollars we need to spend. If we have fire insurance, we don't burn down a room in our house at the end of the year because we didn't have a fire. Yet when it comes to health insurance, we often make unnecessary doctors' visits or perform needless tests at the end of the year just to "spend" our health insurance money.

Finally, I believe a government-run, price-fixing system feeds fraud at all levels because the government simply sets rates for providers and pays claims. The volume of claims is so large, it's nearly impossible to properly manage it on the front end. This puts taxpayers at risk. In Louisiana Medicaid, we process more than 60 million claims each year for more than 25,000 providers. The result is a system designed to pay quickly for volume, but with little ability for the government to determine if what we are paying for is actually appropriate. Extrapolate that to the national level, and you have a serious problem; the Obama administration announced that in 2009, the federal government made around *$50 billion* of "improper payments" in Medicare and Medicaid.[12]

When I was secretary of Louisiana's Department of Health and Hospitals, our program faced a $400 million deficit. There were Medicaid mills operating all around the state that were billing us for fictitious services. Working with the attorney general, we cracked down hard on fraud and sent scam artists to prison. I remember going on a raid in New Orleans where we busted a massive operation which gave candy to dozens of kids a week and offered money to their parents simply to sign off on government forms falsely showing they were receiving health-related services.

For a while it seemed Medicaid fraud was one of the fastest growing businesses in Louisiana. But by adopting reforms including a zero tolerance policy toward fraud, we turned that $400 million deficit into a surplus.

Sunshine is the best disinfectant, as they say, and that's why a transparent healthcare system is crucial to reducing fraud, lowering costs, and improving quality. In Louisiana, we've established www.healthfinderla.gov, a website allowing people to compare quality, patient satisfaction, and cost among hospitals, nursing homes, pharmacies, and health insurance plans. Moreover, we passed a sweeping reform of Medicaid to allow consumers to choose their own insurance rather than being relegated to the once-size-fits-all, fraud-laden, pay-for-volume system. Our reforms also create incentives for coordinated networks of care that help improve metrics we know make people more healthy—like ensuring children get their well-child exams, people with diabetes have their disease managed properly, and women get earlier breast cancer detection. Notably, our Legislature passed these reforms on a bipartisan basis—proving to Washington that vital, market-based reforms can be achieved with broad support.

*   *   *

There is an alternative to the trillion-dollar, top-down, government-driven policies of Obamacare. Here's a list of market-based healthcare reforms that will reduce cost, increase access, and empower consumers:

- FIX THE RISK POOLS. The basic premise of insurance is the spreading of risk. Yet the government keeps creating programs that take healthy people out of the insurance pools and put them into government programs like the children's SCHIP program. This increases the cost of private insurance, because older and sicker people keep their private coverage as younger, healthier people opt out. Called the "death spiral," this trend is a major reason for the rise in premiums. We should leverage what we spend for healthier populations to help improve the risk of the insurance pools. Providing subsidies for private coverage is a far better solution than expanding government programs like Medicaid.

- ALLOW PEOPLE TO "OWN" INSURANCE POLICIES THAT STAY WITH THEM WHEN THEY CROSS STATE LINES OR CHANGE JOBS. By ensuring people keep their policies longer, insurers will invest more to improve their customers' long-term health.

- ALLOW THE CREATION OF VOLUNTARY PURCHASING POOLS. Small businesses, the self-employed, and others should benefit from the economies of scale currently enjoyed by employees of large firms. They should also be allowed to purchase health coverage through their employer, church, or union without tax penalty.

- END THE LAWSUIT CULTURE. We can't ignore the enormous cost of defensive medicine, as doctors order unnecessary tests and procedures solely to avoid lawsuits. Many doctors have even stopped performing high-risk procedures for fear of liability. A study by the American Academy of Orthopedic Surgeons estimated the cost of defensive medicine at more than $100 billion per year.[13]

Approximately half of Texas' doctors are paying lower liability premiums than they were in 2001. Indeed, rates have been reduced by 30 percent or more for about 90 percent of the state's doctors since the 2003 reform. Further, in the years following the reform, Texas has seen thirty rate cuts. And most important, the measure stopped and reversed the outflow of doctors from the state. According to the Texas Medical Association, there has been a nearly 60 percent growth rate in newly licensed physicians in the past two years compared to two years preceding the reform.[14]

- COVER PRE-EXISTING CONDITIONS. We can address the issue of pre-existing conditions by restructuring how we finance care for the poor. Federal-state partnership programs like Medicaid should allow people to use subsidies to purchase private coverage and then provide reinsurance to the plans that take people with pre-existing, high-cost conditions. This type of partnership leverages public spending with already existing private-sector assets and helps keep premiums more stable. We need to guard against the moral hazard risk, but health insurance shouldn't be least accessible when you need it most.

- INCREASE TRANSPARENCY. Consumers have more information when choosing a can of soup than when selecting a healthcare provider. Provider quality and cost should be made available to all consumers by creating websites with continually updated prices and outcomes.

- REFORM THE PAYMENT SYSTEM. Rather than pay for activity, why not pay for performance? About 75 percent of healthcare spending goes toward chronic conditions such as heart disease, cancer, and diabetes. But there is little coordination of care. Today's system results in wide variations in treatment instead of the consistent application of best practices. We must reward efficiency and quality.

- EXPAND DEPLOYMENT OF HEALTH INFORMATION TECHNOLOGY. The current system of paper records threatens patient privacy and leads to poor outcomes, redundant procedures, and higher costs. In Louisiana, we invested in an award-winning initiative to digitally connect our rural hospitals with a major teaching hospital in Shreveport. Now we can provide digital mammography and other diagnostics in the rural community, with a physician in Shreveport reviewing the results. This has improved access and provided a new way to combat the looming physician shortages.

- EXPAND TAX–FREE HEALTH SAVINGS ACCOUNTS. HSAs, which allow individuals with a high-deductible health plan to save pre-tax dollars in a portable account for qualified medical expenses, have helped reduce the costs for employers and consumers. By creating incentives to encourage price and quality comparisons, HSAs encourage people to spend their health care dollars efficiently. Research shows that people with HSA plans are more likely to seek preventative care and routine treatments for chronic illnesses.[15] In fact, some businesses have seen their healthcare costs decrease by double-digit percentages after adopting HSAs.[16] Although millions of Americans use HSAs today, current and proposed regulations are designed to curb their further growth.

- REWARD HEALTHY LIFESTYLE CHOICES. Providing premium rebates and other incentives to people who make healthy choices or participate in managing their chronic diseases reduces costs and improves health. Auto insurance companies give discounts to people with safe driving records—shouldn't we provide the same sort of incentives for healthcare?

- EXPAND PRIVATE COVERAGE. We should provide refundable and advanceable tax credits for the uninsured, and transition

Medicaid toward a subsidy model for private coverage rather than a government-run, fee-for-volume program. This is especially true for the healthy moms and their children who comprise the vast majority of Medicaid beneficiaries. This would put resources in the hands of consumers and help low-income Americans acquire insurance they would own.

- PREPARE FOR THE AGING OF AMERICA. We must start getting ready to provide our mothers and fathers with the dignity of aging in place. Additionally, it is the calling of our time to ensure persons living with developmental disabilities enjoy the opportunity to be independent, self-determined, and successful. For example, while at HHS I helped expand a program called Cash and Counseling that trusts the disabled and their families to have more direct control over healthcare dollars spent on their behalf. We must equip the next generation to be stewards of their own health.

Speaking of the next generation, I should mention that our son, Shaan, came through his surgery in great shape. He still sees his cardiologist regularly, but he's grown into an energetic and healthy boy who likes soccer and basketball. And he has a pretty good sense of humor, too. Recently, a group of politicians came to see me at the governor's mansion. Shaan made them all stand in "time out" before they met with me.

CHAPTER 12

PROPELLING AMERICA FORWARD

As governor of one of America's largest oil producing states, you could reasonably assume that I'm a proponent of fossil fuels. Guilty as charged—and the 2010 oil spill off the Louisiana coast, awful as it is, hasn't changed that. Some people believe that the oil spill means we need to stop offshore oil drilling. But it's completely irrational to halt an entire industry when a tragedy happens. When we suffer the tragedy of an airliner going down, for example, we do not respond by stopping all air travel for six months. Rather, we get to work figuring out the root cause and set about trying to make air travel safer.

But what may surprise you is that along with being a big supporter of fossil fuels, I'm also a big proponent of developing any and all methods of producing energy. I even support pursuing technologies that don't exist yet. Not all of them will succeed, but we have to consider every option in order to make America energy independent.

The problem is that many Washington decision makers are either seriously misinformed or willfully ignorant about energy. It's as if they believe that electricity comes from a light switch and gasoline just magically appears at the pump.

When energy prices skyrocketed during my tenure in Congress, both parties were more focused on using the issue for political gain rather than solving it. Democrats need apocalyptic rhetoric to raise money from environmentalists and from fearful constituents; many of them even believe high energy prices are useful to their environmental agenda, though they won't admit it publicly. Meanwhile, Republicans used the opportunity to attack global warming theories instead of finding common ground to craft a sensible energy policy.

America's enemies benefit from the paralysis of our energy policy. We continue to send billions of dollars to foreign energy producers, including Middle Eastern despots and self-styled revolutionaries like Hugo Chavez who, to say the least, don't have America's interests at heart. All the while, our own tremendous supply of oil and gas lies untapped right here beneath U.S. soil and off our coasts.

Over the past twenty years oil prices have been rising and they will surely jump even higher once growth returns to the global economy. It's simple supply and demand—energy is the lifeblood of a strong economy. What's more, our constant technological progress will not alter this equation. Personal computers, iPads, and other high-tech devices all require electrical power. And high-tech companies need it as much as old industrial companies. You see, it takes a lot of energy to create a wired society. The international demand for energy will also continue to expand with the explosive economic growth of countries like China and India.

At the same time, world energy production is beginning to level off. Countries like Saudi Arabia, which once functioned as swing producers with their excess capacity, can't boost production enough to fix this problem. And many of the biggest oil producing countries have locked up their reserves in national oil companies, leaving Western companies such as ExxonMobil and Shell controlling less than 10 percent of the world's oil and gas reserves.[1]

We have to take control of our energy future. Liberals need to accept that fossil fuels are critical to our national security and to our economy, and that they can be developed in an environmentally responsible way. They are a bridge to the energy future, a necessity as we continue to develop alternative fuels. Conservatives, for our part, need to do more than simply shout "Drill, baby, drill"—we need to aggressively pursue the next generation of renewable and clean energy production technologies.

Republicans seem instinctively to oppose cultivating energy sources favored by the environmental movement, such as solar and wind power. Likewise, Democrats often stridently oppose the expansion of traditional energy sources such as oil, coal, and nuclear power. Here's an idea: how about we do it all? That's not a Republican or Democrat solution. That's an American solution.

Most of us take it for granted that we can easily and affordably fill up our cars and drive 300 miles. Similarly, we assume that on hot Louisiana summer days or cold Minnesota nights, we can adjust the thermostat to a comfortable level for just a few dollars a day. But affordable, reliable energy doesn't just happen by itself. Private companies have made huge capital investments and taken big risks to develop our energy supply. And without affordable energy, it's nearly impossible to develop or maintain a prosperous society. The historical transition from human labor, to animals, to windmills took thousands of years. But with the steady supply of cheap energy delivered by fossil fuels, technological progress has exploded like never before in history.

Securing a plentiful, affordable energy supply is a vital national goal. There are two main plans discussed in Washington today to achieve it: the liberals' all-in bet on "green energy" as an alternative to fossil fuels, and the conservatives' equally one-sided preference for those same fossil fuels. I favor a comprehensive, all-of-the-above approach. We need to unite the public sector, meaning the federal government and our universities, with the private sector behind a common strategy of research and investment. It will be an Apollo mission if you will— except instead of landing on the moon we will try to harness the power of the earth, wind, and sun. Creating and developing a diverse domestic energy supply at low cost should be our unifying goal. The way I figure it: God put oil and natural gas here for us to use. And God gave us creative minds to develop new and better ways to create energy. So let's cut through the ideology and use some common sense.

*   *   *

My mom studied nuclear physics, my dad is a civil engineer, and Supriya is a chemical engineer. Thanks partly to this family environment, I am an enthusiastic advocate of expanding the frontiers of science and technology. From my work in policy, I have also learned that free enterprise, not government planning, is the key to human ingenuity and innovation. It is capitalist innovation, not the heavy hand of government-imposed rationing, that helps our economy grow faster and with comparatively less energy than ever before. In 1973, it took 1,400 barrels of oil to support $1 million worth of gross national product (GNP). By 2003 that number had shrunk by more than half.[2]

So I wouldn't bet against America's ability to develop immense green energy sources. In Louisiana, we're doing our part. We are working on developing cellulosic ethanol (sugar cane stalks) as a source of energy; we have implemented aggressive tax credits for solar panels and compressed natural gas; and our companies are experimenting with harnessing the power of the Mississippi River and manufacturing the modular components for nuclear reactors. Indeed, we announced that Shaw Modular Solutions would be building the first facility focused on constructing components for new and modified nuclear reactors in the United States. An innovative manufacturer named Blade Dynamics has started a factory in New Orleans to produce advanced blades for wind turbines. We actively supported their efforts with performance-based grants and other incentives. Another company named Dynamic Fuels just completed a facility in Geismar, Louisiana, south of Baton Rouge, that will convert animal fats to fuel. We were eager to work with them.

But let's be realistic. A lot of people are portraying green energy as a panacea that will quickly solve our energy problems. Speaker of the House Nancy Pelosi said America needs "an energy policy that will reduce energy prices, reduce our dependence on foreign oil, and reduce pollution."[3] It sounds so easy—one can only wonder why such a simple solution hasn't already been tried. Ask that question, and you'll often hear wild conspiracy theories about Big Oil and Big Coal. In reality, while green energy offers tremendous future potential, the technology is still extremely expensive. Coal costs about 4 cents a kilowatt-hour. Compare that to 12 cents for wind and even more for solar, both of which are far less reliable than coal.[4] Do you really want your utility bills to triple? Over time, technology will narrow this gap in price and reliability, but you can't snap your fingers and make unworkable markets work.

Green energy still needs to overcome other problems as well. For example, wind energy requires enormous landmass—the land covered by a wind power station needs to be about 2,000 times bigger than a nuclear plant to generate the same amount of electricity.[5] While there are some suitable locations for wind farms in small pockets in the Midwest, West, and Southwest, there are relatively few good areas in the eastern half of the United States.

Even where a good location exists, green energy projects are often opposed by their supposed liberal champions. A case in point is the windmill project off Cape Cod, Massachusetts, that was opposed by members of the Kennedy family who reportedly didn't want the view spoiled from their nearby compound. After *eight years* of lawsuits and government studies, the federal government finally approved the project in May 2010.[6] Liberals may support green energy in theory, but in practice they all too often shout NIMBY—Not in My Backyard.

And of course you can't control the wind (just like the hot air coming out of D.C.); it's intermittent and sometimes it completely stops (unlike the hot air coming out of D.C.). So even when you have a wind energy facility, you need back-up capacity, which means building a traditional plant that burns coal or natural gas. Don't get me wrong, I'm all for harnessing wind. But we can't pretend windmills can miraculously power the U.S. economy—no single energy source can.

Solar plants present the same sort of challenges: they only work efficiently in some locations, solar radiation is rarely constant, and the plants require large tracts of land. (To replace a power plant such as California's Diablo Canyon plant, for example, would mean replacing a three square kilometer nuclear plant with a solar plant spanning 687.5 square kilometers.[7]) And while there is great potential for building large solar facilities in the southwest, transporting the electricity long distances through power lines means we will lose a substantial amount in the process through what they call "line-loss."

Technological innovation will make these technologies more efficient, affordable, and marketable. But it's going to take time. The notion that green energy can quickly replace our dependence on fossil fuels is a myth perpetuated by folks who refuse to face reality or who don't care about our prosperity, or both.

Along with solar and wind power, we need to continue research on biomass, geothermal, hydrogen, hydrokinetics, harnessing CO_2 for enhanced oil recovery, converting methane emissions from landfills into energy, clean coal, and other alternative energies. This doesn't mean, however, the government should dictate which sources are developed. Government can help by offering targeted tax credits for a wide range of potential energy sources, but in general the government should let the market decide which of these technologies will succeed and in what form. The market will tell us if solar is best on farms for large-scale generation or on rooftops for use in individual homes or on traffic signals to assist our transportation system. Government bureaucrats should not be picking winners and losers, and should not favor with benefits one technology over another. That inevitably politicizes the process, with the winner being whatever industry has the best lobbyists.

One green technology largely ignored by the Left is nuclear power. You heard me right, nuclear energy is in fact a green technology, and it's one of the best options we have to simultaneously make our country's economy grow and protect our environment. Nuclear power is safe, reliable, emission free, and can create a steady supply of energy. One reactor can produce on average as much power as thousands of wind turbines at a fraction of the cost—and it doesn't threaten birds, as the blades of some windmills do.[8]

The main impediment to expanding nuclear power is what you might call the Three Mile Island Effect. Promoted for thirty years by environmentalists, the Effect cites the 1979 nuclear accident at Pennsylvania's Three Mile Island nuclear plant as proof that nuclear power is unsafe. Of course, public safety has to be paramount in the nuclear industry, as it should be in every energy industry. But the implications of the accident have been grossly overstated for political ends.[9] And don't forget, technology has improved remarkably in the last three decades. Yet, thanks to the myth, no new nuclear reactors have been built in America for thirty years. President Obama's declared support for developing two new reactors is a step forward.[10] But instead of two, we should build a hundred.

There is no excuse for us to be lagging behind many other countries in nuclear power. Today we get about 20 percent of our electricity from America's 104 nuclear power plants. But France gets 79 percent, Sweden 45 percent, South Korea 38 percent, and Belgium 56 percent of their electricity from nuclear reactors.[11] My mom came to America in 1971 to study nuclear physics because we were the worldwide leader in nuclear energy technology at the time. She left the field in the late 1970s because the Carter administration effectively ended the industry's growth.

* * *

While conservatives need to embrace the possibilities of green energy, liberals need to recognize that fossil fuels, particularly those developed in the United States, will dominate our energy supply for the foreseeable future. The Left has to understand that the Alaskan

Wildlife Refuge, ANWR, is not a four-letter word—okay, bad example, because that acronym is four letters. But the bottom line is this: scaling back domestic drilling, and preventing drilling in ANWR, won't cut our use of oil and natural gas. It just means even more of our supply will come from foreign countries.

Today, liberal opposition to the development and use of fossil fuels stems largely from their fears of apocalyptic global warming, or what they now call climate change. (This new phraseology is convenient, of course, since the climate is always changing.) Al Gore has been warning for twenty years that we are on the verge of ecological calamity if we don't dramatically cut our carbon emissions. Back in 1992, in his book *Earth in the Balance*, Gore claimed cars are "posing a mortal threat to the security of every nation that is more deadly than that of any military enemy we are ever again likely to confront."[12] And to think this guy almost became president.

Global warming alarmists claim the science of global warming is settled, though that's far from the truth. We now know, through the leak of thousands of emails from the Climatic Research Unit at the University of East Anglia, the source for much of the information that the United Nations uses for its alarmist climate change reports, that some of the top scientists behind the global warming panic have been suppressing information and trying to blacklist dissenting scientists. Their collusion and suppression of data violated core tenets of the scientific method, which demands open scrutiny and the testing of hypotheses. When someone won't share data, you can only assume they have something to hide. Instead of circling their wagons and attacking their critics, climate researchers should publicize their data. Global warming should not be a faith-based theory.

The science on global warming is far from settled, and we need to continue to debate, measure, and discuss our impact on the environment. But even the true believer in apocalyptic global warming needs to face the fact that we will rely on fossil fuels for the foreseeable future. Hot air from hysterical activists won't heat a single home.

I acknowledge that global warming may in fact be a significant problem for mankind. I certainly believe our economic activities should be balanced by environmental concerns, and that we should harness science and technology to raise efficiency, increase conservation, and reduce our emissions. But, overall these doomsday scenarios are not fact, they're conjecture presented with a bizarre religious fervor. Skeptics of the scenarios are shrilly denounced as modern-day heretics. I for one am not going to be intimidated by this.

Global warming alarmism is often used to further extremist political agendas that are opposed to capitalism, in favor of population control, and even represent a sort of anti-technology Luddism. What all these agendas have in common is an effort to increase government control over the individual. How big your car is, where you live, how much you heat or cool your house, even how many kids you have—these are all areas that should be guarded from government intrusion.

To embrace the current global warming doctrine you need to accept five things:

1. The planet is warming significantly and abnormally.
2. The problem is man-made.
3. Its effects will be catastrophic.
4. The problem can only be solved with massive government intervention.
5. Al Gore tells the truth.

Based on what we know right now in the scientific realm, this requires a modicum of faith.

The liberal attack on fossils fuels doesn't even make sense in the context of global warming—destroying our domestic energy production and manufacturing base and exporting our jobs abroad won't cut the world's carbon emissions. In fact, these jobs will go to countries like Mexico, China, and India, while more of our oil and natural gas will come from countries like Venezuela, Saudi Arabia, and Russia—all of which have much weaker environmental laws than we do. Do you really think a smokestack in Tijuana will produce fewer emissions than one in San Diego?

Keep that in mind next time you hear the Democrats' proposals for a "cap and trade" scheme. In addition to increasing the utility costs of homeowners in America, charging our own companies for releasing carbon will provoke a lot of them simply to relocate to countries that don't charge these fees. Still, at least the Democrats' rhetoric is honest on this issue. Cap and trade *is* a jobs bill—for other countries. It *is* a win/win—for the rest of the world.

The Left, it seems, often opposes fossil fuels purely out of ideology. Take natural gas. Although it's often decried by liberals as a dirty fossil fuel, natural gas in fact is a cleaner-burning energy source. New technologies have allowed us to find more natural gas reserves that could rapidly expand our energy base.[13] We're doing our part in Louisiana, where the Haynesville shale formation was recently discovered. This is one of the largest shale formations in the world, holding up to 200 trillion cubic feet of natural gas. And we'll develop it, creating jobs for Louisianians and fuel for millions of Americans.

The Left's opposition to natural gas, however, pales in comparison to their seething hatred of oil companies. Environmentalists and even some members of Congress portray oil company CEOs as Darth Vader steering the Death Star, with former Vice President Dick Cheney playing the role of the evil Emperor. Tony Hayward, the CEO of BP, played to this stereotype. Although in my experience he seemed far more aloof and less competent than Darth Vader.

Yes, oil companies do try to make a profit; that's what companies do. News flash: solar and wind companies are hoping to make money, too! What critics of the petroleum industry don't seem to understand is that producing energy requires huge investments for locating, drilling, and transporting oil. The average net profit margin for the energy sector, according to Thomson Baseline's examination of the S&P energy companies, was 9.7 percent, compared to 8.5 percent for the entire Standard and Poor's 500. Google has reported net profit margins of 25 percent in some quarters.[14] Does that mean Google is a greedy corporation earning "excess profits"? No, like the oil companies, Google is simply providing a product or service that people want. The only difference is that our entire economy would grind to a halt without oil. These sorts of attacks are useful in raising money for certain politicians and interest groups, but they do nothing to help America's energy future.

Some in Washington want to punish oil companies through so-called "windfall taxes." They forget their history. Jimmy Carter tried a similar approach back in the 1970s, with the predictable result that domestic production fell and our reliance on foreign oil grew. For a lot of reasons, American oil production has already declined from 9.2 million barrels a day in 1973 to 5 million barrels a day in 2007.[15] A basic rule of economics is that if you want less of something, just tax it more.

This self-defeating habit of punishing our own oil companies drives up the price of oil, enriching every oil producing country whether we import from them or not. Russia, with its vast energy wealth, has nearly quadrupled its military spending over the past six years.[16] Iran is putting large chunks of its oil wealth into developing its nuclear capabilities and supporting terrorist groups. In our own hemisphere, Venezuelan dictator Hugo Chavez is using that country's energy wealth to fund his anti-democratic allies throughout Latin America. Even President Obama's six month temporary moratorium in the Gulf has led to rigs being relocated to the Congo and Egypt.

It doesn't have to be this way. America has tremendous energy resources, but a lot of them sit under federal land. And 94 percent of federal land has been put off-limits to energy development.[17] We have more coal than any other country, but we're prevented from accessing a lot of it. We find a similar situation with Congress's ban on oil drilling in the Alaskan National Wildlife Refuge. In Alaska's vast and frozen ANWR, we could produce an estimated 15 billion gallons of oil annually from an area roughly the size of an airport.[18] Within ANWR, that's the equivalent of drilling on an area the size of a postage stamp placed on a football field. That Congress chooses not to ease our reliance on foreign oil by opening up ANWR to drilling is inexplicable—a textbook case of political correctness run amok.

The United States already imports around 62 percent of its oil— and under our current energy policy, this figure will keep rising. While we need to explore all forms of energy production, it will be impossible to improve this situation without more drilling.

We also need to access our offshore oil reserves that are currently blocked by the federal government. The Interior Department estimates the U.S. continental shelf contains 115 billion barrels of oil and 633 trillion cubic feet of natural gas. That's enough oil to fuel our country for sixteen years and enough natural gas for twenty-five years.[19]

I'm not talking about putting oil rigs on Miami Beach—I'm simply calling for balance. Many people will point to the recent oil spill of the Deepwater Horizon rig off Louisiana as a reason to halt new offshore drilling. As one of the governors who has to deal with this mess, I'm not going to sugarcoat it—the oil spill was a tragedy, costing eleven people their lives. Thousands of square miles of ocean have been contaminated, hundreds of species may be affected, and countless fishermen have been cut off from their livelihoods. We will need to focus state and federal agencies to clean it up and make sure those responsible ultimately pay the bill.

However, we shouldn't overreact to the spill with a knee-jerk move to ban new offshore drilling. Creating a "Three Mile Island" Effect from this spill could encumber our oil production for decades, just like the Three Mile Island myth did for nuclear power. As I said before, clamping down on our own drilling will simply make us more dependent on oil from foreign countries with lax environmental standards. It will mean importing more oil, which comes with its own risks—for example, tanker spills like the *Exxon Valdez* disaster. The wise course is to carefully study the cause of the spill and devise strong safeguards to prevent it from happening again.

Without a doubt, the Deepwater Horizon spill shows we need to be more vigilant about drilling safety. Louisiana is the Sportsman's Paradise and home to some of America's most vibrant wetlands. People in my state rely on a healthy ecosystem for their livelihood and a great quality of life. Negligence can put that at risk.

Environmental groups will undoubtedly try to exploit this spill to pressure Congress into banning drilling from more of our coastal

areas. Although this decades-long ban, along with a separate presidential ban, was lifted during the oil price spike of 2008, the Obama
administration only allowed initial steps toward new drilling in the
southern Atlantic coast and in small parts of the Gulf of Mexico and
the Alaskan coast. Meanwhile, drilling effectively remains banned
along the north Atlantic coast, nearly the entire Pacific coast, parts of
Alaska, and most of the eastern Gulf of Mexico.

Canada is drilling off the coasts of Nova Scotia and Newfoundland.
And the Cuban government has contracted with foreign companies to
drill close to the Florida coast. A wide array of countries are drilling
for oil off their shores, including Australia, Great Britain, Sweden,
Norway, Ireland, Brazil, Russia, Singapore, and China—and they're
going to continue drilling whether we do or not. A report issued by
the National Association of Regulatory Utility Commissioners estimates that restrictions on onshore and offshore drilling will increase
consumer energy costs and cut our gross domestic product (GDP) by
$2.36 trillion over the next twenty years.[20]

I say let the people of each state choose whether they want offshore
drilling, and let them share in the royalties if they do. We've been drilling
off the Louisiana coast since 1947 and now produce 91 percent of the oil
and 72 percent of the natural gas that comes from the Gulf of Mexico.
Offshore drilling has its risks, as we've seen firsthand in my state. But for
Louisiana it's meant thousands of jobs and billions in revenue to help
fund schools and to improve our residents' lives in many other ways. And
it's meant more domestically produced energy for all of America.

If we want to keep America strong and prosperous, we need a policy that aims for energy independence. Forget the self-serving cries
from interest groups that want to favor one energy source over the
other. The smart thing is to pursue them all.

CHAPTER 13

OF LIFE AND LOGIC

I had been governor of Louisiana for less than a year before the hurricanes came—first Gustav, then Ike. On the heels of Katrina I was determined that we be ready for the next storms, so we went to inordinate lengths. I personally took a special interest in making sure we were prepared and in understanding every detail. I met with everyone: emergency planners and officials from the National Guard, FEMA, state police, fire and rescue officials, anyone and everyone involved. We went over evacuation plans, conducted drill after drill, and made sure we had adequate supplies. My staff thought I was obsessed—and they were right. When more storms arrived, they inflicted billions of dollars in damage—there was nothing we could do to stop that. But through the heroic efforts of our rescue workers, countless lives were spared.

I'm always in awe of the brave men and women who rescue people in trouble. I remember witnessing the efforts of rescue workers pouring into New Orleans after Katrina to pull people from rooftops. First responders sawed holes in roofs to rescue people who were trapped in their attics as the water level rose. I had a similar sense of awe watching

American rescuers and others save people from certain death after the Haitian earthquake of January 2010. They spent days pulling injured children from collapsed buildings and removing the elderly from piles of debris.

There is just something about a rescue that touches us deeply inside. Rescues are great signs of the human spirit, great testaments to the brotherhood of all mankind. When a person takes risks to rescue another person it makes us all stop and think. You ask yourself, "Why do people do this? Why do people risk their very lives for perfect strangers? Why did firemen run into burning and collapsing buildings on 9/11? Was it because it was their job?" Many firefighters gave that answer after 9/11—"Just doin' my job." And while that is a tremendously humble and gracious answer, we all know there's more to it than that.

People risk all to save others because of the tremendous value we place on human life. One thing we never see in these circumstances is rescue workers walking around and deciding, "That person is not worth rescuing." No one walks around with a clipboard, asking people how old or how injured they are in order to make a cost-benefit calculation. Rescue workers help the young and old, the rich and poor, the Ph.D. and the college dropout. A life is a life. Yound and old, black and white, all are precious in His sight.

In my view there is an easy, universal barometer we can use to evaluate all cultures: how do they treat their most vulnerable members? How do they handle those whom Jesus so aptly referred to as "the least of these"? Do they defend the defenseless? Do they consider all human life to be both sacred and precious? I would go so far as to say that a society that does not do these things is really not a civilized society, at least not in my book. And this is after all . . . my book.

America's Judeo-Christian heritage commands us to help the helpless and demands that we protect innocent human life. Yes, this is a demand, not an option. America is a place that fosters a culture of life, a place that actively strives to protect its most vulnerable members. Undoubtedly, we as a country have made wrong turns over the years—we tolerated slavery after all. But I am an optimist when it comes to the American people. I believe that the great majority of Americans want to affirm life.

And regardless of the mindless political debate we so often hear on the issue of abortion—you know the debate, the one that talks about "choice" and "rights" and "freedom" and "legal precedent" and "settled law" and everything under the sun *except* for abortion itself—regardless of that, I do believe the desire to defend and protect human life extends across party and religious boundaries in America. I believe in America's desire and ability to do the right thing.

In this policy arena we face three fundamental questions: What value do we place on human life at its earliest and most vulnerable point? What value do we place on our young and what lengths will we go to protect them from an ever-coarsening world? And what value do we place on human life when it comes to end of life decisions?

A central component of this is how you view where we came from, who we are, and where we are headed. Put another way: Why? Why all the fuss? Why place such a high value on human life? There are hundreds of practical and utilitarian reasons to place a high value on human life. I agree with all of them. But it all boils down to one basic thing—the Bible teaches that God made mankind in His own image. There is your answer. That's why we place a supreme value on human life.

Again, there are many other reasons to value life. There's always the Golden Rule—do unto others as you would have them do unto you.

There's also common decency, kindness and compassion, and a long-ing to make the world a better place. These are all wonderful senti-ments indeed. But people are fickle. They have good days and bad days, and some folks seem to have a lot more bad days, and sometimes those people wind up being in charge. We can never find ourselves at their mercy. No, the reason we value human life is because God tells us to.

The Bible asks the rhetorical question, "Can man defy God?" or alternately, "Does the clay say to the potter, what are you making?" To refuse to honor and cherish human life is to defy God's laws and His designs for mankind. Incidentally, while discussing this very topic recently, a friend asked me why I was quoting the Bible. I thought that an odd question, so I simply replied, "Why not? You quote Mark Twain's novels and Shakespeare, why can't I quote the Bible?" I went on to tell him, and this really ticked him off, that unlike him, I'm edu-cated. I've read Twain and Shakespeare, but I've also read the Bible. Whether you are a Christian, a believer in some other faith, or even an agnostic, you can't claim to be well read if you haven't read the Bible at least once. So get to it, please.

Back to the question at hand: why value all human life? Let me paint a different scenario, a logical one. If you believe humans are foundationally no different from all other forms of life, or rather, that the only real difference is progress in the evolutionary process, that can lead you to a much different view on life issues than the one we find in the Bible, or at least to several different outcomes. Admittedly, some wonderful people take this view. Many of them are very nurturing of human life simply because they are decent, generous, and kindhearted people who instinctively want to do the right and kind thing. Some who take this view are equally protective of all life, human or animal.

But we have to face the fact that some who take this view—that the only thing separating humans and animals is evolutionary progress—inevitably reach some strange but seemingly logical conclusions. If we have too many deer, it makes sense to thin the herd. Otherwise they eat your flowers and cause car accidents. We do something like that in Louisiana with these things called Nutria. I won't waste your time explaining them to you, but suffice to say they look like overgrown swamp rats on steroids, and they eat everything they see, including vital vegetation that protects and preserves our waterways. They are a menace and have few supporters; their poll ratings are even lower than lobbyists'. In fact, Louisiana has offered a bounty to entice hunters to help exterminate these pests.

It's not far, then, to take a few more logical steps down this pathway of reasoning. Remember, we've already stipulated that humankind and animals are merely separated by positioning on the evolutionary chain, nothing else.

Think about all the poverty in this world and all the problems some regions have with overpopulation. Maybe it's not a good idea to go through with a pregnancy if the child will be born into poverty, or born into a society with a tyrannical government? What if the child has defects? Maybe it would be best to abort? Would that be the compassionate thing to do? Maybe the Chinese have it right—one child per family (preferably a son).

And what of elderly folks who are barely functional and no longer enjoy life? Not to be crass, but let's be honest, they are costing the rest of us a boatload of cash. You want to really solve the healthcare cost problems in this country? Now we're talking big savings. I bet those old timers would rather not be a burden after all. Calling Dr. Kevorkian...

Let me stop right here and make something clear. I have many friends who disagree with me on the origins of man, and some who do not believe in a Creator at all. Most of them are in fact better people than I am. And a great many of them are pro-life, while others are pro-choice. Many of those folks are tremendously compassionate people. I am not in any way attempting to impugn them or anyone else. I am simply making a logical and impassioned plea for the cause of life and the centrality of respect for life in American culture.

For all my pro-choice friends out there, we can agree to keep on disagreeing, and keep on arguing (until I win). Supriya has noted that I like to argue, but that's a topic for another book, one that I hope she never writes.

Now that I have apologized to all of you who disagree with me, let me continue, for those of you who have an open mind and are interested in logic, to press my case.

Once you take God out of the equation, you run a great risk of seeking to solve problems by applying at least some form of "thinning the herd" argument to humankind. It's not that anyone really wants to do it, it's just that it needs to be done in order to preserve the quality of life for the rest of us. Of course, it's all cloaked under the guise of compassion. The proponents of the Chinese one-child policy, on the other hand, are more honest. They are trying to keep the herd under control by any means necessary.

Today, many people attempt to blur our understanding of what human life really is. Daniel Dennett of Tufts University, for example, argues, "At what 'point' does a human life begin or end? The Darwinian perspective lets us see with unmistakable clarity why there is no hope at all of discovering a telltale mark, a salutation in life's process, that 'counts.'" Dennett claims there are "gradations of value in the ending of human lives," that some human lives have more value than others. "Which is worse," he asks, "taking 'heroic' measures to keep alive a severely deformed infant, or taking an equally 'heroic' (if unsung) step of seeing to it that such an infant dies as quickly and painlessly as possible?"[1] This moral relativism is troubling to say the least.

Steven Pinker of Harvard University adopts the same reasoning when he explains the process of having a child. He argues that "nurturing an offspring that carries our genes is the whole point of our existence," and that "a new mother will first coolly assess the infant and her current situation and only in the next few days begin to see it as a unique and wonderful individual." According to Pinker, the mother's love for a new child will grow with the "increasing biological value of a child (the chance that it will live to produce grandchildren.)"[2]

This is ridiculously offensive. Supriya never coolly assessed our kids to see if they met some biological need—nor would any other mother worth her salt. A child is a beautiful creation with an innate value that has little to do with any "biological value." "Biological value" doesn't even really mean anything. This guy should be sent to the Arctic Circle on an independent study program.

Do you see what's happening? When we fixate on the material and the biological, we matter only when we are useful. And I don't know about you, but I've met a number of folks who did not seem all that useful to me. But fortunately, it's not up to me or to you for that matter. "We believe these truths to be self evident, that all men are created equal, that they are endowed by their Creator with certain unalienable rights." Whoever wrote that was really on to something.

If human beings have no inherent value, their value comes solely from being useful, and their existence and right to existence come solely from their usefulness. Not useful? Then not much of a reason to live.

I'm not suggesting everyone who disagrees with me on the issues of abortion and euthanasia takes these views. But I am suggesting that worldviews have consequences. There is no getting around the reality that if you believe human beings are essentially indistinguishable from animals, you run the risk of viewing life and death issues differently from those who believe there is something profound that separates us from the animal kingdom.

Those who promote the concept that some human life is no more valuable than any other life, and therefore advocate abortion, infanticide, and euthanasia, cheapen human life and lay the groundwork for all sorts of destructive behavior. What we need is a culture of life that values human beings as unique creatures who were made by our Creator.

Medical ethics is a difficult subject, but this I can say for sure: where we begin the debate will ultimately determine where it ends. Some of this may strike folks as esoteric. But the origins of our thoughts do in fact matter, as they inevitably dictate our actions.

The Hippocratic Oath is a crucial foundation for over two thousand years of modern medicine. It's a life-affirming oath pledging doctors to sustain life. Among other things, they commit themselves to "neither give a deadly drug to anybody if asked for it, nor make a suggestion to this effect." The Oath helps establish a clear ethical line for doctors, which creates trust with patients. Again, how we treat the weakest and most vulnerable members of our society is a test of our moral character and whether or not we are a civilized society.

Abortion is one of those issues you hesitate to bring up among family and friends, let alone perfect strangers. It's not really a topic for polite conversation for two reasons. First, it's a sad topic. Anyone who has ever had to answer a young kid's question—"Daddy, what is abortion?"—knows exactly what I'm talking about. Secondly, it can turn a nice dinner party into a bitter food fight. "Why bother even bringing it up?" some might say. "I'm not going to face that issue in my life." But how we view human life at its earliest and most vulnerable point can affect the manner in which we will treat life later on. I believe human life is unique in this world, that we have been set aside from all other life by a divine spark. If we say we have the right to end life out of convenience, we are cheapening all human life.

Much as we run to rescue children who are buried under fallen buildings in Haiti or trapped on rooftops in New Orleans, our society's ethics need to be tied to the idea that people have inherent value. Rejecting this view puts us on a perilous path.

* * *

I've occasionally heard liberals say, "You pro-lifers are big on defending the rights of a fetus inside the womb, but you don't do much to protect or help kids after they are born." Ouch. Well, shame on us if that were true.

In my years of public service, I have focused intensely on protecting the lives of the innocent. It's a passion for me, because I believe our country is failing to protect our children. In my view, one of the greatest tragedies of modern life is the rise of sexual predators in America. As the prophet says in Ecclesiastes, "There is nothing new under the sun." Indeed there are many dark corners of this earth where sexual predators thrive and human trafficking still occurs. But this is America. This is the land of the free and the home of the brave. We must not allow this to happen.

America needs to drastically step up our efforts to combat and completely eliminate sexual predators. I'm not interested in any strategy of containment here. I have no patience for those who say it's so hard to end this epidemic that we can only hope to stop it from spreading further. Nonsense. We need to squash it. We need to defend the defenseless, born and unborn, at each and every stage of life.

Unlike Al Gore, I did not invent the Internet, but I'm a big fan of it. Still, we have to acknowledge that each technological advancement creates problems as well as opportunities. And it's no secret that the Internet has become the hub of predators, particularly sexual predators who prey on women and on children.

In Louisiana, we are doing everything we can to make these people miserable. Make no mistake, we are not just trying to stop those who would attack and abuse our young. No, that's far too modest a goal. We mean to do them harm and end their despicable crimes. So we now have some of the toughest sex offender laws in the country. I can tell you this—you really don't want to get caught harming women or children in Louisiana. We have taken steps to double and triple the sentences for anyone in our state who harms a child, but that's merely the tip of the iceberg. We even have chemical castration for sex offenders. Some people think this is a draconian measure. I certainly hope so. I consider chemical castration to be a treatment—and a powerful deterrent at the same time.

The American public is ready for a crushing crack-down on these criminals. During my campaign for governor I had an idea that was widely cheered by Democrats and Republicans, people of all races, men and women, young and old. Let me set it up for you. Every state has a tough prison that is famous in that state. In Louisiana, that prison is Angola. After outlining my plans for tougher laws against sexual predators and for dedicating more resources to combating them, I would declare, "It's great that we can now go online and find out the addresses of all the sexual predators that live in our neighborhoods. But I'm not going to be happy until we can go online and find that they all live at the same address—in the penitentiary in Angola, far away from our children."

Data suggest far more children are being preyed upon and are vulnerable than we even know. The University of Michigan reports nearly two-thirds of parents with children online are concerned about sexual predators. As they should be: studies show 1 in 7 children between the ages of 10 and 17 have received sexual solicitation over the Internet and about 1 in 3 children have been exposed to sexually explicit material.[3]

I remember when I first started working with computers as a young kid there was a popular phrase, "Garbage in, garbage out." Put in bad data or bad code, and you are going to get bad results on the computer. In other words, the system works only as well as what you feed into it. It's the same with our own souls. We have a society today that is saturated with excessive violence and sensuality. Once kept in the dark corners of our society, pornography is being mainstreamed. As people repeatedly expose themselves to this garbage, which is now often called "entertainment," it results in predictably harmful consequences to society. Put garbage in, and you get garbage out.

Plenty of research supports this obvious point. Studies show that rapists and child molesters are heavy consumers of pornography, and that they frequently consume this material while preparing to commit crimes. Studies also show kids who watch porn are more likely to engage in aggressive behaviors. This is a positive development for child abusers, who want kids desensitized to sex and violence because it makes it easier to abuse them.[4] People may not want to admit it, but the rise of sexual predators is not just a criminal problem, it's a cultural one.

Shortly after I became governor, I met a little boy whose parents brought him to spend a day at the Capitol because he really wanted to see the governor's office. I don't think I had ever seen a kid that young so dressed up. He was wearing a blue blazer, khaki pants, and a tie—clearly his Sunday best.

It turns out his parents wanted me to tell him he had done nothing wrong. A monster at his school had sexually abused him, and he had the courage to speak up and tell his parents. Even though the boy had shown incredible bravery far beyond his years in stepping forward, he was still haunted by the abuse, and he frequently woke up in the middle of the night afraid he had done something wrong.

When the boy and his mom left my office, his father stayed behind and took me aside. You could tell he was the kind of man that didn't usually get emotional, but he was about to speak from the bottom of his heart. He told me that not only was his son haunted by what had happened, but that he and his wife were, too. They spent many sleepless nights wondering if they could have done something to protect their child. They assumed that when they sent him off to school he would be safe—but he had been badly hurt and they were left grasping for answers.

I made a promise to that boy's father from which I will never waiver. I told him that I would work to make Louisiana the toughest place in the country for sex offenders in order to help ensure that no other family has to go through the pain his family was enduring.

I also support the use of the death penalty in instances of violent child rape. What? The death penalty for a crime other than first degree murder? Yep, you heard me right. In Louisiana we had a law stipulating that if you violently rape a child under the age of twelve, you might face the death penalty. It was applied in a case in Harvey, Louisiana, a few years ago involving an eight-year-old girl who was violently raped by her stepfather. The case is too awful to describe here, but the girl suffered serious internal injuries and immense psychological trauma. As the prosecutor in the case rightfully put it, child rape is in some ways worse than homicide. For its victims, "It takes away their innocence, it takes away their childhood, it mutilates their spirit. It kills their soul. They're never the same after these things happen."

Patrick Kennedy, the defendant, was found guilty by a jury of his peers and sentenced to death. The decision was upheld in the appeals process, but in June 2008 the U.S. Supreme Court declared the law unconstitutional in a 5–4 decision. The hearing sounded like a meeting of legislators. It was the justices' "independent judgment" that there was a "national consensus" that the death penalty should apply in instances of first degree murder, but not brutal crimes such as child rape.[5]

Funny, I wasn't aware the Supreme Court had begun basing decisions on public opinion polls. One justice declared that child rape was not as heinous as first degree murder. (Tell that to the victim.) What an outrageous example of judicial overreach—the judges were assuming the role of legislators. Instead of making independent ethical judgments, they should have simply evaluated whether the law was consistent with the Constitution. When you violently rape a child you have indisputably devalued them and scarred them for life. You should face death.

At this point, you may be wondering why I'm arguing for the death penalty in a chapter about life. Well, my point is this: we need to value our children by protecting them, nurturing them, and by devising harsh penalties for those who abuse them. It's part of a culture of life. That may sound ironic, but it's true. We value life so much that we'll exact the ultimate penalty upon those who want only to destroy it.

I realize that many people who want to crack down on these predators disagree with me on the death penalty; they'd prefer that we "lock 'em up and throw away the key." I'm fine with that—let your conscience be your guide. But if you believe we should try to rehabilitate these people, that locking them up or executing them will make matters worse, then I don't think we're going to find any common ground. Sexual predators have a high rate of recidivism, and I'm just not going to take any chances with our children.

*   *   *

We need to apply the same standard when it comes to the elderly. This is a particularly vulnerable group, especially because some old folks may deny their own usefulness to society.

Euthanasia is a sure sign of a culture in steep decline. No thinking American is for euthanasia in its starkest and most obvious forms. However, Princeton Professor Peter Singer has argued for infanticide and euthanasia for the severely handicapped or disabled, claiming, "The notion that human life is sacred just because it's human is medieval." He also asserts people with Alzheimer's cease to be people and should have their lives ended prematurely. His argument is so outrageous one is tempted to think he's just trying to attract attention. For those who take him seriously, it should be noted that when it comes to his own mother, who struggles with Alzheimer's, Mr. Singer rejected his ethic and hired a group of healthcare workers to look after her.[6]

But the stark views that Singer and other academic types espouse are not the real threat, since the majority of Americans would never approve of killing Alzheimer's patients. The bigger problem is presented by the more subtle forms of euthanasia, when the issue becomes cost control at the end of life. For example, are there any limits on the interventions we should take to prolong life? Maybe so, but one thing is clear: these decisions are difficult and must *not* be made by the government or some group of experts, but by the immediate family, the people who genuinely care for the patients.

In the debate over nationalized healthcare, the challenge of euthanasia is a real one. It's presented as a cost problem, and in a nationalized system healthcare cost will be the principal driver of decisions. When you think about it, all life is a cost problem. A patient-centered healthcare system is far more fair and compassionate in arbitrating these questions. When you are ninety-four years old with a long list of ailments and a prescription drug list to match, God help you if you are at the mercy of a faceless, heartless bureaucracy of a centralized government healthcare plan.

But the main question here is not cost but control: who has the right to control end of life decisions? I have a simple answer: individuals should have the final say, as long as they are of age and of sound mind—period! If they are not of age or sound mind, then their immediate family members should make the decision. With the input and guidance of their doctors, who are bound by the Hippocratic Oath and are directly involved with their treatment, this is the best way to make these decisions.

Who should never be involved in these decisions? The government. It's that simple. Not in America. Ever.

* * *

So how does our culture currently measure up on the "defense of the defenseless" barometer? Right now the gauge is in the red zone. Some people believe *Roe v. Wade* caused our current situation where we have turned our backs on the defenseless. But that's not really true. That is merely a symptom, a result of a society where some people, particularly the elites, no longer believe in the innate value of human life.

But I'm no pessimist. While some Americans no longer believe in the sanctity of human life, I think deep down most still do. Call it the shadow of our Judeo-Christian heritage or call it the ember of a divine spark in all of us, but most Americans still want to believe that human beings are of eternal value.

In fact, there is strong evidence that shows Americans are gradually becoming more pro-life in their point of view. Polling by Gallup shows a ten-point increase in the number of Americans who consider themselves to be pro-life over the past decade. Fifty-one percent of Americans now consider themselves pro-life, the first time Gallup has ever reported a pro-life majority.[7]

Scientific advancements and logic are at least partially the cause of this shift. Twenty years ago, when a young couple saw an ultrasound picture of their first child, it was a blurry scan that was almost impossible to decipher. With today's technology, however, you know exactly what you are looking at. You see the form of your child, you see the wonder that has been created. In fact, I signed a bill as governor that requires providers to give an ultrasound to mothers before any decisions are made. It's just common sense. It's hard to see anything other than a precious little baby, *your* precious little baby. Suddenly it doesn't matter whether you once were persuaded by the poll tested slogans of "reproductive freedom" or "freedom of choice"—that's all a distant memory. You know what you are looking at, and you wonder at the marvel of this new creation, and you begin to think of the boundless opportunities that lie in the near future.

We cheer and our hearts are warmed when people are pulled from the wreckage of a building. We don't care how old they are or whether they are "useful to society." It's the rescuing of human life that matters. We have to fight to nurture that spark back to a flame and struggle against the devaluation of human life and the cultural coarsening it inevitably causes.

CHAPTER 14

SAVING MEDICARE

Let's face it: railing against big government without proposing specific ways to reduce costs can make for pretty good politics. But of course, it accomplishes very little. So let's discuss a simple reform that could save a program that is now one of our biggest looming budgetary disasters.

The growth in entitlements is the most serious fiscal challenge we face today. People might denounce foreign aid or defense spending, but the promises the federal government has made to the poor, retired, and elderly in the form of Social Security, Medicare, and Medicaid dwarf other spending. In 2009, entitlements and other mandatory government spending comprised more than half the federal budget. If we are going to close the budget deficit instead of just talking about it, we'll need to reign in entitlements. And by far the biggest and most challenging of these is Medicare, where spending is expected to triple by 2050.[1]

The best way to defuse a ticking time bomb like Medicare is to reform it early, before we're forced to take really disruptive measures. Congress had a chance to do that in 1997...and blew it. But the reform proposals that emerged back then point to a viable way to shore up Medicare's long-term financing.

Although Washington commissions don't typically accomplish much, Congress had a real shot at reforming Medicare when the National Bipartisan Commission on the Future of Medicare was created in 1997. Republicans, who controlled Congress at the time, wanted to reign in exploding entitlements, and Democrats were showing a willingness to tackle what had long been a liberal sacred cow. President Clinton had conveyed to Democratic Senator John Breaux of Louisiana, who was a co-chairman of the commission and a close personal friend of the president, that he was serious about reforming the program.

Congress and the president had just cooperated in overhauling welfare to cut dependency, reduce teenage pregnancies, and save money. That effort had forced both parties to make uncomfortable political decisions; Republicans had to commit to spending on child care, transportation, education, and other government programs, while Democrats had to reform their cherished Great Society programs by instituting work requirements for welfare recipients. But both parties had a stake in reform as well. This was especially true of President Clinton, for whom welfare reform became the political equivalent of Nixon going to China.

Medicare reform posed an even bigger challenge than welfare reform. The federal government's approval of Medicare, which offered to help pay for the healthcare of nearly all Americans aged sixty-five and older, was an essential reform for the elderly, about half of whom had no health insurance when the program was approved in 1965. Understandably, the program was modeled on the typical employer-sponsored health plan of the 1960s. The problem is that the program has hardly changed in more than forty years. As Senator Breaux said more than a decade ago, "Throwing more money into this 1965 program is like putting more gas in an old car, it still runs like an old car. . . . Above all, we need to give this car a major overhaul first."[2]

Medicare's costs exceeded expectations from the beginning. Washington developed archaic and confusing stopgap plans to plug the holes, including price controls, payment schedules, and complex formulas for paying doctors, hospitals, and other providers. A core problem is that Medicare is designed as a pay-as-you-go system, meaning today's taxpayers have to finance the benefits that are now being paid out. That might work fine when lots of young people are supporting a smaller group of retirees, but as Americans' life expectancy has risen and the population has aged, the program has become unsustainable.

The Medicare Commission began as a good-faith attempt to solve these problems, though it still featured some typical partisan bickering. Even before the commission was named, there was a weeks-long fight over who would be chairman—it seemed like Congress would need a commission to appoint the commission. Eventually, both sides agreed the commission would have eight Republican and nine Democratic members. John Breaux served as chairman, while Republican Congressman Bill Thomas was named administrative chairman.

Knowing my track record of reform as head of the Louisiana Department of Health and Hospitals, Thomas asked me to serve as the commission's executive director. The timing wasn't great, coming just weeks after I had married Supriya. The job would last just one year—not exactly what you call job security. And we didn't really want to live in Washington, so suddenly you are talking about one heck of a commute. But it was a great opportunity to help bring about long-term reform. This was the sort of thing I had studied in graduate school—transforming large systems—and had been working on ever since in business and healthcare. I would have understood if Supriya had opposed the move, but as always she was incredibly supportive. She likes a good challenge as much as I do. So I took the job, packed my bags, and headed to Washington, while Supriya held down the fort back home in Baton Rouge.

I quickly realized my biggest task was keeping the chairmen working together. Breaux and Thomas are as different as you could imagine. Relying on loud, angry shouting to motivate his staff, Thomas had been voted the meanest member of Congress by staff and colleagues several years in a row. But he was also one of the smartest congressmen I've ever met. He would read your memo and then tell you why footnote number twenty-three was wrong, and he would correct lobbyists about their own industries. Democrats considered him a worthy opponent, a man both feared and respected in Washington.

John Breaux, in contrast, earned a reputation as every president's favorite senator. He had managed to become good friends with George H. W. Bush, Bill Clinton, and later George W. Bush. He was a back-slapping moderate who voted for the creation of SCHIP under Clinton in 1997 and the Bush tax cuts in 2001. It was hard to find anyone who would say anything bad about him.

In short, Thomas and Breaux needed a buffer...and that would be me.

In the end, the two men actually complemented each other quite well as part of a well-balanced commission. The commission's seventeen members comprised elected officials and bureaucrats, including some strong-willed members such as Senators Phil Gramm and Jay Rockefeller, Congressmen Jim McDermott and John Dingell, economist Stuart Altman, and former Clinton administration official Laura

Tyson. Eleven of seventeen votes were needed on the commission in order to make official recommendations.

I watched with a mix of bemusement and frustration as an early dispute broke out over where the commission would meet. Various people and groups offered us office space, but commission members feared we'd be beholden to whoever gave us space. There was also a big fight over whether to use House or Senate space. (There's an old saying in Washington that the other party is the opposition, while the other chamber is the enemy.) Someone even suggested renting space downtown just to avoid the issue. I said that was ridiculous; we were not going to waste taxpayer money just because some people were acting like children. Eventually we ended up working behind stacks of books at the Library of Congress. It was the quintessential Washington solution—split the difference to fix a problem that should not have existed in the first place.

Once we got down to work, Republicans and Democrats quickly agreed Medicare was on an unsustainable path, as the ratio of workers to retirees was expected to decline from 4–1 to 2–1. That would force the Part A trust fund into insolvency even before the baby boomers retired. In 1997, 37 percent of Medicare funding was coming from general tax revenues and other sources, because the payroll taxes or premiums that people paid into the system weren't covering the costs. Everyone on the commission knew the situation would get worse without major reform, and I think we've been proven right in the thirteen years since then. By 2007, Medicare was taking $179 billion from general revenues to cover the shortfall; that's equivalent to about half the federal corporate income tax receipts the government takes in every year. The Medicare Trustees calculate that as of 2009, Medicare's total excess costs are an astonishing $85.6 trillion.[3]

The government was keeping the program alive, as it still is today, through short-term budgeting gimmicks that allowed Medicare to limp on for another five- or ten-year budget window. Instead of structural reform, it considered band-aid solutions such as means-testing, raising the eligibility age, price controls, and arcane payment rules. Government planners dictated how much to spend on a particular service or procedure, and then cut the volume necessary to meet that line in the budget. As economist Len Nichols put it at the time, Medicare was setting 10,000 prices in 3,000 different counties. Senator Breaux and others realized how ridiculous this was. "I never went to medical school," Breaux said. "Why are elected officials determining how medical decisions are made?"

In 1997 Medicare still closely resembled 1960s-era private insurance, having failed to incorporate new technologies, procedures, and private-sector benefits. Over time, the program was covering fewer and fewer healthcare costs. You still had separate hospital insurance and medical insurance, there was a nearly $800 hospital deductible, and there was no real coverage for outpatient medicines, no limit on out-of-pocket spending, and limited coverage of preventative care. Seniors were still left paying for half their healthcare, causing 89 percent of them to enroll in some other program such as Medicaid, Medigap, private Medicare plans, or employer-provided coverage. This resulted in duplication and a lack of coordination.

Overall, we found Medicare to be an inefficient, wasteful system that was mired in red tape. Mayo Clinic president Dr. Robert Waller testified to the commission that more than 130,000 pages of laws, regulations, guidelines, rulings, and other stipulations applied to Medicare procedures and services. The American Hospital Association reported that because of Medicare and other regulations, nurses were often spending as much time filling out paperwork as they were tend-ing to patients.[4]

This created bizarre and frightening situations for some patients. A retired judge told our staff how he had been rushed to the hospital with chest pains. The doctor wanted to perform a certain procedure, but he suddenly withdrew the recommendation after the judge said he had Medicare. The judge quickly figured out the doctor had changed his mind simply because Medicare would not cover the pro-cedure. But when the judge offered to pay for the procedure out of his own pocket, the doctor informed him it was illegal for Medicare members to pay for separate procedures! (Congress did try to fix this problem in its typical head-scratching way—it allowed providers to collect private payments from Medicare patients if the providers quit Medicare for two years.) The judge's story was an aggravating reminder of the dysfunction of Medicare; if you are a Medicare mem-ber, you can pay for a vacation, but you may not be able to pay for your own healthcare.

We also heard an ambulance driver discuss the obstacles erected by the Medicare bureaucracy. Because rules were determined by fiscal intermediaries based on geography, the driver could only pick up patients in certain areas who had certain conditions. It was madden-ing to imagine having to decide which patients to pick up and which to leave behind based on geography, not their medical conditions. Beneficiaries had their own frustrating stories about Medicare paying more to rent equipment than it would cost to buy the same equip-ment, or paying for the treatment but not the cheaper cost of pre-venting many ailments.

The more complex you make a program or system, the easier it is to exploit the confusion and swindle people. Thus, it wasn't a complete surprise that we discovered it was incredibly easy to rip off Medicare. As one convicted felon told the U.S. Senate, "The government actually made it easy for me to steal. I became rich very fast billing the Medicare system." The guy was a Miami nightclub owner who knew nothing about healthcare, but he got a Medicare provider number over the phone for a fake medical supply company. He collected more than $32 million from Medicare over six years using 2,000 senior citizens' Medicare insurance numbers.[5]

When I joined the commission, I knew something about medical fraud from my two-year stint as head of the Louisiana Department of Health and Hospitals. In Louisiana we had identified fifteen psychiatric hospitals that had been overpaid in Medicaid funds and had gotten sweetheart political deals. There was a lot of squealing when we went after them and others—these included politically connected providers with ties to a former lieutenant-governor and other important officials. Billing Uncle Sam or some state for medical reimbursements was a very profitable business.

*　*　*

Medicare reform may not be the most fascinating topic, but the commission's meetings were livened up by some strong, animated personalities. Republican Senator Phil Gramm from Texas was an extremely intelligent economist who habitually cited his mother as an example for every absurdity in the system; one day she couldn't get a surgical procedure, the next day she couldn't find a specialist who accepted Medicare. (We discovered later she was, in fact, quite healthy. She passed away in 2008 at the age of ninety-one.) When I met Gramm and he learned I was from Louisiana he asked me, "How could somebody so smart come from Louisiana?" It seemed he had not yet forgiven Louisiana for not supporting him in the 1996 Republican presidential primary.

Another committee member was Democratic Senator Bob Kerrey from Nebraska. Kerrey was a likeable, courageous figure. Liberal Democrats were pressing him to defend the status quo in Medicare and to reject all reforms aside from raising payroll taxes. When I told Senator Breaux I was concerned Kerrey wouldn't support reform, Breaux told me not to worry. Senator Kerrey had served his country in Vietnam, and Breaux claimed when Kerrey was really determined to get something done, he'd get a certain look in his eye, like he was ready to take a hill in 'Nam. And he had that look when it came to Medicare reform, Breaux said. He was right; in the end Kerrey bucked the pressure from his own party and voted for change.

The commission had serious leadership that kept our proceedings from degenerating into a political sideshow. Bill Thomas quickly rejected suggestions from several commission members that we raise the commission's media profile by inviting celebrities to testify. Thomas even resisted the idea of holding Medicare field hearings around the country. In the end we held only one, in Minneapolis, Minnesota. We were greeted by protestors there, but it needs to be said that Minnesota protestors are extremely polite. Kevin McCarthy, now a congressman and then a member of Thomas's staff, invited them in for some food and lemonade. By the time the meeting started the protest had ended—they were all eating and drinking.

Commission members were struck by the contrast between the inefficient Medicare system and the well-functioning Federal Employees Health Benefits Program (FEHBP). FEHBP is not perfect, but it is less bureaucratic and more responsive to its enrollees than Medicare. (This helps explain why members of Congress who write the Medicare rules and the bureaucrats who run the program are enrolled in FEHBP, not Medicare.) Instead of paying for services, FEHBP allows recipients to choose from hundreds of health insurance plans, and then it pays for a large portion of the premiums. Far from being a top-down system, FEHBP encourages competition among insurers for federal employees.

In light of FEHBP's success, commission members proposed applying the FEHBP model of "premium support" to Medicare in order to spur competition, increase quality, and reduce costs. (Those who preferred the traditional Medicare system, however, would be allowed to stay in it.) Premium support would link the federal government's contribution for each health option to the weighted average premium. If you selected lower-cost plans, a larger share of the premium would be subsidized by Medicare. If you wanted a Cadillac plan, Medicare would pay a smaller share and you would have to pay more. The reform would help solve a core problem of the Medicare system: there is no relationship between pay and performance, and no incentive to compete on price. With the premium support model, health plans would be given flexibility to compete by either reducing premiums or enhancing benefits.

We expected this reform would reduce the growth in Medicare spending by a modest amount up front, and by a significant amount in the long term through "the magic of compound interest," as Senator Gramm was fond of saying. The commission estimated that premium support would shave between one-half and 1 percent a year off the program's long-term cost. That might not seem like much, but it would amount to billions of dollars over the long term. In short, we found a way to expand choice within Medicare while significantly cutting costs. Dan L. Crippen, the Director of the CBO, argued the proposed reforms "should enhance efficiency—the productive use of medical resources." Our agenda for reform was endorsed by a broad coalition of organizations, including the American Medical Association, Democratic Leadership Council, Healthcare Leadership Council, the Mayo Clinic, the United Seniors Association, and the *Wall Street Journal.*

President Clinton complained after he left the White House that he never had the opportunity to be a great president. (Let's ignore the narcissism for a minute.) But when it came to saving Medicare, he had his chance. He could have supported these bipartisan reforms and helped us to avert a looming fiscal nightmare while improving the lives of millions of American seniors. But instead, he chose to play a different role.[6]

The chairmen delayed the end of the commission just as it appeared tantalizingly close to agreeing on specific reform proposals. The main sticking point was the amount of prescription drug subsidies to be added to the Medicare program. Holdouts among President Clinton's appointees seemed willing to endorse reforms, especially the centerpiece premium support reform, if the subsidies were high enough. Though the Republican members wanted to keep the subsidies low, both sides seemed to be negotiating their way to an agreement.

And then, suddenly, the holdouts became intransigent and the discussions ground to a halt. The abrupt change in atmosphere is hard to explain without knowing the wider political context; namely, the commission was operating during the Monica Lewinsky scandal. Some Democrats on the commission, like John Breaux and Bob Kerrey, bravely voted for reform. But President Clinton, who at a private White House meeting in 1998 had told the commission he wanted real reform and had praised premium support, now backed away. We can only guess why, but the reason probably relates to Clinton surviving impeachment with the support of House liberals who opposed our Medicare reforms, favoring instead a hike in payroll taxes. Some have speculated these liberals pressured Clinton to reject Medicare reform as repayment for supporting him during impeachment.[7] His appointees to the commission, including economists Laura Tyson and Stuart Altman, who had initially supported reform, now voted against it. (Altman would later express regret for not supporting the commission's proposed reforms.) The final vote was 10–7 for the reforms—one vote less than we needed.

Ironically, Republicans under President Bush years later would spend far more on the prescription drug subsidy than the holdouts had demanded back in 1997—and without getting any comprehensive reforms in return.

The ideas that formed the basis of that Medicare Commission are still sound. Medicare may have lower administrative costs than FEHBP, but a single-payer system like Medicare is good at hiding its true costs and shifting them to you and me. At any rate, regardless of its finer qualities, the current Medicare system is simply not sustainable. In Washington we need to get control of entitlement spending and give our grandparents more choices regarding their healthcare. A premium support system would encourage competition and choice and drive down costs. We conservatives need to tackle the problem of entitlements head on. Let's start by ensuring Medicare is viable and responsive to the needs of our children and grandchildren.

CHAPTER 15

FREEDOM ISN'T FREE

As governor of Louisiana, I've met with soldiers as they headed off to war and greeted them when they returned. I've met with widows and children who lost loved ones serving their country. Although I'm known as a real talker, the heroism of our soldiers often leaves me speechless.

One of my great privileges as governor has been awarding the Louisiana Veterans Honor Medal, which has given me the opportunity to meet some of the most extraordinary American patriots. I met a man who lied about his age so he could fight in World War II. I met a brave mother whose oldest son was killed in combat and whose younger son was seriously wounded—I met her when she was welcoming her grandson back from his service overseas. I gave a Vietnam vet his medal as he wept and told me how, when he returned from Vietnam, he hid his uniform in his closet because of all the animosity directed at vets back then.

I'm amazed at how many vets come from families with a tradition of serving—grandfathers, fathers, uncles, brothers, and sisters all serving in the military of this great country. And it's striking how vets from any war respond nearly identically when they receive the medal. When I thank them for their service and their commitment to our country, more often than not they humbly reply, "I just did what I was supposed to." If only we had more of that sense of duty and humility in Washington.

War is an ugly thing—ask any vet who has seen combat. But tyranny and oppression are even uglier. Americans have been fighting for this country for more than 200 years because we know freedom isn't free. And as strange as it might sound, peace is something for which you must fight.

You hear a lot of fashionable theories these days about how we can achieve peace. The Obama administration wants to focus on disarmament. Like those who argue that guns cause crime, President Obama's team seems to believe that simply reducing the number of military weapons—including the weapons we ourselves possess—will reduce conflict. But weapons, whether hunting rifles or tanks, are inanimate objects. I'm not worried about the objects themselves, but about who controls them and where they're being pointed. If Canada announces it is building a new missile, I wouldn't be too concerned. But when Iran or North Korea do it, I'm a lot less sanguine. We can abolish as many of our missiles as we want, but that's just not going to convince international miscreants to do the same. That's why President Obama's decision to drastically scale back our missile defense program was ill-advised.

The real cause of war and international conflict is not the existence of weapons, but authoritarian leaders trying to expand their power. If someone is willing to murder and oppress his own people, do you really think he would hesitate to break a treaty he might sign with us? We've had this debate before. After the carnage of World War I, a powerful disarmament movement arose both in the U.S. and abroad. Walter Lippmann summed up the results in 1943, during World War II: "The disarmament movement has been tragically successful in disarming the nations that believed in disarmament."

Treaties can be useful, but we need to "trust but verify," as Reagan said. And treaties by themselves will not make aggressors more peaceable. Only the prospect of countervailing force will do that.

I'm convinced many people focus on inanimate objects as the source of violence because they can't bring themselves to blame people for their actions. They're uncomfortable using "judgmental" words like good and evil or right and wrong. Their moral confusion prevents them from identifying evil and confronting it. We saw one stunning example after 9/11, when former Vice President Al Gore was asked whether the hijackers who flew the planes into the twin towers were evil. The best he could muster was moral mush. "What is 'evil' anyway? I do not pretend to have the answer to such a question but my faith tradition teaches me that all of us have the potential inside of us for both good and evil."[1] I'll tell you what my faith tradition and good old common sense tell me: terrorists who fly planes into buildings are evil.

In these politically correct times, it's even too much to ask that our own government refer to Islamic terrorists as "Islamic terrorists." Instead we hear the deliberately vague expression "extremists." This is nonsense. People who root for Alabama Crimson Tide to beat LSU in football are extremists. People who want to kill Americans are terrorists. We should not be afraid to call it like it is. Apparently even the word "terrorism" is too judgmental, since Janet Napolitano announced shortly after being named secretary of homeland security that she preferred the ridiculous term "man-caused disasters."[2]

I'm alarmed at how often we hear arguments of moral relativism, which hold that we aren't any more moral than the terrorists we're fighting. President Obama doesn't go that far, but he certainly doesn't help establish moral clarity by infusing his foreign policy speeches with abject apologies for America's supposed past sins.

Those who assert moral equivalence point to abuses like those that occurred at Abu Ghraib. But the fact that a handful of U.S. soldiers have committed infractions does not erase the huge distinction between us and the terrorists. Put simply, terrorists are fighting for death, we are fighting for life. It's that simple. We have profoundly different views on the value of human life—we believe all life is intrinsically valuable and therefore all people deserve to live in freedom.

Here's an example: NBC reported not long ago that a U.S. helicopter shot and wounded two terrorists who were placing an IED explosive device on an Iraqi road in hopes of killing U.S. soldiers. A U.S. Army medical team arrived shortly afterward and worked hard to save their lives. One of the terrorists was severely wounded and needed thirty pints of blood for surgery. At Camp Speicher near Tikrit, dozens of U.S. GI's showed up to donate blood—to save the life of a man who was trying to kill them. As one soldier, Brian Suam, put it, "A human life is a human life."[3] When the terrorists stop blowing up innocent people and shooting at our soldiers and instead start organizing blood drives for Americans and Israelis, I'll be glad to revisit the issue. In the meantime, don't tell me that some moral equivalence exists between America and her enemies.

A common refrain we heard after 9/11, especially from the media, was "Why do they hate us?" The question itself implies we are somehow responsible for provoking the terrorists' hatred. I don't waste a lot of time with this view, because history is full of murderers and aggressors who claim they are victims and had no choice but to attack and kill innocent people. Adolf Hitler stormed into Czechoslovakia and

Poland after accusing those countries of persecuting their German minorities. The Soviet Union claimed it was defending its allies from foreign-backed counterrevolutionaries when it invaded Hungary in 1956 and Czechoslovakia in 1968. The point is that all aggressors claim legitimate grievances are behind their violent actions. Sociopaths and psychopaths are always full of explanations and justifications. It's pretty rare to hear some tyrant proclaim, "I attacked that country because it's weak and I thought I could get away with it."

Al Qaeda claims they are fighting us because we are imperialists and we hate Muslims. They don't seem impressed that the United States supported the Islamic Afghan resistance against the Soviet invasion, or that we've sacrificed many lives and billions of dollars to defend Muslims in Kuwait, Afghanistan, Iraq, Bosnia, Kosovo, and Somalia. Far from being anti-Muslim, the United States has done more for peace-loving Muslims that any other country on the planet.

Yes, there are peace-loving Muslims: we all know that. But let's not be confused. There are also war-loving, murderous Muslims who believe it is their religious duty to destroy America. Although political correctness demands we ignore this inconvenient truth, we can't forget that history is littered with the corpses of those who fail to recognize a real threat when they see it.

*   *   *

Our current therapeutic approach to national security is dangerous. I'm just not interested in empathizing with the "grievances" of our sworn enemies. Let's figure out where they're vulnerable and destroy them. FDR didn't agonize over what we may have done to provoke the Japanese attack on Pearl Harbor. He just developed a plan to defeat them. Likewise, Harry Truman and Ronald Reagan didn't wring their hands wondering what we'd done to anger the Soviets; they simply fig-ured out a strategy to beat them.

To defeat Islamic terrorism, we should develop a practical strategy based on American ideals. First, we need to act as if we're at war—because we are. It seems obvious that when networks of terrorists are try-ing to kill thousands of people by blowing up buildings and airplanes and cars in our homeland, this amounts to war. But the Obama admin-istration prefers to handle terrorism mostly as a criminal matter. This is misguided. When a foreign enemy is trying to attack us on our own soil, we are facing a military situation and the armed forces, not law enforce-ment, should play the primary role in hunting down the terrorists, inter-rogating them, detaining them, and when necessary, killing them.

I don't see any reason to continue giving Miranda rights to foreign terrorists, as we did to Umar Farouk Abdulmutallab, the would-be bomber of Flight 253. As Senators Collins and Lieberman wrote to Attorney General Eric Holder, the decision to treat Abdulmutallab as an ordinary criminal "almost certainly prevented the military and the intelligence community from obtaining information that would have been critical to learning more about how our enemy operates and to preventing future attacks."[4] This is just common sense; intelligence is our first line of defense in war. That's why I voted in Congress to amend the Foreign Intelligence Surveillance Act (FISA) so the presi-dent and the attorney general could authorize electronic surveillance of foreign agents without a court order. Extending full legal protec-tions to foreign terrorists will simply mean more dead Americans.

Our national security strategy should aim to achieve one thing: defeating our enemies. Some say this is an unrealistic goal, and that we can only hope to manage, not eliminate, problems like terrorism and rogue states. I think this attitude short-changes America's abilities.

Winning World War II was so difficult that at the time many pessimists believed it would take us decades to win, if we ever could. And during the Cold War, most scholars and Washington experts assumed the Soviet bloc was a permanent fixture in global affairs. The simple fact is that history is moved and shaped by the actions of leaders and by the courage of nations. As Reagan said, "Evil is powerless if the good are unafraid."

Adopting a defensive strategy toward terrorism simply won't work. Think about it: the terrorists are not going away. They are not going to abandon the fight because we try to reason with them or indulge their grievances. If we don't hunt them down, destroy their networks, and kill their leaders, we will cede the field of battle to them. They will get to pick when and where to attack us. Sitting back passively and waiting for an attack is not a strategy. And relying on civilian passengers to restrain a terrorist on a plane, or alert passers-by to notice a car bomb in Times Square, is not a strategy. Eventually our luck will run out.

Instead of staying on the defensive, we need to put the terrorists on the defensive. We should relentlessly hunt them and kill them so they have to spend all their time just trying to stay alive. That strategy requires us to give our armed forces the leadership and financial and material resources they need to win. I'm not interested in parity; I want to guarantee U.S. military superiority. As the late Senator Henry "Scoop" Jackson put it, "International peace and security depend not on a parity of power but on a preponderance of power in the peace-keepers over the peace-upsetters."[5]

* * *

Above all else, our national security policy should aim to protect America. But that mission is clouded when President Obama and others blur the lines between the United States and the rest of the world. They emphasize the need for "consensus" among the "international community." Apparently finding his U.S. citizenship too limiting, then-Senator Obama in 2008 proclaimed in Berlin that he was "a proud citizen of the United States and a fellow citizen of the world." Along the same lines, when asked if he believed in American exceptionalism, Obama replied that he believed in it "just as I suspect that the Brits believe in British exceptionalism and the Greeks believe in Greek exceptionalism."[6] Our president seems to think it would be intolerant to believe that America is more exceptional than any other country.

Consistent with its internationalist approach, the Obama administration puts far too much faith in the United Nations to solve problems and guarantee world security. The UN is simply a collection of governments—many of them tyrannical—that all pursue their own interests. So it made little sense, in the name of furthering international cooperation, for the Obama administration to join the discredited UN Human Rights Council, where paragons of civil rights such as Cuba and China deflect scrutiny of their own miserable human rights records by indulging in the Islamic world's favorite pastime: denouncing Israel. In May 2010, a majority of UN members elected Libya—a country run by an oppressive, mentally unstable dictator whose government was implicated in the horrific Lockerbie plane bombing and other bloody terrorist activities—to the Human Rights Council. That vote came shortly after the misogynist, theocratic government of Iran was elected to the leading UN women's rights agency, the Commission on the Status of Women.

Because UN membership is open to any two-bit despot, the organization has become corrupt and dysfunctional. So it's quite disturbing to see the Obama administration rely on the UN to take a leading role in tackling some of the major national security challenges of our time, such as keeping the Iranian mullahs from developing nuclear weapons. While I was in Congress I voted for the U.S.—which pays more of the UN budget than any other country—to withhold funding for the UN in order to encourage transparency, anti-corruption measures, and other reforms. But I'm not sure if any reforms could fix the UN's dysfunctions.

We would do much better to put our faith in our allies rather than in some nebulous body filled with autocrats. Senator John McCain has proposed creating a League of Democracies. Comprising only democracies, it would better reflect our values and better protect U.S. security. Although such a league would present a valuable way to coordinate our actions with our allies, we also have to be prepared to go it alone. No one—no person, country, or international organization—should have veto power over American security. Ever.

History teaches that democracies are more peaceful than tyrannies and are extremely unlikely to wage war against other democracies. So, for our own benefit and for the international good, we should work to spread democracy. But we cannot be naïve about this undertaking. For democracy to flourish you need more than elections and the basic infrastructure of representative government. You need cultural values that reinforce democratic instincts. One thing we've learned in Iraq is that it takes a lot of effort to spread notions of individual rights and democratic norms in cultures that are less individualistic.

But I do know our ideals inspire people everywhere in the world. Perhaps some people want to live in oppressive societies—especially the people who are doing the oppressing—but the vast majority of people everywhere would live in freedom if given the opportunity.

And it is our duty to provide the world's best example of a free society. As Abraham Lincoln put it, "[The authors of the Declaration of Independence] set up a standard maxim for free society, which should be familiar to all, and revered by all; constantly looked to, constantly labored for, and even though never perfectly attained, constantly approximated, and thereby constantly spreading and deepening its influence, and augmenting the happiness and value of life to all peoples of all colors everywhere."[7]

In light of the difficult battles we've faced in Iraq and Afghanistan, a new kind of isolationism has gained adherents in both parties. The thinking is that if America would stop standing up for dissidents, speaking out for human rights, and trying to spread freedom, we would become safer by making ourselves inconspicuous. This, of course, is a revival of the kind of thinking that became popular in America after World War I. But what we learned with the outbreak of World War II was that world events affect us and draw us in, whether we like it or not. This is especially true today in light of globalization and the spread of nuclear technology—any country capable of manufacturing or obtaining a nuclear device could directly threaten the United States. This suggests two possible approaches: we could "be nice" to regimes like the Iranian Ayatollahs and hope they'll be nice back to us once they get nukes; or we could use all available means to keep them from getting nukes in the first place. I would opt for the second course—it's never a good idea to leave your fate in the hands of your enemies.

Moreover, isolationism contradicts America's national character. We have traditionally responded to threats by taking the offensive, by confronting and defeating our enemies head on. This tradition runs deep in our history. President Thomas Jefferson dispatched Americans to

North Africa more than 200 years ago to deal with Barbary pirates. As Yale historian John Lewis Gaddis points out, this tradition started with John Quincy Adams, who laid the foundations for the expansion of America, and it continues today.[8]

This does not mean America needs to maintain a modern day empire, as some critics claim we are doing. We do not have an empire, nor do we seek one. We are not called to be the world's policeman or to necessarily engage in nation-building around the world. In countries where we fight, our goal is to attain freedom for the people living there and then to bring our troops home. We only keep troops long-term in places like Germany, Japan, and South Korea at the request of those governments. They are there to preserve those nations' freedom and independence, not to enslave those peoples to any mythical American empire. Once again, this is a tradition that goes back to the earliest days of our nation. John Quincy Adams reminded us that America "goes not abroad, in search of monsters to destroy." If we did so, he warned, "she might become the dictatress of the world" and would "be no longer the ruler of her own spirit."[9]

*   *   *

We are threatened by murderous ideologies—namely radical Islam—which spring from evil in the human heart. But it's hard to develop a sound national security strategy when the administration is too paralyzed by political correctness to even name the ideology that threatens us or to acknowledge the existence of evil. They instead want to focus on the "root causes" of terrorism, which are often identified as poverty and ignorance. With this view, fighting terrorism becomes less a military battle and more a grand attempt at international social work. As Barack Obama wrote in the *Hyde Park Herald* shortly after the 9/11 attacks, terrorists suffer from an "absence of empathy" that "grows out of a climate of poverty and ignorance, helplessness and despair."[10] This view was again evident in 2008 when Obama, then a presidential candidate, called for increasing our security through a new Marshall Plan that would double our foreign aid for efforts such as fighting global poverty and eradicating diseases.[11]

These views are echoed by President Obama's Ambassador to the UN, Susan Rice. In an academic article published in 2005, Rice and co-author Corinne Graff posit that terrorism is "a threat borne of both oppression and deprivation." Wars are largely the result of poverty, they say. "The risk of conflict onset rises and its average duration increases with decreasing per capita GDP, rates of economic growth, and secondary school enrollment, or with higher child mortality rates."[12]

Unfortunately for Obama and Rice, empirical research shows the modern Islamic terrorist is not typically some poor, ignorant soul. Professor Marc Sageman of the University of Pennsylvania, a psychiatrist formerly with the U.S. Navy and CIA, analyzed 500 al Qaeda members. He discovered most of these terrorists are "well-educated, married men from middle- or upper-class families, in their mid-20s and psychologically stable." In his book *Understanding Terror Networks*, Sageman reports that three-quarters of the al Qaeda members he studied are from the upper or middle class and fully 63 percent went to college, "compared with the 5-6% that's usual for the third world. These are the best and brightest of their societies in many ways." As he puts it, "The typical recruit to al-Qaeda is Western-educated and has a wealthy, professional background."[13]

Most of the terrorists came from a small number of wealthy Arab countries or from immigrant groups living in the West. Many were like British-born terrorist Omar Sheikh, who was educated at a private school before heading to Afghanistan.

Terrorism scholar Peter Bergen has also studied the demographics of terrorists and found no evidence that poverty or lack of education play any role. "We found that a majority of them are college-educated, often in technical subjects like engineering," he wrote with Swati Pandey in the *New York Times*. "In the four attacks for which the most complete information about the perpetrators' educational levels are available—the World Trade Center bombing in 1993, the attacks on the American embassies in Kenya and Tanzania in 1998, the 9/11 attacks, and the Bali bombings in 2002—53% of the terrorists had either attended college or had received a college degree. As a point of reference, only 52% of Americans have been to college. The terrorists, in our study thus appear, on average, to be as well-educated as many Americans."[14]

Strangely enough, Islamic terrorists often hail from the richest Middle Eastern nations—fifteen of the nineteen 9/11 hijackers came from Saudi Arabia—while dirt poor Muslim countries like Mali, Bangladesh, and Niger produce few if any terrorists.[15]

Scott Atran, in a more narrow investigation of suicide bombers, found that most suicide bombers are well-educated and have a generally higher socio-economic status. Many had graduate degrees and well-paying jobs before they chose to murder innocent civilians in suicide attacks.[16]

Nevertheless, the Obama administration continues to cling to the "poverty causes terrorism" theory because it supports the social work approach to national security that it favors. They sometimes call this "soft power." While I'm all for using every aspect of our strength to fight terrorism, soft power alone is not going to protect us from regimes and terrorist organizations that want to destroy us. Ronald Reagan would really have gotten a good laugh at the notion of "soft power." He knew that "soft power" is only effective in containing evil regimes when you have the credible threat of hard power to back it up.

If the Obama administration were to admit that Islamic terrorists are not motivated by poverty but rather by an evil ideology, that would require a paradigm shift in the way it approaches terrorism. They'd have to admit the existence of evil, name the enemy, and acknowledge that military power rather than more anti-poverty programs must be the central means to fight and win.

As we engage and defeat our enemies on the battlefield, we also need to win the battle of ideas by projecting confidence in our values, history, and our way of life. Our president has made a bad habit of apologizing to foreign audiences for America's supposed transgressions. This groveling needs to end—now. The American president must proudly represent the world's greatest democracy to the world. It is naïve to think these apologies gain us respect—they simply convey a dangerous lack of confidence. We also need to begin making it clear that our words mean something. If we threaten Iran with consequences when it continues developing nuclear weapons, it should not mean, "Oh, okay, you crossed that red line, but here's a new one, and hopefully you'll respect our wishes this time." If we draw a line in the sand, we need to be willing to follow it up with action.

We won the Cold War without firing a shot because we projected strength and stood up to the Soviet Union on every front. We countered its expansion everywhere, supported dissidents and freedom fighters, and perhaps most importantly, we proudly proclaimed the superiority of western individualism and liberty. Today, we need to say loudly and clearly that America harbors no ill will against Muslims, but that we will fight radical Islam everywhere until it no longer threatens us.

The president should also declare much more emphatically our solidarity with dissidents suffering in Iran, North Korea, and Cuba. I recall a story about Natan Sharansky, a Soviet dissident who later became interior minister and deputy prime minister of Israel. He was in a Soviet prison when he heard that President Ronald Reagan had called the Soviet Union an "evil empire." Although Reagan's remarks sent American liberals into fits of apoplexy, Sharansky leapt for joy—Reagan's speech emboldened him and other dissidents behind the Iron Curtain. I have no doubt there are Sharanskys in Cuba, North Korea, and Iran who would benefit from knowing that America stands with them.

Terrorism gives a small group of motivated, educated, and well-funded fanatics the potential for sowing massive destruction in the United States. To steal a phrase from Winston Churchill, never have so many had so much to fear from the actions of so few. But we need to remember that resorting to terrorism is actually a sign of weakness. They have to use fear, terror, and mass murder to advance their agenda because most people around the world reject it. America has to be confident we are on the winning side and stop apologizing for being there. As Dean Acheson once warned, "No people in history have ever survived, who thought they could protect their freedom by making themselves inoffensive to their enemies."[17]

I believe America is freedom, and therefore the American ideal is the hope of people all across this planet. I will never apologize for America. And I know that the American people still believe in the power and promise of America. Once, while I was waiting at the airport to meet some of our soldiers returning from Iraq, I saw an older man standing by himself on the tarmac. I walked up to him, shook his hand, and asked what he was doing there. He explained that when he had returned from serving in Vietnam, no one greeted him at the airport. And he had vowed then and there that he would turn out to that airport whenever soldiers were returning from war, to make sure someone was there to thank them. That's America.

CHAPTER 16

IT'S THE CULTURE, STUPID

Remember the slogan "It's the economy, stupid"? It was a Clinton-era homage to the notion that one must reduce all political comments to the eighth grade level. We hear the same argument from political strategists today. And just like in the 1990s, it's not true.

I've spent a lot of my life in public service worrying about budgets, money, waste, taxes, and the economy. All these issues are vitally important. And make no mistake, when the economy is suffering, as it is today, that is the only thing on the voters' minds. As marketing and campaign strategy goes, "It's the economy, stupid" is genius. After all, it helped get a president elected.

In fact, I often gather my entire cabinet and staff for a leadership series where we hear from leaders in industry, politics, government, and the arts. We recently had a session with the inventor of the "It's the economy, stupid" phrase, Democratic strategist James Carville, one of Louisiana's favorite sons and a brilliant political strategist. Our session with Carville and his wife, former Republican strategist Mary Matalin, was fascinating and informative.

But step outside the world of campaign strategists—which is a parallel dimension in time and space if you ask me—and look at reality. What you discover is that this view simply doesn't reflect the real world. The theme of this chapter is going to be regarded as heresy by both Republican and Democrat strategists, but here it goes: there are more important things than the economy.

During political campaigns, both parties divide people's interests and concerns into neat little categories. Well-paid pollsters discern people's attitudes by splicing and dicing. They poll about healthcare, foreign policy, defense, the economy, and moral issues. Our political dialogue is conducted in much the same way. Pundits go on the cable networks and pontificate on some narrow subject, then give way to other pundits sharing their expertise on some other narrow subject.

But that is not how real life works. All these issues are interconnected. Like spokes in a wheel, they are all linked to one central hub: America's culture.

The word culture comes from the Latin word *cultura*, which means to cultivate. Our culture—our shared set of values, goals, and attitudes—defines who we are as a nation. And everything else—foreign policy, social policy, and yes, even the economy—springs from it. Culture is not merely the social issues or the moral issues that pollsters and pundits discuss. Culture is much more than that. Our culture defines what we strive for, what we value, and how we conduct ourselves as a people.

The beauty and promise of America is not our economic system—even though it has helped us to generate amazing prosperity. The beauty of America is not our political system—great as our form of government is. The beauty of America is not our military superiority—even though it can really come in handy.

The beauty of America is our culture. Our culture is the glue that keeps us together and the engine that makes the American Dream possible.

* * *

Let's take these assertions one at a time, beginning with the first—that the beauty of America is not in our economy. Now, if you've read this far in the book, you have probably noticed that I'm a zealous proponent of free enterprise and an unapologetic advocate of American capitalism. I have written for the *Wall Street Journal* and spoken at the Hoover Institution and the Heritage Foundation. I even own an Adam Smith tie.

In fact, since I became governor of Louisiana we have cut taxes several times, including the largest income tax cut in our state's history, and we have eliminated over 6,000 government positions. We aren't just talking about fiscal responsibility and conservative economic principles; we are actually applying them to solve problems. In short, I'm an economic conservative if there ever was one, not just in theory, but in practice.

But I'll be honest with you: I wouldn't give you a plug nickel for capitalism and free enterprise in a country where people don't play by the rules, don't respect the rule of law, don't share a common view of the dignity of all mankind as God's creation, or generally don't care for one another. Capitalism in such a society will fail. Even my tie tells me so, or at least the man on my tie.

Adam Smith wrote his masterpiece, *The Wealth of Nations*, to describe the power, morality, and efficiency of a market economy. He explained how the profit motive—the desire to make money—created incentives to be productive. In other words, selfishness was a good thing because it motivates people. But Smith also wrote *The Theory of Moral Sentiments*, which he considered his most important work. Smith argued here that the free market system would not work well—and could even bring out the worst in some people—in a society that lacked a strong moral foundation. Values like propriety, prudence, and benevolence are needed to check our inherent selfishness, Smith argued. And he didn't just preach this—he actually lived it, becoming famous in his native Scotland for his charitable efforts. Although he made a fortune during his lifetime, when Smith died his estate was minuscule because he had given away so much of his wealth.

America was founded on strong Judeo-Christian moral values, but some of these have weakened in recent years. This has given us a bitter taste of the consequences of embracing Smith's economic theory without the moral prerequisites. The economic meltdown our nation experienced was in large part brought on by unchecked avarice. Adam Smith would have seen it coming.

We now know, for example, that subprime lenders were selling loans they knew were toxic. The Securities and Exchange Commission has released the email records of Angelo Mozilo, the CEO of Countrywide, as part of a civil suit that was filed against him. In those emails we discover that while Mozilo was pushing subprime loans and crowing publicly about how good they were, privately he was telling a colleague, "In all my years in business I have never seen a more toxic product." In another email he wrote that the no-money-down mortgage—another instrument he was touting publicly—was "the most dangerous product in existence and there can be nothing more toxic."[1]

Numerous other examples abound. According to the *Wall Street Journal*, in late 2006 Goldman Sachs executives were already convinced that the "sub-prime market was heading for trouble." So what did they do? They sold off their "stockpile" of mortgage-backed securities and effectively started selling short, that is, betting that the market would go down. But what did they tell their clients? They encouraged them to keep buying these toxic investments. Goldman Sachs made $4 billion from selling these securities. Their clients didn't do so well.[2]

Other reports looked at the leadership at Bear Stearns, the investment house that imploded and had to be bought out in March 2008. It explained how the CEO, in the months leading up to the crisis, spent a lot of time playing golf, enjoying bridge tournaments, and even smoking dope, all the while being well compensated for his efforts.[3]

I once read somewhere that the love of money is the root of all evil.

But let's not stop there. Banks made loans to people they knew could not afford them. There were so-called liar loans (where they didn't even ask to see proof of your income) and even NINJA loans (no-income, no-job loans). Handing out these disastrous loans became a common practice in an industry focused more on earning fast commissions and fees than doing due diligence and responsibly handling its business. The greed was so extensive it was almost comical. Washington Mutual, once the sixth largest bank in the country, gave a loan to a non-English speaking strawberry picker in California earning $14,000 a year. The loan was for $720,000.[4] Did I mention Washington Mutual had to file for Chapter 11 bankruptcy?

Politicians played their part in stoking the crisis. In hopes of appealing to specific demographic groups, they pressured banks to give risky mortgages to homeowners who were extremely unlikely to pay them back. Regulations like the Community Reinvestment Act (CRA) forced banks to make loans based not on the applicants' merits, but because they had to strike agreements with radical "community" groups such as ACORN. In fact, the federal government sued banks to force them to make risky mortgage loans. Andrew Cuomo, secretary of Housing and Urban Development during the Clinton administration, bragged at a 1998 press conference about reaching a settlement with a major lender worth billions of dollars. Cuomo even admitted he knew some of these loans would not be paid back.[5] Nice thing to do with other peoples' money.

Some of the blame also belongs to consumers, who borrowed money they knew they couldn't repay. Interest rates were low and mortgages were easy to get, and lots of people jumped at the opportunity to buy a bigger house than they could really afford. So they traded up and borrowed more than they could handle because, well, we all deserve a big house, don't we? Owning a home is part of the American Dream. But getting it through an interest-only adjustable rate mortgage is more like a nightmare.

Predictably, after the meltdown liberals called on the government to adopt strict new regulations to ensure it will not happen again. (Good luck with that.) But more regulations can't solve what is largely an ethical problem within the culture. Unchecked avarice at every level has taken its toll on our economy.

I have no doubt we will overcome the economic crisis. But if we want to prevent a similar crisis from erupting in the future, we need to recommit our nation to the bedrock values that keep us committed to doing the right thing. We cannot serve both God and Mammon.

MSNBC anchor Contessa Brewer recently advised Republicans to "focus away from morals and values into things that affect people's lives." Her guest, *New York Times* reporter John Harwood, agreed:

"Well, bingo, Contessa, that's exactly right."[6] This couldn't be more wrong—morals and values affect everything in people's lives. Republicans taking campaign advice from the media is like a chef getting culinary advice from cannibals—it won't end well. Still, some Republicans are tempted by this argument. They believe we'll get more votes by focusing on free market economics and ignoring all that "divisive" talk about values and morality. The trouble is that the world doesn't naturally divide into neat categories. If we focus narrowly on political strategy and ignore more fundamental issues of right and wrong, we will fail. That great campaign consultant Confucius had some applicable thoughts: "The superior man understands what works; the inferior man understands what sells."

Think about why America, the wealthiest nation in world history, still suffers from social ills such as child poverty. The truth is, economics alone are not to blame. Studies consistently show children in broken homes are four times more likely to live in poverty. The poverty rate for children of married couples is 8.2 percent, compared to 35.2 percent—four times higher—for children of single parents.[7]

While recognizing the heroic work done by single moms across the country, we cannot ignore the evidence that families matter, that children of two parent households tend to do better, and that the family unit is the foundation of society. When America launched the war on poverty in 1965, the child poverty rate was 20.7 percent. More than forty years later, the rate is only slightly lower.[8] We have spent trillions of dollars to fight poverty with meager results. Why? Because simply throwing money at the problem will not fix it. Poverty, like so many other economic problems, is not simply about money. It's about values that work.

*   *   *

I also said the beauty of America is not in our political system. Most of us are taught at an early age about the glories of our system of government. And there is no question that the elegant brilliance of our Constitution is to be marveled at. It is the best system of government ever created.

But our republic rests on self-government. That requires people to share a common commitment to virtue, to mutual respect, to core values, to doing unto others as you would have them do unto you, to self-lessness, and to "peace, patience, kindness, and self-control." (I took that from a certain ancient manuscript.) Our Founding Fathers understood that we can't put our trust in our structure of government alone. George Washington in his Farewell Address recognized morality, faith, and our values as essential to our political survival. "Of all the dispositions and habits which lead to political prosperity, religion and morality are indispensable support." He concluded by observing that "virtue or morality is a necessary spring of popular government." Note that he didn't say *helpful*; he said *necessary*.

Samuel Adams argued that if you want to see America prosper, you will devote your time and energies to promoting virtues and values. "He therefore is the truest friend to the liberty of his country who tries most to promote its virtue, and who, so far as his power and influence extend, will not suffer a man to be chosen into any office of power and trust who is not a wise and virtuous man." Personally, I'd rather take the advice of Sam Adams than those talking heads on MSNBC.

Democracy simply won't work among a people characterized by selfishness, greed, malice, or lawlessness. Fortunately, America has traditionally been kept on the right path thanks to our commitment to faith and religious values. Alexis de Tocqueville visited America in the nineteenth century and wrote his celebrated book *Democracy in America*. As he described it, "On my arrival in the United States the religious aspect of the country was the first thing that struck my attention; and the longer I stayed there, the more I perceived the great political consequences resulting from this new state of things." He continued,

> Religion in America takes no direct part in the government of society, but it must be regarded as the first of their political institutions. . . . I do not know whether all Americans have a sincere faith in their religion—for who can search the human heart?—but I am certain that they hold it to be indispensable to the maintenance of republican institutions. This opinion is not peculiar to a class of citizens or to a party, but it belongs to the whole nation and to every rank of society.[9]

De Tocqueville noted that at the time the "enlightened" philosophers in Europe were turning their backs on faith and arguing that religion and freedom were incompatible. (Sound familiar?) But de Tocqueville saw that America was proving them wrong. "Unfortunately facts by no means accord with their theory," he wrote. "There are certain populations in Europe whose unbelief is only equaled by their ignorance and debasement; while in America, one of the freest and most enlightened nations in the world, the people fulfill with fervor all the outward duties of religion."[10]

What de Tocqueville described still holds true today. As the late-Harvard professor Samuel P. Huntington put it, "Religion has been and still is a central, perhaps the central, element of American identity. America was founded in large part for religious reasons, and religious movements have shaped its evolution for almost four centuries.

By every indicator, Americans are far more religious than the people of other industrialized countries."[11] If we are feeling lost and wondering what our national purpose and direction should be, Huntington argued that we will find the answers by looking at our faith and culture.

Our faith, values, and culture bind us together. If we lose our commitment to common values, the country will inevitably fragment. Aristotle understood this and believed it to be the hub in the wheel. Without a common morality, he warned, a political community would become "a mere alliance."[12]

This makes the United States unique among the nations of the world. As I mentioned earlier in this book, most national identities are tied to geography or ethnicity. Americans are different. We recognize the beauty of our country, but we don't call ourselves Americans because of the soil beneath our feet. Back in 1849 a European visitor noted that an "American exhibits little or none of the local attachments which distinguish the European. His feelings are more centered upon his institutions than his mere country. He looks upon himself more than in the light of a republican than in that of a native of a particular territory. . . . Every American is thus, in his own estimation, the apostle of a particular political creed."[13]

Nor is it simply our common history that makes us Americans. We should be inspired by what occurred at Plymouth Rock and Gettysburg, but these events are examples of what it means to be an American—they don't make us Americans. There are millions of Americans such as myself who don't have any familial link to those historical events but who are touched by them because they reveal values.

What defines us are our values and ideals, our commitment to individualism, a spirit of independence, limited government, and the

American spirit. The Founding Fathers identified these values for us in the Declaration of Independence and the Constitution. They also selected three Latin phrases to define our republic. The first is well known: *E pluribus unum* ("From many one"). The other two, which you don't hear much about anymore, speak to the Founders' sense of the historic nature of the American project. One phrase was *Annuit coeptis* (Providence has favored our undertakings); the other was *Novus ordo seclorum* (A New Order for the ages).[14] Clearly, from the very beginning our Founders were motivated by a sense of American exceptionalism. And what make us exceptional are our culture and our national ideals.

Our political system has worked brilliantly for more than two centuries because it could rely on a culture in which people share a common commitment to doing the right thing. As John Adams warned, "Our Constitution was made only for a moral and religious people."[15] Without that, even a democracy could simply become the will of the mob.

* * *

Finally, the beauty of America is not our military superiority.

We live in a dangerous world, and America needs to be strong. U.S. Senator Phil Gramm used to say that if the lion and the lamb are going to lie down together, I'd just as soon that America be the lion. That's a good point—and I'd add that the lion and the lamb are not likely to lie down together in this lifetime.

We must remain not just strong, but the strongest power in the world, and we should make no apologies when we must use our military strength from time to time. But this is not where our true strength lies. Military might is a means to an end, not an end in itself.

A strong military in the hands of a corrupt, wicked, or oppressive regime does not make that regime great.

Both George Washington and Abraham Lincoln were effective and successful leaders because they held core values that kept them focused on right and wrong and also kept them humble. Both of them proclaimed various days of thanksgiving and fasting. The goal was, in the words of Lincoln, to create "a day of public humiliation, prayer and fasting, to be observed by the people of the United States with religious solemnities." Both leaders accepted their accountability to God and showed the humility that flows from it.

Having military superiority is great—but it has to be tethered to a culture that promotes goodness, freedom, and justice. Without that, we would be no better than the old Soviet Union.

To sum up, American capitalism is great, American democracy is great, and American military power is great. Put me down as being for all three. But the success of America does not rely on these things alone.

The success of America and the realization of the American Dream rely on our common sense of culture, a culture that admits some things are right and some things are wrong, a culture that respects and honors the dignity of the individual, a culture that defends the defenseless, values human life, and remains true to our Judeo-Christian ethic.

My parents came from a country that is quite similar to our own—India embraces free enterprise, it is a democracy, and it possesses substantial military strength. Certainly India is a great country and a good American ally. I have fond memories of visiting my grandparents there—but I'm only interested in visiting. My parents didn't move to America for nothing. They were attracted to American culture, to our unique sense of unbridled freedom and opportunity.

There's a quote, sometimes attributed to de Tocqueville, that says, "America is great because it is good. If America ceases to be good, America will cease to be great." This is something we have to come to grips with as a people. The free enterprise system and democratic governance are gifts to mankind, but their goodness can always be undone by men behaving badly.

Simply put, our culture is crucial to our success as a nation. It's not merely a luxury item that we can dispense with when our society becomes rich enough that we think we no longer need it.

You may also have heard another line attributed to de Tocqueville: "Liberty cannot be established without morality, nor morality without faith." This of course is an unfashionable sentiment in today's society. We like to believe that free enterprise and democracy will lead to success regardless of the status of the cultural underpinnings. Not true.

Good or harm will come to our country depending on what we value and what we reject. A robust economy, a brilliant political system, or unrivaled military strength can't protect us from ourselves if we make bad moral choices.

Now What?

So you say, "Nice book Bobby. Now what?" I'll tell you what—now go out there and take your government back. Or take it over. Take up whatever rallying cry you like. Just don't take it for granted.

Conservatives are at a political disadvantage today. We tend to build our lives around chasing the American Dream, which to most of us means starting our own business, launching our careers, or raising our families. For most of us, it does not include running for office or working for the federal government. And there is a reason for that. We believe in citizen government. We believe in the old-fashioned notion that the government which governs best governs least. We think the Republic is most secure when the Legislature is out of session and the president is on vacation. We believe local government allows us to govern ourselves more efficiently than the federal government.

We think the greatness of America is found in the freedom to do whatever we want and in creating our own destiny. Our goal is to become the best rocket scientist or doctor or plumber or restaurant manager or musician or parent or teacher or soldier that we can possibly be. As conservatives we think of creating something with our own hands, or working our way up in the private sector. We think of creating wealth, not living off the wealth of others. For conservatives, it is the private sector that grows our economy, creates opportunity and jobs, generates wealth, and is responsible for America's strength and vitality.

To put it in a more personal context, very few conservatives think of chasing the American Dream by going to work at the Louisiana Department of Health and Hospitals, the National Bipartisan Commission on the Future of Medicare, the University of Louisiana System, the U.S. Department of Health and Human Services, the U.S. Congress, and the Louisiana governor's office.

The view from the Left, however, is radically different. For most young liberals there is scarcely a higher calling than pushing your ideological agenda via government service. It's right at the top of the queue, rivaled only by a career in journalism or higher education. (Before I get into trouble here, I will note that I know many reporters, or some, or a few anyway, who are not liberals.)

For most liberal ideologues the prospect of burrowing into the government and pushing their agenda is a dream come true. Government is doing more than ever, it is growing bigger than ever, it is costing more than ever, and it is spending more than ever. It has an insatiable appetite that will not diminish by itself. Government will never volunteer to be "The Biggest Loser."

There will always be someone else with a new idea for government to try, and nine times out of ten that idea will cost money. There will always be another wrong for the government to set right. There will always be another snail darter to save, another study to fund, another regulation to pass, and another tax to raise. There will always be another government building to build and to name after someone who is very important, or who at least was very important in securing the funds to build the building.

While recessions, technological advancements, and other events sometimes reduce the size of the private workforce, there is no such downsizing pressure in the public sector. We seem to need more and more staff to collect more and more taxes to run more and more programs that spend more and more money.

So today, it takes far fewer Americans working on an assembly line to make a car, but it takes far more Americans to manage our incredible exploding government. The guy at the car plant is not thinking up ways to spend more of your money. If anything, he's hoping to get a raise or a promotion by devising a way to make a better car. For the liberal working in the bowels of the Department of Education, it's a different story. He's trying to invent a new government program that will suck in more federal dollars and give him a chance to pursue some big idea. He may have the best intentions, but rest assured, the program he designs will cost money. And rest assured that you, the taxpayer, will pay for it.

Actually, that's not quite right. You will not pay for that new federal program. You don't have nearly enough money. We have amassed a debt so large that you will not live long enough to pay for it. But, if you have kids, and if they have kids, *they* will probably pay for it, unless of course China and the Middle Eastern countries call in the promissory notes before that. I don't really want to think about what happens then.

This dichotomy—that liberals are drawn to public service while conservatives are repelled by it—is nothing new. But the result is that most of the bureaucracy is controlled by people who are ideologically vested in expanding the government. So the question is what to do about it. I have two suggestions. The first conservatives will like, the second they may not.

First, we need to insist that our government functions in the way it was originally intended. We need a government, composed of part-time citizen legislators, that is not seen as the answer to every problem. Too many people today are asking the question, "How can the government solve our problems?" Here is the answer: it can't.

Don't get me wrong, I think competent, efficient government is essential. That's what I strive for every day. But even the most well-functioning government cannot guarantee our nation's success. It's entirely possible to have a great government and a lousy country. American greatness is not defined by our government. America is an idea based on freedom. When government grows too large, it begins threatening freedom. It has always been that way, everywhere.

The folks in Congress need some outside-the-beltway thinking on our problems. In fact, if the Republican Party really wants to reconnect with the American people and regain their trust, it needs to commit itself to something I call the Grandchildren Debt Relief Package, but that you could just as well call A Promise to the American People. That promise would be that every Republican elected to Congress would work to restore America's future with a seven-step recovery program. Here it is:

1. INSTITUTE TERM LIMITS, to force members of Congress to think of our nation's future rather than their own reelection.
2. MAKE CONGRESS A PART-TIME LEGISLATURE. Congress does less harm when it's not in session, so it should be out of session more often.

3. PASS A BALANCED BUDGET AMENDMENT TO THE CONSTITU-
TION. Nothing threatens our future more than Washington's
runaway spending, which is bleeding America's financial
lifeblood and weakening our national security. It has got to stop,
and this would help.

4. GIVE THE PRESIDENT A LINE-ITEM VETO, to prevent the sneaking in of pork barrel projects. Most governors have it, so should
the president.

5. FORCE CONGRESS TO HAVE SIMPLE UP OR DOWN VOTES ON
SINGLE-ITEM LEGISLATION, to prevent Congress from hiding bad
policy in "must pass" legislation. These are more than infuriat-
ing examples of government waste; they are placing unbearable
burdens of debt on our economy and our children's future.

6. LEGISLATE PAY-AS-YOU-GO BUDGETING, so that every government program doesn't dig us into a deeper hole. Politicians pay
lip-service to this principle; it needs to be put into law in a way
that makes it unavoidable.

7. REQUIRE A SUPER MAJORITY TO RAISE TAXES. We didn't get into
this economic mess by *not* taxing the American people enough;
we got into it by letting Washington become Fedzilla, a wealth-
eating monster of unimaginable proportions.

If we commit ourselves to enacting these seven reforms, it would be
the greatest act of improving our children's future since Ronald Reagan won the Cold War.

Sure there are other important reforms, many of which I have
detailed in this book. But I am convinced these seven simple steps would
put Congress on a radically different path than the irresponsible

course it's on now. And since Congress has the power of the purse, once we turn Congress around, we can turn the government around.

So we should demand that our elected officials adhere to these minimum steps. Democrats really should get behind this program since it is geared toward saving America from fiscal oblivion. But since they're leading us into the abyss, it's doubtful they'll get on board. Our best hope is for Republicans to reclaim the mantle of limited, competent, results-oriented government they once upheld.

Nevertheless, I have to point out that the Republican Party failed to pass these reforms when they had the chance in the 1990s. Still, they took a good shot at many of them. Most notably, Congress fell just one vote short of passing a Balanced Budget Amendment in 1995. Just think about that. The amendment passed the House with more than the necessary two-thirds margin, and the Senate fell a single vote short of a two-thirds majority. Think of how different things would be today if they had found one more vote.

On the whole, the Republican Revolution of 1994 will go down in my book as a great movement that yielded some fruit, but which ultimately fell short of its promise. That does not mean we have to fail again, however. We can learn from our mistakes, and I believe we will.

My second proposal to fight big government may not be welcomed by many conservatives. As we move our policy proposals forward, I believe conservatives should adjust an important aspect of our philosophy. As much as I lament of the growth of government, I do not believe conservatives should roundly condemn the very concept of government service, as is often the case today. We should consider the possibility that government service might in fact be a *noble* calling. It shouldn't be viewed as a way to get rich or to make a comfortable life-long career with great employment benefits. But there are many noble and worthwhile public service callings that some people really do enter with selfless motives. Teaching and public health are two that come to mind.

We need conservatives in government positions who are devoted to changing government without letting government change them. We need people of strong resolve who will resist the temptation to go native in Washington, D.C. You don't have to do it as a career, but you might consider giving some time to it. Consider it missionary work.

* * *

A top-down, command style organization works in the military but not in government. Whether the issue is education, healthcare, energy, you name it—a one-size-fits-all solution is rarely the best one in a nation of 300 million people. Enhancing local power, promoting the free market, and allowing people to make their own meaningful choices—in other words, expanding freedom—is the traditional American way because it's the way that works best.

We are trying to live this way and govern this way in Louisiana. It's not easy—old habits die hard, as they say. And quite often the complex rules and regulations coming from Washington tie the hands of local government and make it even harder to change.

President Obama won election in 2008 with a brilliant campaign that convinced people that change was on the way, that he was going to do things differently. There was a sense of newness, of freshness, a sense that the little guy was going to get a chance to help in a grand effort of national improvement. The campaign fed off grassroots energy and the idea that no one needed to wait for instructions from central command.

Less than two years into the Obama administration, reality has set in. Betraying his people-power rhetoric, this president has ushered in the biggest expansion of the old, top-down, centralized government model our country has ever seen. More than ever, power is concentrated in a few hands in Washington. Obama's young campaign workers and grassroots enthusiasts, it turns out, were not empowered at all.

The biggest change we've seen, in fact, is that it almost seems like you can add another zero to everything—to the number of jobs lost, to the deficit, to the debt, to our foreign obligations. Instead of "change you can believe in," it's "change you hoped you'd never see." The Democrats, seemingly to their own surprise, are discovering the government can't spend us into prosperity.

Americans have a certain tolerance for ideology and rhetoric, but underneath it all they expect to find policies that work. So it's up to us to turn our conservative principles into practical solutions that empower people and that will keep America the greatest and freest nation on earth.

I believe government can and should function at an extremely capable level. We need to root out the casual toleration of mediocrity in government. It should be embarrassing that the phrase "It's good enough for government work" has become the ultimate slacker motto. We would often feel blessed just to get basic competence out of government—ask anyone in line at the Post Office or at the DMV. But that is setting the bar too low. We must demand from government not just competence, but something more—a commitment to excellence.

*   *   *

I'd like to end this book by asking you to do something: I want you to get in the game.

There are many ways you can make a difference. You can run for office; serve in government; volunteer on a campaign; donate to a candidate who wants to get our country on the right track; start going to townhall meetings and tea parties; or just talk to people you know about ways to get this country moving forward again.

This much I know: we will not take our government back by sitting on the sidelines.

My mom and dad had a simple goal for their kids: to make whatever sacrifices necessary to ensure that we had more opportunities than they did. Millions of American parents have made and kept that same promise. But my generation of Americans could be the first to leave fewer opportunities for our children than we enjoyed. It's hard to think of a bigger example of national failure. We must not let that happen.

Let me close by recalling a scene from the movie *Hoosiers*. A kid on a high school basketball team is called up from the bench by the coach and told to go into a big game. The kid is a reserve who hadn't received much playing time, but this is a crucial time, and his team needs him. The kid, being of strong faith, stops on the sidelines and kneels down to pray. The coach walks up to him and says, "Son, God wants you in the game."

There you have it. It's time to get in the game. Do it now—your country needs you.

[Let's continue the conversation. Visit me at bobbyjindal.com]

ACKNOWLEDGEMENTS

First of all, even though they don't know it, the people of Louisiana helped me write this book. From my neighbors growing up, to my teachers in school, to the many good folks I have met in my thirty-nine years, the people of Louisiana have helped to form and shape me as a person. I thank them.

Let me first point out how much I appreciate the input I received from folks who work on my staff. They work long hours for the people of Louisiana, and it was really above and beyond the call of duty for them to give me a few of the precious hours of free time they have to provide feedback. Timmy Teepell, Melissa Sellers, Stephen Waguespack, and Kyle Plotkin all provided excellent suggestions and criticism. I also want to thank their families for letting them help out.

Many others agreed to look over the initial drafts and give suggestions, and I even listened to some of their ideas. Among those are Wes Anderson, Alex Castellanos, Ben Domenech, Garret Graves, Blaise Hazelwood, Alan Levine, Brad Todd, and Sam Van Voorhis. Well done, and thank you all.

Curt Anderson and Peter Schweizer were crucial to this book. Peter is an accomplished author in his own right, and Curt is a close friend who knows how I think.

My brother Nikesh is irreplaceable in my life, many thanks to him for his friendship and assistance. My parents, Amar and Raj Jindal, are responsible for me. If you don't like me, take it up with them. I could not have written the book without their help.

My children, Selia, Shaan, and Slade, did not help on this book, and at times did their best to stop the process altogether. But what they have done is give me a much better understanding of what life and love are all about.

What can I say about Supriya? We are inseparable, we do everything together. She's my biggest defender, and in private my best check and balance. To say that she helped me on this project is an enormous understatement.

NOTES

CHAPTER I

1 "Whiteboard Archives," Politico.com, May 2, 2010; available at: http://www.politico.com/politico44/wbarchive/whiteboard05022010 .html [accessed September 14, 2010].

2 I think Alexander Hamilton got it right in the Federalist Papers, no. 70: "Energy in the executive is a leading character in the definition of good government. It is essential to the protection of the community against foreign attacks; it is not less essential to the steady administration of the laws; to the protection of property against those irregular and high-handed combinations which sometimes interrupt the ordinary course of justice; to the security of liberty against the enterprises and assaults of ambition, of faction, and of anarchy." Quentin P. Taylor, The Essential Federalist: A New Reading of The Federalist Papers, Constitutional Heritage Series, Vol. 3 (Lanham, MD: Rowman and Littlefield, 1998).

3 Clifford Krauss, "Oil Spill's Blow to BP's Image May Eclipse Costs," New York Times, April 29, 2010; available at: http://www.nytimes .com/2010/04/30/business/30bp.html; Tim Webb, "BP boss admits job on the line over Gulf oil spill," The Guardian (UK), May 14, 2010; available at: http://www.guardian.co.uk/business/2010/may/ 13/bp-boss-admits-mistakes-gulf-oil-spill; Christopher Helman, "In His Own Words: Forbes Q&A with BP's Tony Hayward," Forbes, May 18, 2010; available at: http://www.forbes.com/2010/05/18/oil-tony-hay-

ward-business-energy-hayward.html; Jessica Durando, "BP's Ton Hayward: I'd like my life back," *USA Today,* June 1, 2010; available at: http://content.usatoday.com/communities/greenhouse/post/2010/06/bp-tony-hayward-apology/1?loc=interstitialskip; and Emily Loftis, "Spill Workers Get Sick, Chemicals Get a Pass," *Mother Jones,* June 2, 2010; available at: http://motherjones.com/blue-marble/2010/06/chemical-regulation-gulf-workers-sickness [accessed September 14, 2010].

4 "Oil Cleanup Crews Rest More Than Work," wapt.com, July 14, 2010; available at: http://www.wapt.com/r/24256040/detail.html [accessed September 14, 2010].

5 *Hornbeck Offshore Services, LLC* vs. *Kenneth Lee "Ken" Salazar,* United States District Court, Eastern District of Louisana; available at: http://www.laed.uscourts.gov/GENERAL/Notices/10-1663_doc67.pdf [accessed September 21, 2010]. See also Laurel Brubaker Calkins and Margaret Cronin Fisk, "Deepwater Drilling Ban Lifted by New Orleans Federal Judge," Bloomberg, June 23, 2010; available at: http://www.bloomberg.com/news/2010-06-22/u-s-deepwater-oil-drilling-ban-lifted-today-by-new-orleans-federal-judge.html [accessed September 14, 2010]. A recording of the oral arguments in the case can be found here: http://www.ca5.uscourts. gov/OralArgRecordings/10/10-30585_7-8-2010.wma.

6 David Hammer, "Jindal says Obama still doesn't get moratorium's economic impact," Nola.com, June 10, 2010; available at: http://www.nola.com/news/gulf-oil-spill/index.ssf/2010/06/jindal_says_obama_still_doesnt.html [accessed September 14, 2010].

7 Stephen Power and Leslie Eaton, "U.S. Saw Drilling Ban Killing Many Jobs," *Wall Street Journal,* August 21, 2010; available at: http://online.wsj.com/article/SB10001424052748704488404575441760384563880.html [accessed September 14, 2010].

8 Editorial, "Protests from experts show drilling moratorium based on politics, not science: An editorial," nola.com, June 11, 2010; available at: http://www.nola.com/news/gulf-oil-spill/index.ssf/2010/06/protests_from_experts_show_dri.html [accessed September 14, 2010].

CHAPTER 4

1 Dr. Jennifer Patico, Georgia State University, Department of Anthropology; bio available at: http://www.cas.gsu.edu/anthropology/ 2255.html [accessed September 14, 2010].

2 Quoted in Clinton Bolick, *Voucher Wars: Waging the Legal Battle over School Choice* (Washington, D.C.: Cato Institute, 2003).

3 See for example "Learning for Tomorrow's World," OECD Programme for International Student Assessment; available at: http://www.oecd.org/document/5/0,3343,en_32252351_322361 73_33917573_1_1_1_1,00.html [accessed September 14, 2010].

4 Thomas Jefferson, Correspondence to Charles Yancey, January 6, 1816, Thomas Jefferson Encyclopedia, http://wiki.monticello.org/ mediawiki/index.php/Quotations_on_Education#_note-6 [accessed September 23, 2010].

5 Trevor Colbourn, ed., *Fame and the Founding Fathers: Essays by Douglass Adair* (Liberty Fund, 1974).

6 Alexis De Tocqueville, *Democracy in America* (Regnery Gateway Editions, 2002).

7 See Jay P. Greene's excellent *Education Myths* (Lanham, MD: Rowman and Littlefield, 2005).

8 Jay P. Greene, *op. cit.*

9 Editorial, "Can Louisiana education reform survive teachers' union assault?" *Washington Post*, May 1, 2010; available at: http://www.washingtonpost.com/wp-dyn/content/article/ 2010/04/30/AR2010043002132.html [accessed September 14, 2010].

10 Paul Ciotti, "The Wrong Approach," *Tampa Tribune*, March 30, 1996; and John Taylor Gatto, *The Underground History of American Education* (New York: Oxford Village Press, 2000).

11 See Kathryn G. Newmark and Veronique De Rugy, "Hope After Katrina," *Education Next*, Fall 2006; available at: http://educationnext.org/ hope-after-katrina/ [accessed September 14, 2010].

12 Ibid. See also "New Orleans Schools Before and After Katrina Hit," PBS *News Hour with Jim Lehrer*, November 1, 2005; available at: http://www. pbs.org/newshour/bb/education/july-dec05/neworleans_11-01.html [accessed September 14, 2010]. See also Joanne Jacobs, "F Is For Valedic-

torian," Fox News, August 17, 2003; available at: http://www.foxnews.com/story/0,2933,94864,00.html [accessed Septmber 23, 2010].

13 Paul E. Peterson, "Learning from Catastrophe Theory: What New Orleans Tells Us about Our Education Future," *Education Next*, vol. 6, no. 4 (2006); available at: http://educationnext.org/learning-from-catastrophe-theory/ [accessed September 14, 2010]; and Kathryn Newmark and Veronique de Rugy, "Hope after Katrina: Will New Orleans Become the New City of Choice?" *op. cit*. See also, Kathryn G. Newmark and Veronique De Rugy, "Hope after Katrina," *Education Next*, Fall 2006; available at: http://educationnext.org/hope-after-katrina/ [accessed September 23, 2010].

14 Sarah Carr, "Higher LEAP scores add fuel to debate over charter schools," *New Orleans Times Picayune*, May 30, 2009; available at: http://www.nola.come/news/index.ssf/2009/05/higher_leap_scores_add_fuel_to [accessed September 23, 2010]. See also Brian Thevenot, "New Orleans Charter Schools Operator Plans Expansion," nola.com July 24, 2009; available at: http://www.nola.com/ education/index.ssf/2009/07/kipp_schools_a_leading_charter.html [accessed September 14, 2010]; and Lesli A. Maxwell, "In New Orleans, University's Charter School Makes Gains," *Education Week*, May 21, 2008; available at: http://edweek.org/ew/articles/2008/05/21/39wrightcharter_web.h27.html [accessed September 23, 2010].

15 Bernie Pinsonat, "Louisiana, Baton Rouge Public Schools Need Discipline for Success"; available at: http://www.bayoubuzz.com/News/Louisiana/Business/Louisiana_Baton_Rouge_Public_Schools_Need_Discipline_For_Success__8031.asp [accessed September 14, 2010].

CHAPTER 6

1 John Coyne and John Fund, *Cleaning House: America's Campaign for Term Limits* (Washington, D.C.: Regnery, 1992).

2 David Morgan, "Bayh: No Chance I'll Switch parties," CBSNews.com, February 16, 2010; available at: http://www.cbsnews.com/8301-503544_162-6212208-503544.html [accessed September 14, 2010].

3   Dan Greenburg, "Cutting Congress Down to Size: How a Part-Time Congress would work," Heritage Foundation Backgrounder, 1009, November 2, 1994; available at: http://www.heritage.org/Research/Reports/1994/11/Cutting-Congress-Down-to-Size-How-a-Part-Time-Congress-Would-Work [accessed September 14, 2010].

4   Walter Mondale, S. Hrg. 103–158, p. 7; available at: http://www.archive.org/stream/testimonyofhonwa00unit/testimonyofhonwa00unit_djvu.txt [accessed September 14, 2010].

5   See Budget of the United States Government, fiscal year 2000; available at: http://www.gpoaccess.gov/usbudget/fy00/pdf/budget.pdf [accessed September 14, 2010]; Mark Knoller, "National Debt to Top 100 Percent of GDP," CBS News, Political Hotsheet, July 23, 2010; available at: http://www.cbsnews.com/8301-503544_162-20011546-503544.html [accessed September 14, 2010]; *2010 Budget Chart Book: The Federal Budget in Pictures*, Heritage Foundation, http://www.heritage.org/BudgetChartbook/PDF/All-Budget-chart-book-2010.pdf [accessed September 14, 2010].

6   Bruce Bartlett, "The 81% Tax Increase," Forbes, May 15, 2009; available at: http://www.forbes.com/2009/05/14/taxes-social-security-opinions-columnists-medicare.html [accessed September 14, 2010].

7   Mwangi S. Kimenyi and Robert D. Tollison, "The Length of Legislative Sessions and the Growth of Government," *Rationality and Society*, Vol. 7, No. 2, April 1995.

8   Michael Ferguson and Hugh Douglas Witte, "Congress and the Stock Market," Social Science Research Network, Working Paper Series, 2005.

9   See House of Representatives, Conference Report, 1st Session, 111th Congress; available at: http://www.house.gov/billtext/hr1_legtext_cr.pdf [accessed September 14, 2010]; and "1,073 Pages," *Wall Street Journal* Review & Outlook, February 15, 2009; available at: http://online.wsj.com/article/SB123456958734386181.html [accessed September 14, 2010]. See also, "Cutting Congress Down to Size: How a Part-Time Congress Would Work," Heritage Foundation Backgrounder, November 2, 1994; available at: http://s3.amazonaws.com/thf_media/1994/pdf/bg1009.pdf [accessed September 23, 2010].

10 Joseph Russell, "GOP Congressman: Not Enough Time To Read Health Care Reform Bill," Talk Media News, July 17, 2009; available at: http://www.talkradionews.com/news/2009/7/17/gop-congress-man-not-enough-time-to-read-health-care-reform-b.html [accessed September 27, 2010].

11 Senator Stevens' conviction was overturned by the courts, but the fundamental facts of the case were not challenged.

12 David Kocieniewski, "For Rangel, Four Rent-Stabilized Apartments," *New York Times*, July 11, 2008; available at: http://www.nytimes.com/2008/07/11/nyregion/11rangel.html?_r=2 [accessed September 14, 2010]; and Jennifer Fermino and Carl Campanile, "Rep. Charlie Rangel defends himself again, says he wants to 'get back to work,'" *New York Post*, August 12, 2010; available at: http://www.nypost.com/p/news/local/work_charlie_rangel_defends_himself_eLZIkIlwC3iqTAs1WOVkAK [accessed September 14, 2010].

13 Lobbying Database, OpenSecrets.org, http://www.opensecrets.org/lobby/index.php [accessed September 27, 2010].

14 Raquel Meyer Alexander, Stephen W. Mazza, and Susan Scholz, "Measuring Rates of Return for Lobbying Expenditures: An Empirical Analysis under the American Jobs Creation Act," Social Science Research Network, Working Paper, May 26, 2009.

CHAPTER 7

1 See the Coast Guard release here: http://www.deepwaterhorizon response.com/go/doc/425/119926/ [accessed September 21, 2010].

2 Amanda Ripley, "In Case of Emergency," *The Atlantic Monthly*, September 2009; available at: http://www.theatlantic.com/magazine/archive/2009/09/in-case-of-emergency/7604/ [accessed September 14, 2010].

CHAPTER 8

1 George Washington, "Address to the Members of the Volunteer Association and Other Inhabitants of the Kingdom of Ireland Who Have Lately Arrived in the City of New York," PBS, *Rediscovering George Washington*, December 2, 1783; available at: http://www.pbs.org/

georgewashington/collection/other_1788dec2.html [accessed September 14, 2010].

2 Quoted in Thomas Ricento, *Ideology, Politics, and Language Policies* (Impact, 2000).

3 Marshall Smelser, "George Washington and the Alien and Sedition Acts," *American Historical Review*, January 1954.

4 David M. Kennedy, "Can We Still Afford to be a Nation of Immigrants?" *The Atlantic*, November 1996; available at: http://www.theatlantic.com/magazine/archive/1996/11/can-we-still-afford-to-be-a-nation-of-immigrants/4835/ [accessed September 14, 2010].

5 Matt Richtel, "Tech Recruiting Clashes with Immigration Rules," *New York Times*, April 11, 2009; available at: http://www.nytimes.com/2009/04/12/business/12immig.html [accessed September 14, 2010].

6 Ibid. See also, Paul Kedrosky and Brad Feld "Start-up Visas Can Jump-Start the Economy," *Wall Street Journal*, December 2, 2009; available at: http://online.wsj.com/article/SB10001424052748704402404574525772299940870.html [accessed September 14, 2010].

7 Philip Martin and Peter Duignan, *Making and Remaking America: Immigration into the United States* (Stanford, CA: Hoover Institution Press, 2003).

8 Robert Rector and Christine Kim, "The Fiscal Cost of Low-Skill Immigrants to the U.S. Taxpayer," Heritage Foundation Special Report, May 21, 2007; available at: http://www.heritage.org/research/reports/2007/05/the-fiscal-cost-of-low-skill-immigrants-to-the-us-taxpayer [accessed September 14, 2010].

9 Charles A. Ferguson and Shirley Brice Heath, eds., *Language in the USA* (NY: Cambridge University Press, 1981), 15.

CHAPTER 9

1 William Ivy Hair, *The Kingfish and His Realm: The Life and Times of Huey P. Long* (Louisiana State University Press, January 1997).

2 Harnett Thomas Kane, *Huey Long's Louisiana Hayride: The American Rehearsal for Dictatorship: 1928-1940* (LA: Pelican, 1971).

3 Caitlin Ginley, "Louisiana, Mississippi Movin' Up; 20 States Still Flunk," The Center for Public Integrity, States of Disclosure, June 24, 2009;

available at: http://www.publicintegrity.org/investigations/states_of_disclosure/ articles/entry/1428 [accessed September 15, 2010].

4 "2008 BGA-Alper Integrity Index shows New Jersey, Louisiana have strongest ethics and transparency laws; Vermont, South Dakota at the bottom," Better Government Association, October 27, 2008; available at: http://www.bettergov.org/IntegrityIndexRelease.aspx [accessed September 15, 2010].

CHAPTER 10

1 Quoted in Peter Schweizer, *Makers and Takers* (NY: Doubleday, 2008).

2 Quoted in Howell V. Williams, "Benjamin Franklin and the Poor Laws," *The Social Service Review*, March 1944.

3 Jeremy Schaap, *Cinderella Man: James Braddock, Max Baer, and the Greatest Upset in Boxing History* (Boston: Houghton Mifflin, 2005).

4 Paul Johnson, *Intellectuals* (NY: Harper Perennial, 1988), 340.

5 Pamela Villarreal, "Social Security and Medicare Projections," National Center for Policy Analysis, June 11, 2009; available at: http://www.ncpa.org/pdfs/ba662.pdf [accessed September 15, 2010].

6 FDR, quoted by David M. Kennedy in Cynthia M. Koch, "Historians, Teachers, Authors Take a Fresh, Sometimes Critical, Look at Roosevelt," The National Archives, *Prologue*, Winter 2006, Vol. 38, No. 4.

7 "Health Costs and History," *Wall Street Journal*, October 20, 2009; available at: http://online.wsj.com/article/SB10001424052748703746604574461610985243066.html [accessed September 15, 2010]; and Chris Edwards, "Government Schemes Cost More than Promised," Cato Institute *Tax & Budget Bulletin*, No. 17, 2003; available at: http://www.cato.org/pubs/tbb/tbb-0309-17.pdf [accessed September 15, 2010].

8 Michael Novak, "Tocqueville at 200," *National Review,* December 21, 2005; available at: http://old.nationalreview.com/novak2005/22/0809.asp [accessed September 23, 2010].

9 Milton Friedman, *Capitalism and Freedom* (University of Chicago Press, 2002), 9.

10 Mark Steyn, "It's the Demography, Stupid," *Wall Street Journal*, January 4, 2006.

11 Barack Obama, *Dreams from My Father.* "Eventually a consulting house to a multinational corporation agreed to hire me as a research assistant. Like a spy behind enemy lines, I arrived every day at my mid-Manhattan office and sat at my computer terminal."

12 The data come from Michael Cembalest, the chief investment officer at J.P. Morgan bank, "Obama's Business Blind Spot," Forbes.com, November 24, 2009; available at: http://www.forbes.com/2009/ 11/24/michael-cembalest-obama-business-beltway-cabinet.html [accessed September 15, 2010].

13 Steve Montgomery and Steve Farrell, "Politically Correct Butchers of the 20th Century," newsmax.com, September 24, 2001; available at: http://archive.newsmax.com/archives/articles/2001/9/23/235930.sht ml [accessed September 23, 2010].

14 Arthur C. Brooks, *Who Really Cares* (Basic Books, 2006); and James T. Lindgren, "Testing Social Dominance: Is Support for Capitalism and Opposition to Income Redistribution Driven by Racism and Intolerance?" Northwestern Law and Economics Research Paper, no. 6–10.

15 Jerry Bruce Thomas, *An Appalachian New Deal* (The University Press of Kentucky, 1998).

16 See Paul R. Ehrlich, *The Population Bomb* (Sierra Club/Ballantine, 1968); and Paul R. Ehrlich and Anne H. Ehrlich, *The End of Affluence: A Blueprint for Your Future* (NY: Ballantine Books, 1974). See also, Gary Demar, "The 40th Anniversary of Paul Ehrlich's The Population Bomb," American Vision, June 30, 2008; available at: http://americanvision.org /1702/the-anniversary-of-paul-ehrlichs-population-bomb/ [accessed September 23, 2010].

17 From Reagan's First Inaugural Address, January 20, 1981.

CHAPTER II

1 Associated Press, "Almost $50 billion in 'Questionable' Medicare," *New York Post*, November 14, 2009; available at: http://www.nypost.com/p/news/politics/medicare_fraud_almost_billion_growing_lA6Gt 32D5rrvbAV0Z3ljpO [accessed September 15, 2010].

2 David Doyle, "Hope in Sight for Richard," *Ealing Times* (UK), May 29, 2007; available at: http://www.ealingtimes.co.uk/archive/

2007/05/29/Health 1 %28news_health%29/1433305.Hope_in_sight_
for_Richard/ [accessed September 15, 2010].

3 Sarah Boseley, "Patients Pull Own Teeth As Dental Contract Falters," *The Guardian* (UK), October 15, 2007; available at: http://www.guardian.
co.uk/uk/2007/oct/15/health.healthandwellbeing; "I Rip Out My Teeth With Pliers," BBC News, October 15, 2007; available at: http://news.bbc.co.uk/2/hi/health/7045143.stm; Jenny Hope, "Patients Turn to DIY Dentistry as the Crisis in NHS Deepens," *Daily Mail* (UK), October 15, 2007; available at: http://www.dailymail.co.uk/news/article-487621/Patients-turn-DIY-dentistry-crisis-NHS-care-deepens.html; "Brits Resort to Pulling Own Teeth," CNN, October 15, 2007; available at: http://edition. cnn.com/ 2007/WORLD/europe/10/15/england.dentists/; and Jo Willey, "The Patients Forced to Pull Out Their Own Teeth," *Daily Express* (UK), October 15, 2007; available at: http://www.express.co. uk/posts/view/22071/The-patients-forced-to-pull-out-their-own-teeth [accessed September 15, 2010]. See also, "I took my teeth out with pliers," BBC, September 8, 2004; available at: http://news.bbc.co.uk/2/hi/3696758.stm [accessed September 23, 2010]; and Laura Barton, "Grin and bare it," *The Guardian*, March 2, 2006; available at: http://www.guardian.co.uk/lifeandstyle/2006/mar/02/healthand wellbeing.health [accessed September 23, 2010].

4 Scott Edmonds, "Tories Hit Emotional Health Issue," *Portage Daily Graphic* (Canada) May 23, 2003.

5 Unnati Gandhi, "Twins, Times Two, Born To Calgary Mother," *Globe and Mail* (Canada), August 17, 2007; and Amy Ridenour and Ryan Balis, *Shattered Lives: 100 Victims of Government Health Care* (Washington, D.C.: National Center for Public Policy Research, 2009).

6 "MRI Wait for Son Too Long, Mother Says," CBC News (Canada), January 13, 2005.

7 Lisa Priest, "Long wait forces cancer patient to buy operation in land he fled," *Globe and Mail* (Canada), January 31, 2007; available at: http://www.theglobeandmail.com/life/article76725.ece [accessed September 15, 2010].

8 Jennifer LaRue Huget, "Canadian official has heart surgery – in the U.S.," *Washington Post*, February 25, 2010; available at: http://

voices.washingtonpost.com/checkup/2010/02/canadian_premier_has _heart_sur.html [accessed September 15, 2010].

9 Fact Sheet on Older Americans, Civic Ventures, http://www. civicventures.org/publications/articles/fact_sheet_on_older_americans .cfm [accessed September 15, 2010].

10 Janice Lloyd, "Doctor Shortage Looms as Primary Care Loses its Pull," *USA Today*, August 18, 2009; available at: http://www.usatoday.com/ news/health/2009-08-17-doctor-gp-shortage_N.htm [accessed September 15, 2010].

11 Maggie Mahar, "The state of the nation's health," *Dartmouth Medicine*, Spring 2007; available at: http://dartmed.dartmouth.edu/ spring07/html/atlas.php [accessed September 15, 2010].

12 Carla Engle, "Feds to review Medicare and Medicaid error rate data," *Healthcare Finance News*, December 11, 2009; available at: http://www.healthcarefinancenews.com/blog/feds-review-medicare-and-medicaid-error-rate-data [accessed September 15, 2010].

13 Stuart L. Weinstein, "The Cost of Defensive Medicine," American Association of Orthopedic Surgeons Now, November 2008; available at: http://www.aaos.org/news/aaosnow/nov08/managing7.asp [accessed September 15, 2010].

14 "Proposition 12 Produces Healthy Benefits," Texas Medical Association, January 19, 2010; available at: http://www.texmed.org/Template. aspx?id=5238 [accessed September 22, 2010].

15 "Health Savings Accounts and Preventive Care," Council for Affordable Healthcare Issues & Answers, April 2009.

16 See for example Jennifer Gill, "Cut Your Health Care Costs Now," *Inc.*, April 1, 2005; available at: http://www.inc.com/magazine/ 20050401/ health-care.html [accessed September 15, 2010].

Chapter 12

1 "The Role of National Oil Companies in International Energy Markets," The Baker Institute Energy Forum, April 2007; available at: http://www.rice.edu/energy/publications/nocs.html, p. 1.

2 James L. Sweeney, "An Energy Policy for the Twenty-first Century,"
   Hoover Digest, no. 1, 2005; available at: http://www.hoover.org/ pub-
   lications/digest/2993911.html [accessed September 15, 2010].

3 http://www.house.gov/pelosi/press/releases/July05/energy.html

4 U.S. Energy Information Administration, *Electric Power Monthly*, September 2010 edition, http://www.eia.doe.gov/cneaf/electricity/
   epm/epm_sum.html [accessed September 21, 2010]. See also, David
   Frum, *The Comeback: Conservatism That Can Win Again* (NY: Double
   Day, 2008), 120–21.

5 "Wind," Institute for Energy Research, http://www.instituteforenergy
   research.org/energy-overview/wind/ [accessed September 23, 2010].

6 Jay Lindsay, "Gov't OKs 1st US offshore wind farm, off Mass.," Associated Press, May 3, 2010.

7 "Facts on Energy: Solar," Institute for Energy Research, June 11, 2009;
   available at: http://www.instituteforenergyresearch.org/2009/06/11/
   facts-on-energy-solar/ [accessed September 23, 2010].

8 Gregory   Murphy,   "The   Non-Science   of   Wind   Energy,"
   http://portbayny.org/files/Download/The%20Non-Science%20of%20
   Wind%20Energy.pdf [accessed September 23, 2010].

9 American Nuclear Society, Frequently Asked Questions—Three Mile
   Island   Accident—March   28,   1979,   http://www.ans.org/pi/
   resources/sptopics/tmi/faq.html [accessed September 15, 2010].

10 Sam Youngman, "Obama announces $8.3 billion program for two
   nuclear power plants," *The Hill*, February 16, 2010; available at:
   http://thehill.com/homenews/administration/81183-obama-announces
   -30-billion-for-new-nuke-plants [accessed September 15, 2010].

11 Data from the Institute for Energy Research, http://www.institutefor
   energyresearch.org/ [accessed September 21, 2010].

12 Al Gore, *Earth in the Balance: Ecology and the Human Spirit* (New York:
   Plume, 1993).

13 Ben Cassleman, "U.S. Gas Fields Go From Bust to Boom," *Wall Street
   Journal*, April 30, 2009; available at: http://online.wsj.com/ arti-
   cle/SB124104549891270585.html [accessed September 15, 2010].

14 Paul R. LaMonica, "In defense of oil companies," CNN Money, April 29, 2008; available at: http://money.cnn.com/2008/04/29/markets/ thebuzz/ [accessed September 15, 2010].

15 U.S. Energy Information administration, Petroleum Basic Statistics, September 2008, http://www.eia.doe.gov/energyexplained/index.cfm ?page=oil_home#tab2 (October 28, 2008). See also, "U.S. Crude Oil Production," US Energy Information Administration, http://tonto.eia. doe.gov/dnav/pet/hist/LeafHandler.ashx?n=PET&s=MCRFPUS2&f =A [accessed September 23, 2010].

16 Russian Military Budget, http://www.globalsecurity.org/military/ world/russia/mo-budget.htm [accessed September 15, 2010].

17 Institute for Energy Research, Issue Focus: Oil and Gas Leasing on Federal Lands, June 25, 2008, http://www.institutefor energyre-search.org/2008/06/25/truth-about-ocs/ [accessed September 15, 2010].

18 Jonah Goldberg, "The horror of 'ANWR,' the American elite's favorite hellhole," National Review, March 18, 2005; available at: http://old.nationalreview.com/ flashback/goldberg200503180758.asp [accessed September 15, 2010]. See also, "Drill here. Drill now. Drill ANWR." anwr.org; available at: http://www.anwr.org/Latest-News/Drill-here.-Drill-now.-Drill-ANWR.php [accessed September 23, 2010].

19 Michael Janofsky, "Cuba Plans Offshore Wells Banned in U.S. Waters," New York Times, May 9, 2006; available at: http://www.nytimes.com/ 2006/05/09/washington/09drill.html [accessed September 15, 2010].

20 Ben Geman, "Report: Oil-and-gas drilling bans will cut GDP by $2.36 trillion," The Hill, February 15, 2010; available at: http://thehill.com/blogs/e2-wire/677-e2-wire/81091-oil-and-gas-drilling-bans-will-cut-gdp-by-236-trillion-report [accessed September 15, 2010].

CHAPTER 13

1 Richard Weikart, "Does Darwinism devalue human life?" The Human Life Review, March 1, 2004; available at: http://www.discovery.org/ a/2172 [accessed September 15, 2010].

2   Ibid.

3   "Internet predators, privacy, porn: Are parents concerned?" University of Michigan Health Care System, November 19, 2009; available at: http://www2.med.umich.edu/prmc/media/newsroom/details.cfm?ID=1382 [accessed September 15, 2010].

4   See, e.g.: Daniel Lee Carter, Robert Alan Prentky, Raymond Knight, Penny Vanderveer, and Richard Boucher, "Use of Pornography in the Criminal and Developmental Histories of Sexual Offenders," *Journal of Interpersonal Violence*, vol. 2, no. 2; Eileen Alexy, Ann Burgess, and Robert Prentky, "Pornography Use as a Risk Marker for an Aggressive Pattern of Behavior Among Sexually Reactive Children and Adolescents," *Journal of the American Psychiatric Nurses Association*, Vol. 14, no. 6; Michele Elliott, Kevin Browne, and Jennifer Kilcoyne, "Child sexual abuse prevention: What offenders tell us," *Child Abuse and Neglect*, Vol. 19, No. 5; and W. L. Marshall, "The Use of Sexually Explicit Stimuli by Rapists, Child Molesters, and Nonoffenders," *The Journal of Sex Research*, Vol. 25, No. 2.

5   *Kennedy v. Louisiana*, Supreme Court, June 25, 2008, http://www.law.cornell.edu/supct/html/07-343.ZO.html [accessed September 15, 2010].

6   Jeff Sharlet, "Why Are We Afraid of Peter Singer?" *Chronicle of Higher Education*, March 10, 2000; available at: http://chronicle.com/article/Why-Are-We-Afraid-of-Peter/11979; and Peter Berkowitz, "Other People's Mothers," *New Republic*, January 10, 2000; available at: http://www.peterberkowitz.com/otherpeoplesmothers.htm [accessed September 15, 2010]. See also, Donald Demarco, "Peter Singer: Architect of the Culture of Death," Catholic Education Resource Center, 2003, http://www.catholiceducation.org/articles/medical_ethics/me0049.html [accessed September 23, 2010].

7   Lydia Saad, "More Americans 'Pro-Life' Than 'Pro-Choice' for First Time," Gallup, May 15, 2009; available at: http://www.gallup.com/poll/118399/more-americans-pro-life-than-pro-choice-first-time.aspx; see also: Associated Press, "Majority of Americans now pro-life, poll says," MSNBC.com, May 15, 2009; available at: http://www.msnbc.msn.com/id/30771408/ [accessed September 15, 2010].

Chapter 14

1 "Entitlement Spending Will More than Double by 2050," Heritage Foundation 2010 Budget Chart Book, http://www.heritage.org/ budgetchartbook/entitlement-spending-double [accessed September 16, 2010].

2 "Clinton Proposes Drug Coverage in Medicare Plan," *St. Louis Post-Dispatch*, June 30, 1999.

3 J. D. Foster, "Medicare Reform: Setting Attainable Goals for Sustainability," Heritage Foundation Backgrounder, no. 2251, March 18, 2009; available at: http://www.heritage.org/Research/Reports/2009/03/Medicare-Reform-Setting-Attainable-Goals-for-Sustainability [accessed September 16, 2010].

4 "Chairman's Recommendations, National Bipartisan Commission on the Future of Medicare," p. 27.

5 "Jindal right person to reform Medicare," *American Press*, March 5, 1998

6 "The President's New Clothes," *Wall Street Journal*, March 18, 1999.

7 "Monica, or Medicare?" *Wall Street Journal*, January 15, 1999.

Chapter 15

1 Al Gore, "A Commentary on the War Against Terror: Our Larger Tasks," Remarks at the Council on Foreign Relations, February 12, 2002; transcript available at: http://www.cfr.org/publication/4343/commentary_on_the_war_against_terror.html?id=4343 [accessed September 16, 2010].

2 Bret Baier, "Terrorism Is a 'Man-Caused Disaster'?" Fox News, March 17, 2009; available at: http://www.foxnews.com/story/ 0,2933,509597, 00.html [accessed September 16, 2010].

3 Robert Bazell, "A Human Life Is a Human Life: At U.S. military field hospitals, care and compassion for wounded enemies," NBC News, March 2, 2007; available at: http://www.msnbc.msn.com/id/17406009/ [accessed September 16, 2010].

4 "Congress and Terror Trials," *Wall Street Journal*, January 29, 2010; available at: http://online.wsj.com/article/SB10001424052748703906 204575027320751100574.html [accessed September 16, 2010].

5   Robert Gordon Kaufman, *Henry M. Jackson: A Life in Politics* (WA: University of Washington Press, 2000), 184.

6   "Analysis: What has Barack Obama's First Foreign Tour Really Achieved?" *Daily Telegraph*, April 7, 2009; available at: http://www.telegraph.co.uk/news/worldnews/northamerica/usa/barackobama/5120797/Analysis-What-has-Barack-Obamas-first-foreign-tour-really-achieved.html [accessed September 16, 2010].

7   Quoted in Glen E. Thurow, *Abraham Lincoln and American Political Religion* (State University of New York Press, 1976), 49.

8   John Lewis Gaddis, *Surprise, Security and the American Experience* (Harvard University Press, 2004).

9   John Quincy Adams, Speech to the U.S. House of Representatives on Foreign Policy (July 4, 1821); transcript available at: http://millercenter.org/scripps/archive/speeches/detail/3484 [accessed September 27, 2010].

10 *Hyde Park Herald*, September 19, 2001.

11 See Obama's July 15, 2008 speech, "Senator Barack Obama's New Strategy for a New World," http://my.barackobama.com/page/content/newstrategy [accessed September 16, 2010].

12 Susan Rice and Corinne Graff, "Can 'Freedom Only' Secure Our Future?" *McGill International Review*, Fall 2005.

13 Marc Sageman, *Understanding Terror Networks* (University of Pennsylvania Press, 2004). See also, Marc Sageman, "Understanding Terror Networks," Foreign Policy Research Institute, November 1, 2004; available at: http://www.fpri.org/enotes/20041101.middleeast.sageman.understandingterrornetworks.html [accessed September 23, 2010].

14 Peter Bergen and Swati Pandey, "The Madrassa Myth," *New York Times*, June 14, 2005; available at: http://www.nytimes.com/2005/06/14/opinion/14bergen.html [accessed September 16, 2010].

15 Michael Rubin and Suzanne Gershowitz, "Political Strategies to Counterterrorism," Middle East Forum, July 12, 2006; available at: http://www.meforum.org/974/political-strategies-to-counterterrorism [accessed September 16, 2010].

16 Scott Atran, "Discover Dialogue: Anthropologist Scott Atran," *Discover*, October 2003; available at: http://discovermagazine.com/2003/

oct/featdialogue [accessed September 16, 2010]. See also, Scott Atran, "Understanding How the Priveleged Become Violent Fanatics," *The Huffington Post*, May 7, 2010; available at: http://www.huffingtonpost.com/ scott-atran/how-to-even-the-privelege_b_568489.html [accessed September 28, 2010].

17 Quoted in Joe Lieberman, "Democrats and Our Enemies," *Wall Street Journal*, May 21, 2008.

CHAPTER 16

1 Floyd Norris, "There Can Be Nothing More Toxic," *New York Times*, June 4, 2009; available at: http://norris.blogs.nytimes.com/ 2009/06/04/there-can-be-nothing-more-toxic/ [accessed September 16, 2010].

2 Ben Stein, "The Long and Short of It at Goldman Sachs," *New York Times*, December 2, 2007; available at: http://www.nytimes.com/ 2007/12/02/business/02every.html [accessed September 16, 2010]. See also, "How Goldman profited by the subprime meltdown," MSN Money, December 17, 2007; available at: http://articles.moneycentral. msn.com/Investing/Extra/HowGoldmanProfitedFromSubprimeMeltd own.aspx [accessed September 23, 2010]; and Kate Kelly, "How Goldman Won Big on Mortgage Meltdown," *Wall Street Journal*, December 14, 2007; available at: http://online.wsj.com/article/ SB119759714037228585.html [accessed September 23, 2010].

3 "25 People to Blame for the Financial Crisis," *Time*; available at: http://www.time.com/time/specials/packages/article/0,28804,1 877351_1877350_1877327,00.html [accessed September 16, 2010].

4 Prmia.org Case Studies, Washington Mutual, Christopher Whalen and the Professional Risk Managers' International Association, http://www.prmia.org/pdf/Case_Studies/WaMu_-_090911.pdf, p. 3; see also, Anne Coulter, "Can't we at least get a toaster?" *World Net Daily*, January 27, 2010; available at: http://www.wnd.com/ index.php?pageId=123377 [accessed September 16, 2010].

5 Andrew Cuomo Press conference, April 6, 1998, CSPAN; excerpts available at: http://www.youtube.com/watch?v=ivmL-lXNy64&feature =player_ embedded [accessed September 16, 2010].

6 Kyle Drennen, "MSNBC's Brewer: GOP Should Abandon 'Morals and Values,'" NewsBusters.org, June 15, 2009; available at: http:// news-busters.org/blogs/kyle-drennen/2009/06/15/msnbcs-brewer-gop-should-abandon-morals-values [accessed September 16, 2010].

7 Robert Rector, Kirk Johnson, and Patrick Fagan, "The Effect of Marriage on Child Poverty," Heritage Foundation, April 15, 2002; available at: http://www.heritage.org/Research/Reports/2002/04/The-Effect-of-Marriage-on-Child-Poverty [accessed September 16, 2010].

8 Child Poverty, National Center for Children in Poverty, http://www.nccp.org/topics/childpoverty.html [accessed September 16, 2010].

9 Alexis de Tocqueville, "Religion Considered as a Political Institution Which Powerfully Contributes to the Maintenance of a Democratic Republic among the Americans," chapter XVII, *Democracy in America*; chapter available at: http://xroads.virginia.edu/~HYPER/DETOC/religion/ch1_17.htm [accessed September 16, 2010].

10 Michael Ledeen, *Tocqueville on American Character: Why Tocqueville's Brilliant Exploration of the American Spirit Is as Vital and Important Today as It Was Nearly Two Hundred Years Ago* (Truman Talley Books, 2000).

11 Samuel P. Huntington, *Who Are We? The Challenges to America's National Identity* (New York: Simon & Schuster, 2004), 20.

12 Quoted in "Review: Community without Politics," *Harvard Law Review*, February 1989, p. 913.

13 Ibid.

14 "Annuit Coeptis—Origin and Meaning of the Motto Above the Eye," http://www.greatseal.com/mottoes/coeptis.html [accessed September 16, 2010].

15 Quoted in J. Clifford Wallace, "Resolving Judicial Corruption While Preserving Judicial Independence: Comparative Perspectives," *California Western International Law Journal*, Spring 1998.

Index

Can't Get Enough Regnery Books?

Follow us on...

FACEBOOK.COM/
REGNERYBOOKS

TWITTER.COM/
REGNERY

DIGG.COM/
REGNERYPUB

And learn more about our **authors**, **upcoming titles**, and the latest in **conservative news**.

Since 1947
**REGNERY
PUBLISHING, INC.**
An Eagle Publishing Company • Washington, DC